Languages and Jargons

Languages and Jargons

Contributions to a
Social History of Language

EDITED BY PETER BURKE AND
ROY PORTER

Polity Press

Copyright © this collection Polity Press 1995
Each chapter © the contributor

First published in 1995 by Polity Press
in association with Blackwell Publishers Ltd.

2 4 6 8 10 7 5 3 1

Editorial office:
Polity Press
65 Bridge Street
Cambridge CB2 1UR, UK

Marketing and production:
Blackwell Publishers Ltd
108 Cowley Road
Oxford OX4 1JF, UK

Blackwell Publishers Inc.
238 Main Street
Cambridge, MA 02142, USA

ISBN 0–7456–1279–2

A CIP catalogue record for this book is available from the British Library.

Library of Congress Cataloguing-in-Publication Data

Languages and jargons: contributions to a social history of language / edited by Peter Burke and Roy Porter.
    p.   cm.
Includes bibliographical references and index.
Contents : Introduction / Peter Burke – The jargon of the schools / Peter Burke – Perplex't with tough names : the uses of medical jargon / Roy Porter – Anti-language or jargon? : canting in the English underworld in the sixteenth and seventeenth centuries / Lee Beier – Caló : the 'secret' language of the Gypsies of Spain / John Geipel – Masonics, metaphor, and misogyny : a discourse of marginality? / Marie Mulvey Roberts – Jargon of class : rhetoric and leadership in British labour politics, 1830–1880 / Timothy R. Burns – The jargon of Indostan : an exploration of jargon in Urdu and East India Company English / Javed Majeed.
    ISBN 0–7456–1279–2 (alk. paper)
    1. Jargon (Terminology) 2. Languages, Secret. I. Burke, Peter.
II. Porter, Roy, 1946–
P409.L36   1995
306.4'4–dc20
                                        95–35965
                                          CIP

Typeset in Times 10 on 12pt
by Wearset, Boldon, Tyne and Wear
Printed in Great Britain by TJ Press Ltd, Padstow, Cornwall

This book is printed on acid-free paper.

P409
.L36
1995

Contents

Notes on Contributors

Lee Beier is Professor of History at Illinois State University. He has published *Masterless Men: The Vagrancy Problem in England, 1560–1640* (1985) and several articles on early modern social history. He was a co-editor of and contributor to *London 1500–1700: The Making of the Metropolis* (1986) and *The First Modern Society: Essays in English History in Honour of Lawrence Stone* (1989).

Peter Burke is Reader in Cultural History at the University of Cambridge, and Fellow of Emmanuel College, Cambridge. His more recent publications include *The Italian Renaissance* (1987), *The French Historical Revolution* (1990), *History and Social Theory*, 2nd edn (1992), *The Art of Conversation* (1993), *Venice and Amsterdam*, 2nd edn (1994) and *The Fortunes of the Courtier* (1995). He is the co-editor *of Language, Self and Society* (1991) and editor of *New Perspectives on Historical Writing* (1992).

Timothy R. Burns, formerly at Birkbeck College, University of London.

John Geipel researched the interaction between Castilian and Caló while working in Mérida, Estremadura, in 1990–1991. His previous publications include *The Europeans: An Ethno-historical Survey* (1969), *The Viking Legacy: Scandinavian Influence on English and Gaelic* (1970), *Anthropologie de l'Europe* (1971), *Mame Loshn: The Making of Yiddish* (1982) and numerous articles on anthropological linguistics for such journals as *History Today*.

Javed Majeed is Lecturer in the Department of South Asia at the School of Oriental and African Studies, University of London. His D. Phil. thesis was published by Clarendon Press as *Ungoverned Imaginings: James Mill's 'The History of British India' and Orientalism* (1993). He is now working on aspects of language politics in British India with special reference to Urdu and Persian.

Roy Porter is Professor of the Social History of Medicine at the Wellcome Institute for the History of Medicine. He is currently working on the history of hysteria. Recent books include *Mind Forg'd Manacles: Madness in England from the Restoration to the Regency* (1987); *A Social History of Madness* (1988); *Health for Sale: Quackery in England, 1660–1850* (1989); and with Dorothy Porter, *In Sickness and in Health: The British Experience, 1650–1850* (1989), and *Patient's Progress* (1989). He is the co-editor of *Language, Self and Society* (1991) and editor of *Myths of the English* (1992).

Marie Mulvey Roberts is Senior Lecturer in Literary Studies at the University of the West of England and is the author of *British Poets and Secret Societies* (1986) and *Gothic Immortals* (1990). She has edited *Out of the Night: Writings from Death Row* (1994) and has co-edited *Literature and Medicine During the Eighteenth Century* (1993), *Sources, Perspectives and Controversies in the History of British Feminism* (1993–1995) and is the general editor of three series, *Subversive Women, For Her Own Name* and *Her Write His Name*.

Introduction

PETER BURKE

This is the third successive volume of a series of studies in the social history of language, initiated by the editors because they found much earlier work on language two-dimensional (if it was historical in approach, it generally lacked the social dimension, while if it was indeed social, it was not historical). Like other forms of social history, this history of language is concerned with both solidarities and conflicts, continuities and changes. More distinctively, the project is inspired by the work of sociolinguists and ethnographers of communication, as well as by the traditions of the historian's craft.[1] This particular volume, unlike its predecessors, concentrates on one main theme, the relations between languages and jargons.

What is a jargon? Since the term is used both in everyday language and in the professional discourse of linguists, sometimes to describe and sometimes to censure, it is unlikely that any single definition will satisfy everyone, and no attempt has been made to impose any single definition on the contributors to this volume. Jargon is as much in the ear of the listener as on the tongue of the speaker, and the history of language offers many examples of words once condemned as jargon which later come to be considered inoffensive or even indispensable.

All the same, it may be worth making a few preliminary remarks on the history of the word 'jargon', and of some other words with which it is frequently associated, with special reference to a few Western European languages. These languages do not exhaust the subject of jargon – far from it. They simply mark the limits of the present writer's communicative competence. For similar reasons, the majority of the examples which follow will be taken from the early modern period, with which I happen to be most familiar.

The concept of jargon

Jargon is a medieval word, already to be found in Provençal and French in the twelfth and thirteenth centuries and in English a little later. Chaucer used it to describe the twittering of birds. The term was used to refer to unintelligible speech, a sort of gargling in the throat ('gargle' and 'jargon' are derived from the same root): in other words, mere 'gibberish' or 'gabble', as the English called it by the sixteenth century. By that time the word had spread to Italian (*gergo* or *zergo*), Spanish (*jerga, jerigonza*) and Portuguese (*gerigonça*).

As it spread from one language to another, the word 'jargon' changed its meaning and came to refer primarily to the language of the underworld, a kind of slang (as we might say today) which helped to keep the activities of beggars, thieves, confidence tricksters and so on secret from ordinary citizens. It was an 'anti-language' of a counter-culture, or a marginal language for marginal people.[2] Thus a gang of thieves discovered at Dijon in 1454, the so-called *Coquillards*, had 'a certain jargon' (*certain langaige de jargon*), as well as certain signs for members to recognize one another by. The term *Coquillards* was part of the jargon, suggesting that the group explained their nomadic life by pretending to be pilgrims to the shrine of Santiago de Compostela, whose symbol was a shell (*coquille*).[3]

By the sixteenth century, if not before, there was an impressive series of synonyms for this language of the underworld. In Spanish, for instance, it was called *germanía*, referring to a corporation or brother-hood, or sometimes *gringo*, apparently a corruption of *grego* (Greek), a term which was destined to make its fortune in the New World. It was also called Caló, the language of the Gypsies discussed by John Geipel (see below, pp. 102–32), since Gypsies were assumed to be thieves and thieves Gypsies. In Portuguese it was called *calão*.[4] In German it was known as *Rotwelsch*, and in French, by the year 1600 or thereabouts, as *argot* (or sometimes as *baragouin*, *blesquin* or *narquois*).[5] In Italian it was sometimes known as *furbesco*, after its primary users, the rogues (*furbi*). In English, from the late sixteenth century onwards, a common term was 'cant' (apparently derived from singing – *chanter*, *cantare*, etc.). For a rich variety of synonyms, we may turn to Cotgrave's *French–English Dictionary*: '*Jargon*. Gibridge, fustian language, Pedler's French;

a barbarous jangling.' *'Jargonneur*. A chatterer, gibridgemonger, counterfeit rogue that speaks fustian, or a language which either himself or
his hearers understand not.'[6]

The language of the underworld was, however, only the most noticeable, the most audible of the many slangs invented for themselves by
particular social groups – ethnic groups, for example, especially marginal ethnic groups like the Gypsies and the Jews. In German and Polish
the term *Jargon* or *zargon* refers primarily to Yiddish, which was
presumably as difficult for other Germans or Poles to follow as the
language of the underworld. Some people, including Luther, believed
that the language of the beggars was derived from that of the Jews.

Awareness of these special languages or slangs is increasingly evident
in the seventeenth and eighteenth centuries. In England, for instance,
the term 'cant' came to refer not only to the language of the confidence
tricksters or 'cony-catchers' of Elizabethan London (discussed by Lee
Beier, pp. 64–101), but also to that of scholastic philosophers, perhaps
because they were coming to be considered a kind of confidence
trickster (p. 73). The term was extended, apparently for similar reasons,
to religious groups such as Puritans and Friends. As one writer
complained at the end of the seventeenth century, 'Really to understand
the Quaker-Cant is learning a new language.'[7] Or at least a new 'lingo',
another pejorative term for usages deviating from plain English and one
which made its début, on the stage anyway, in 1700, in William
Congreve's *Way of the World* (Act 4 Scene 4).

By then the words 'cant' and 'jargon' were employed still more widely
to refer to the 'terms of art' or 'technical words' used by different
occupational groups.[8] As chapter 1 will demonstrate, the phrase 'the
jargon of the schools' has been in use since 1688 at the latest. Swift wrote
in 1704 of 'the cant or jargon of the trade'; Addison, in 1712, of 'the cant
of particular trades'; and Bullock, in 1717, of 'the jargon of the law'.

An alternative description for these usages, in English at least, was
'dialect', as in the phrase 'the lawyer's dialect', attested by the 1740s, or
even 'the court gibberish', a phrase penned by the novelist-magistrate
Henry Fielding.[9] By this time, incidentally, the language of the London
underworld was known by other names, such as 'flash lingo' or 'the
slang' (the original context of this term).[10]

A final twist, or extension, in the meaning of the word 'jargon' also
dates from the eighteenth century. It was employed to describe the
various kinds of lingua franca which enabled different language groups
to communicate with one another. Thus Defoe wrote of 'the Levant
jargon which we call lingua Frank' and Johnson of 'the jargon which
serves the traffickers on the Mediterranean and Indian Coasts', while

George Hadley described Hindustani in his grammar of that language as 'the current corrupt dialect of the jargon of Hindostan'.[11] I shall return to this topic towards the end of this introduction.

In other European countries there appears to have been a similar widening in the meaning of the term 'jargon' and its synonyms, revealing an increasing awareness of the variety of technical terms and forms of slang used by different social groups. The word *Rotwelsch*, for example, which originally referred to the language of professional beggars, came to signify technical terms in general, what eighteenth-century Germans called by the Latin phrase *termini artis*.[12] Again, the meaning of the French word *baragouin* shifted from the language of the underworld to the lingua franca of the Caribbean. Jean Jacques Rousseau was perhaps the first to refer to the 'jargon' of journalists in the preface to a periodical of his own, *Le Persifleur* (1749). In Italy the word *gergo*, once a description of the vocabulary of thieves and beggars, came to be used to describe – and to condemn – the technical terms used by members of professions such as lawyers, physicians (discussed by Roy Porter below, pp. 42–63), philosophers and diplomats. In Portugal the word *calão* followed a similar trajectory. The current Czech word for jargon, *hantyrka*, is unusual in referring originally to the language of artisans, as well as in its derivation from Danish or Swedish.

The historiography of jargons

The history of language thus reveals growing interest in the varieties of language spoken by different subcultures. There is further evidence of this interest, on the part of men of letters at least, from the fifteenth century onwards. François Villon, for instance, an early example of the bohemian intellectual, wrote six *ballades* in the jargon of the *Coquillards*, poems which modern critics have been able to decode only thanks to the discovery of the records of a trial of these *Coquillards* in Dijon in 1455.[13] In Italy the poet Luigi Pulci's glossary of thieves' language, or 'counter-point' as its users called it, was made just a few years later.[14] So was Knebel's brief dictionary of *Rotwelsch*.[15]

In the sixteenth and seventeenth centuries these forms of language would continue to fascinate men of letters, from the dramatist Pietro Aretino to the picaresque novelist Johann Michael Moscherosch, and the glossaries would lengthen, proliferate and appear more and more often in print, thus making private languages relatively public.[16] A comparative study of languages by the Swiss humanist Conrad Gesner discussed the languages of beggars and Gypsies as examples of what he called 'invented languages' (*linguae fictitiae*).[17] The Polish poet Sebastian Klonowic inserted examples of thieves' slang into his poem *Worek Judaszów* (Judas's bag; 1600). In the case of Italian, one thinks of the *Nuovo modo de intendere la lingua zerga* (New way of understanding jargon; 1545); in that of Dutch, *Der Fielten Vocabulaer* (The rogues vocabulary; 1563); in the case of English, of Thomas Harman's *Caveat for Common Cursitors* (1566) and R. Head's *Canting Academy* (1673; discussed below); in that of Spanish, of the vocabulary in Juan Hidalgo's *Romances de germanía* (1609); in that of French, of *Le Jargon de l'argot réformé* (1628).[18] As these examples suggest, it was the language of the underworld which men of letters and their readers found most glamorous. Trade and craft vocabularies were published rather later, from the eighteenth century onwards.

These glossaries and others like them are precious evidence of both the spread and the continuity of certain terms. *Coquillards*, for instance, turns up in 1628 as in 1455. 'Dupe', a victim, goes back to the late seventeenth century in English, but it is attested in French as early as 1426, and is also known in Spanish.[19] 'Cove', a person, was in use in London from the sixteenth century to the twentieth. *Poilu*, a hairy man, described the French soldier long before the First World War, in the 1830s if not earlier.[20] An American term for money, 'bread', is reminiscent of *grano* (grain), which was sixteenth-century Italian slang for a ducat.

Up to the nineteenth century jargons were studied essentially as curiosities, whether by writers (including Cervantes, Balzac, Dickens and Victor Hugo), by antiquarians, like Francis Grose or the 'London Antiquary' who published a *Dictionary of Modern Slang* in 1859, or by other amateurs. Eugène Vidocq's account of the language of French thieves and Friedrich Avé-Lallemant's investigation into the language of German beggars were both the work of retired police officers.[21]

With the rise of linguistics as an academic discipline, however, the study of jargons and slangs of all kinds became more professional. Several classic works in this field go back to the beginning of the century or thereabouts. One thinks of Rafael Salillas in Spain, Alfredo Niceforo of Lazare Sainéan in Italy and Albert Dauzat in France and of Ludwig Günther in Germany.[22] It seems that the study of the jargons of delinquents, which attracted most attention, was still not considered quite respectable unless it was wrapped up in the jargon of turn-of-the-century criminology of the school of Lombroso (stuffed with references to 'pathology', 'degeneration' and so on). All the same, the frequent reprints of some of the leading studies suggest a growing public interest, from the 1920s to the present, in slangs and jargons of all kinds, defined as 'parasitic' or 'partial' languages – in other words, a supplement to the vernacular, not an alternative to it.[23]

Underworld languages have received the lion's share of attention from linguists and sociologists alike, thanks perhaps to the thrill for sedentary academics of vicarious participation in a forbidden, secret world of sex, trickery and violence. Yet interest gradually spread to other 'sociolects' (a term coined on the model of 'dialect') or 'special languages', as they have come to be known in linguistic circles since the beginning of the century (*Sondersprachen, langues spéciales, lingue settoriali*, etc.).

For example, the language of the early Christians was the subject of two of the earliest sociolinguistic studies, carried out by Jozef Schrijnen and his pupil Christine Mohrmann at the University of Nijmegen (well before the invention of the label 'sociolinguistics' and the institutionalization of the subject in the 1950s).[24] Again, the First World War led to a series of studies of soldiers' slang in the various languages of the combatants.[25] Another series of studies was devoted to the jargon of students – though not, curiously enough, to that of their professors.[26] A concern with what linguists in the 1930s still called 'trade jargons' led to the current distinctions between 'pidgins' and 'creoles', to be discussed further below.[27] Today there is a Centre d'argotologie at the Université René Descartes in Paris, a sign that the study is not only on the way to academic respectability, but also in the process of creating a jargon of its own.

Varieties of jargon

All the same, despite the fascination of other people's secrets, the study of jargon appears to have remained almost as marginal as jargon itself, for social historians if not for linguists. More's the pity, because the history of jargon is quite well documented, and this from earlier periods than is commonly realized.

In the paradigm case of the languages of European beggars and thieves the evidence of plays offers a few examples from the thirteenth century, while systematic attempts to compile glossaries go back, as we have seen, to the fifteenth century. In the case of soldiers, attention has focused on the two world wars, but, thanks to literary sources, it is possible to go back much further and resuscitate the *Feld-Sprache* used in the Thirty Years' War (*Glid* for whore, *Joham* for wine and so on), and even the 'pidgin' Italian employed by the German *Lanzknechts* in the early sixteenth century.[28] It is also possible to study the history of the language of sailors in Britain and elsewhere.[29]

The languages of particular trades and crafts can sometimes be reconstructed, at least in part, not only for the nineteenth century, but for more remote periods as well.[30] The *argot typographique*, as Balzac called it (in other words, the jargon of printers), is particularly well documented, at least in the case of eighteenth- and nineteenth-century France, and there is some evidence for it as early as the sixteenth century.[31] The linguist Albert Dauzat printed vocabularies of several itinerant trades, notably masons and chimney-sweeps, and in that of the bell-makers of Lorraine was able to find abundant evidence of eighteenth-century usage.[32] The language of German hangmen has been the subject of a special study.[33] The *linguaggio arsenalesco*, the slang used by workers in the Venetian Arsenal (carpenters, caulkers and the like), is recorded in a manuscript dating from the sixteenth century.

The slang of many generations of students can also be recovered. The dialects of Oxford and Cambridge, the public schools and the *école normale* and *École polytechnique* have all been the object of investigation, and even the uninitiated now know, or can easily discover, the meaning of 'fag' and 'prep', 'sporting one's oak', *cacique, khagne* and so on.[34] *Burschensprache*, the vocabulary of German students – for example at the universities of Giessen, Halle and Jena in the eighteenth century – has also been reconstructed in some detail, and its links with both Latin and *Rotwelsch* pointed out.[35] Before this point in time it is necessary to be a little more speculative, but Pantagruel's famous encounter with a Limousin student in Paris would lose most of its point if the undergraduates of the period had not been in the habit of Latinizing their speech in this way. 'Nous transfretons la Sequane au dilucule et crépuscule . . . Et si, par forte fortune, y a rarité ou pénurie de pécune dans nos marsupies et soyent exhaustés de métal ferruginé, pour l'escot nous dimittons nos codices . . .'[36]

The jargon of the professions can also be traced back a few centuries. Doctors are studied by Roy Porter in a later chapter in this book, so it may be more useful to take another example here, the language of civil servants, known since 1884, according to the *Oxford English Dictionary*, as 'officialese', and in the mid-eighteenth century as 'the language of the secretary's office'.[37] Officialese has, perhaps appropriately, attracted particular attention from historians of the German-speaking world, from Austria to Prussia, whether they concern themselves with the *Ärärisches Deutsch* of the Habsburg Treasury or the euphemisms and metaphors employed by the civil servants in the age of Hitler. Indeed, what was then called the *Geschäftsstyl* or *Curialstyl* of the bureaucrats was already an object of interest in the later eighteenth century.[38]

All the same, it might be interesting to study 'administrative idioms', as Javed Majeed calls them (pp. 182–205), from a comparative point of view, from the *prikaznyi jazyk* (Chancery language) of Muscovy to the *Guan hua* of the Chinese mandarins or the 'bureaucratese' of the Romans (the object of a pioneering study in the early sixties by the ancient historian Ramsay MacMullen).[39] Multilingual empires might be particularly worth studying in this respect, since the jargon of the bureaucrats might serve as a kind of lingua franca between rulers and ruled. In Milan one can observe the Hispanicization of the language of administration in the period of Spanish domination, in the sixteenth and seventeenth centuries.[40] When India was part of the British Empire, a hybrid administrative language developed which owed a good deal to that of the previous imperial administration, that of the Mughals. Thus the minister of finance was known as the 'Dewaun', while an office and its documents was called a 'Dufter' (cf. the Ottoman 'Divan', and 'Defter'). The jargon of diplomacy should not be forgotten, whether attention focuses on its Latino-French vocabulary (*casus belli, status quo, ultimatum, démarche, entente, doyen*, etc.) or on structural characteristics such as the propensity for ambiguity and understatement.[41] The jargon of communist regimes, or 'double-talk' – studied by political scientists, mainly for polemical purposes, during the cold war – deserves a more profound examination.[42]

A wide variety of occupational groups develop their own jargon, but not all do so. For instance, craftsmen have a tendency to produce jargon, but factory workers apparently do not. Another problem is that of class. Although the middle class frequently criticize the working class for faulty English, while the working class reject the accent and vocabulary they stigmatize as 'BBC', it is far from clear whether or not social classes generate jargons in the strict sense of the term. Timothy Burns discusses one aspect of this problem in his contribution to the volume (pp. 155–81).

It seems that small face-to-face groups are necessary to the formation of private or semi-private languages. Among the crafts, some occupational groups have produced much more jargon than others. Can these differences be explained? The linguist Albert Dauzat noted how often *argots* developed among nomadic occupational groups.[43] Examples include beggars, thieves, masons (who passed on some of their terms to the Masons), chimney-sweeps, Gypsies, soldiers, sailors and also actors, who were for a long time treated with contempt and even denied Christian burial. No wonder, then, that they developed their own terms for insiders ('de la banque', in eighteenth-century France) and outsiders ('lof').[44]

Less rooted than most people in a local culture, the occupational culture of these groups was doubtless more important to their lives. The nomad explanation does not always work. It does not fit the case of prisoners, or of schoolboys. Hence it may be useful to supplement it by suggesting that people confined to what the sociologist Erving Goffman called 'total institutions', in other words, organizations which exercise unusually close control over their inmates (prisons, monasteries, asylums, boarding-schools, barracks, ships and so on), are equally likely to create semi-private languages.[45] Monasteries are the obvious exceptions here, thanks to the rule of silence, unless one counts their sign languages as jargons.[46]

Studies of the languages of soldiers, sailors and students have already been mentioned. Prisons too have caught the attention of students of language on both sides of the bars, from the United States to Poland.[47] What the nomads and their apparent opposites, the confined, have in common is, of course, their isolation from the rest of the world, physical or psychological. The same goes for secret societies like the Masons, discussed by Marie Roberts (see below, pp. 133–54). This sense of isolation will be discussed further in the section on functions below.

If jargon of some kind has not always been with us, some forms of it have been around for a very long time. However, the nineteenth and twentieth centuries have witnessed an extraordinary proliferation of jargons, at least as far as Europe is concerned, in large part the result of a proliferation of occupations through the increasing division of labour which accompanied the rise of industrial society.

All the same, we should not link jargon too closely to occupations. The world of leisure generates jargon as well as the world of work, and has done so especially since the later eighteenth century, when a number of sports were institutionalized, commercialized and formalized. Obvious examples come from the worlds of racing and boxing in England around the year 1800, a world vividly evoked for us by sporting writers such as John Badcock and Pierce Egan: the 'turf' for the racecourse, 'round-betting' for what would later be called 'hedging' one's bets, 'levanting' for what would be called 'welshing' on them, a 'floorer' for what we call a 'knock-out', a 'miller' for a second-rate boxer and so on.[48] In France the language of 'le turf' was a variety of *franglais*, and members of the Jockey Club ('le Jockey') could be heard commenting on 'le yearling', or 'le meeting'.[49]

The critique of jargon

So far we have been discussing the word 'jargon' and its synonyms as descriptive terms, and jargon as a linguistic phenomenon like any other. To complete the picture, or at least to make this introductory sketch somewhat less sketchy, it is necessary to examine 'jargon' as a pejorative term and to discuss the way in which the sociolects of some groups have been criticized by other groups. After all, the word 'jargon' had been coined to express the idea that the language of others was as unintelligible as gargling in the throat, much as the ancient Greeks coined the term *barbaroi* to describe other people who were unable to speak Greek, and hence unable to produce more than unintelligible sounds such as ba, ba.

From the beginning of the sixteenth century onwards, criticisms of different jargons abound. Some of them express xenophobia, as in the case of the German rejection of the jargon of the Jews. Others emphasize the unintelligibility and mystification of these special languages. This latter point may be illustrated from the language of bureaucracy, which twentieth-century writers are far from the first to criticize. Nineteenth-century Americans censured their administration for the use of what they stigmatized as 'Washington Choctaw', as unintelligible to the public as the language of the Indians, while Charles Dickens referred to Whitehall as the 'Circumlocution Office'. In the previous century Frederick the Great ordered his civil servants to avoid the use of Latin phrases and other jargon. A century earlier the Swedish statesman Axel Oxenstierna was already rebuking administrators for writing a Swedish stuffed with German and other foreign phrases.[50] Over a hundred years before that Martin Luther, who wrote in a direct, vigorous German, objected to the pompous style of the chanceries.[51]

An even more common critique of jargon emphasized affectation or pretentiousness, such as the employment of what sixteenth-century Englishmen sometimes called 'inkhorn terms' or 'inkhornisms', and others 'hard words'.[52] For example, a late fifteenth-century English play, *Mankind*, criticized preachers for their use of a 'clerical manner' full of 'Latin words'.[53] In the early sixteenth century the Latinate Italian of such writers as Mario Equicola and Battista Pio was already condemned as a *jergo mariopioneo*.[54] In the seventeenth century Guy Miage included what he called 'made words' alongside archaisms and provincialisms in his dictionary of 'barbarous French'.[55] The Latinate French mocked by Rabelais in the passage quoted above may allude to this linguistic debate as well as to the slang of students.

The debate was certainly a lively one in sixteenth-century France.

Rabelais's contemporary, the printer Geoffroy Tory, denounced the corruption of French by *jargonneurs*, defined in this case as 'skimmers of Latin' (*escumeurs de Latin*), who added unnecessary whipped cream to solid French fare. Later in the century Jacques Tahureau complained of 'affected Latinizers' who 'produce jargon' (*jargonnent*).[56] A similar criticism was levelled by Henri Estienne (like Tory, a scholar-printer) against the language of courtiers, 'ce jergon si sauvage Appelé courtisan langage'.[57]

In these cases the term 'jargon' may well have been chosen not only because the form of language criticized is unintelligible to most people, but also because it is a linguistic mixture, either of French and Latin or, as with Estienne's courtiers, French and Italian. (Remember that by the seventeenth century, if not before, the term 'jargon' was sometimes applied to a lingua franca.)

The language of women was not exempt from this kind of criticism. The poet Francisco Quevedo wrote a satire on 'jargonizing ladies' (*las damas jerigonzas*), who larded their Spanish with words borrowed from Latin, while Molière mocked their French sisters in similar style in *Les Précieuses ridicules* (1659), in which a plain bourgeois, Gorgibus, on hearing his daughter and his niece conversing in the fashionable high style, explodes with 'Quel diable de jargon entends-je ici?' (Act 1 Scene 4). One gentleman went so far as to compile a dictionary of the jargon of the *précieuses*, in other words, the literary ladies who frequented the *salons*. If his description of their speech habits is at all faithful, rather than a satire on what the compiler calls their linguistic 'extravagance', then it is clear that these ladies were addicted to euphemisms and other circumlocutions. Fortune becomes 'la déesse des courtisans'. Seats are not seats but 'commodités de la conversation'. One does not say 'j'aime', but 'j'ai un furieux tendre pour . . .'.[58]

In its article on 'Jargon' Diderot's *Encyclopédie* (1751–80), more generous – or more patronizing – declared that the ladies could be pardoned for using these special or eccentric words or turns of phrase, but claimed that they were 'unworthy of a man'. On the other hand, a seventeenth-century defender of women, Poullain de la Barre, praised them precisely for avoiding technical terms. 'On ne leur entend point prononcer ces termes de sciences, qu'on appelle consacrés.'[59]

In fact, almost all the forms of jargon discussed in this essay are predominantly male, though future research on nuns, prostitutes and schoolgirls may require this generalization to be modified, while a late nineteenth-century study devoted a few fascinating pages to the language of dressmakers – not technical terms so much as slang enabling the girls to talk freely about sexual experiences without their employer noticing.[60]

At this point we ought to turn to the assumptions underlying the criticism of jargon. Readers of this essay may themselves feel a strong distaste for jargon, or at least some forms of jargon, whether on aesthetic grounds or because it is a hindrance to effective communication. So, for that matter, do I. Indeed, I very much hope to have managed to avoid employing academic jargon – as opposed to the essential technical terms of linguistics – in the course of this essay. All the same, criticisms of jargon should not be assumed to be nothing but expressions of common sense, impervious to change over time and unrelated to social solidarities and conflicts. The task of a social historian of language is, after all, to reveal the many links between language and society.

In early modern Europe, for example, the rise of criticisms of jargon is associated with self-conscious movements for the reform of language, the exemplary cases being those of sixteenth-century Italy and seventeenth-century France. In both these cultures critics and poets such as Pietro Bembo and François de Malherbe attempted to raise the status of the vernacular, to give it the same dignity as ancient Greek and Latin. To do this it was necessary to 'purify', or 'purge', ordinary language of recurrent and revealing metaphors. Erasmus's *Moriae Encomium* (*Praise of Folly*) censured scholastic theologians for speaking not only 'barbarously', but also 'in a filthy manner' (*spurce*).[61] One seventeenth-century man of letters, Paul Pellisson, condemned the language of lawyers as 'les impuretés de la chicane'.[62] Other metaphors are also recurrent and revealing. Good language has to be 'chaste'. It must be a legitimate, not a 'bastard' language. It must be independent, not 'parasitic'; healthy, not 'diseased'.[63]

So out went foreign words, for a start, since they violated or adulterated a vernacular perceived as 'pure' (the link between criticisms of jargon and xenophobia has already been mentioned). Out too went the technical terms of trades, crafts and even professions, 'low' words associated with 'low' people, reminding us that the social group associated with these reforms was aristocratic, or at least presented itself as such. It is in this context that we should place the story of two French aristocrats of the mid seventeenth century, who are said to have disliked the jargon of the schools and the law so much that they fined anyone who employed it in their households. 'The late Prince of Condé with the Duke of Orleans that now is, were used to have a censor in their houses, that if any of their family spoke any word that savoured of the Palace or the Schools he should incur an amercement.'[64]

Words current in provincial dialects were also banned from a language which was supposed to follow the usage of the metropolis, Florence or Paris. The first of three definitions of 'jargon' offered by the *Encyclopédie* was 'a corrupt language, of the kind spoken in the provinces'. In France as in Italy a literary academy was founded to maintain standards and to produce dictionaries of correct usage. The name of the Florentine academy is revealing. It was the *crusca*, the sieve, used to separate the linguistic wheat from the chaff of vulgar usage, 'to purify the dialect of the tribe'.

When we condemn jargon, we are appealing, whether we are aware of this or not, to a canon or standard of purity of this kind, be it formal or informal. In language, as elsewhere in their culture, the British continue to prefer case law and an unwritten constitution, but unofficial condemnations of Americanized English, for instance, run parallel to official French condemnations of Anglo-Americanized French (better known as *franglais*).

Beneath these attempts to reform language lies 'anxiety', as it does beneath other purification movements, from Puritanism to Temperance. They are examples of what the American historian Daniel Boorstin once called 'defensive purism'.[65] Here the anxiety might be defined more precisely as a fear of loss of identity. Linguistic academies have something in common with ethnic cleansing. To be fair to both parties, one might say that while many groups of people define their identity by using jargon, one group, the critics, define theirs by rejecting the jargon of the others.

The functions of jargons

Like a sociologist or a social anthropologist, a social historian faced with a particular phenomenon is always well-advised to ask questions about its possible uses or functions. In the case of jargon several possible uses or functions immediately spring to mind.

The first function is that of practical convenience. As the Italian linguist Alfredo Niceforo once put it, 'to exercise different occupations means speaking differently'.[66] It means using technical terms, abbreviations and allusions rather than spelling everything out, in other words, 'talking shop' (a favourite nineteenth-century term which combined contempt for jargon with contempt for trade). 'Shop' has some of the characteristics of what the sociolinguist Basil Bernstein has called a 'restricted code', notably the dependence of meaning on a particular context.[67] The result is to communicate more quickly and effectively

than otherwise to the initiated. Outsiders will not understand, but then
this kind of talk does not concern them.

This 'shop' theory blends into a second theory, that of secrecy. Secret
societies like the Masons need secret languages, including, of course, the
gestures studied by Marie Roberts (p. 143). Descriptions of the jargon of
the underworld have traditionally emphasized this function. The language of beggars, thieves and so on is not only different, it is private, a
means of communication which the public, including possible victims
and the police, might overhear but will be unable to decode. A
remarkable formulation of this theory of jargon as a defence mechanism
can be found in a document claiming to record the interrogation of a
certain Girolamo, arrested for begging in Rome in 1595, in which the
prisoner speaks of a general assembly of beggars called 'to change the
jargon' (*mutare il gergo del parlare*) because it had become known to too
many people. Whether or not it is a genuine trial record, the document
at least bears vivid witness to the leading early modern theory of
jargon.[68]

This theory in turn blends into what might be called the 'imposture' or
'mystification' theory of jargon. John Wilkins for one, a leading language reformer of the seventeenth century (see below, p. 33), complained that the language of scholastic philosophers was full of
pseudo-profundities 'whereby some men set up for reputation'. The
language of bureaucracies in particular has often been criticized as
'designed to mystify, to intimidate and to create a sense that the present
arrangement of society is immutable'.[69]

So far, the explanations offered have been utilitarian. Historians,
however, have learned to be suspicious of attempts to reduce the
explanations of social and cultural phenomena to what is useful, efficient
or convenient. Language is, after all, a symbolic system, and we should
at least ask ourselves about the possible symbolic functions of jargon. It
may, for example, be used playfully, as it often has been by children or
by students.

Again, as the linguist Walter Nash recently put it, jargon is not only
'shop talk' but also 'show talk', a means of impressing the uninitiated.[70]
The Latinate vernacular of physicians and the Italianate vernacular of
Renaissance courtiers furnish two striking examples. What is being
shown off may be knowledge, but it may also be one's membership of a
group from which the listener is excluded. The use of jargon by a social
group is one of the most potent means of inclusion and exclusion. It both
expresses and encourages an *esprit de corps*, a form of bonding which is
usually, though not universally, male. It is no accident that this form of
language is so richly developed in total institutions, in which the

inhabitants feel extremely distinct from the rest of the world – described by them in a series of colourful contemptuous expressions such as 'civvies', 'landlubbers', 'suckers' or whatever. Indeed, there is evidence that in some of these total institutions, from prisons to public schools, the use of the local jargon is compulsory. It is both a means and a sign of their initiation into a new community, truly a 'second life' (*drugie zycie*), as Polish prisoners call it.[71] A final example in favour of the thesis that jargon expresses a social or psychological isolation rather than a physical isolation from the rest of society is that of drug addicts, 'junkies' 'hooked' on their 'rock', 'snow' or 'grass'.

The content of jargons as well as their very existence carries symbolic meanings. Jargons are rich in figures of speech, notably metaphor and euphemism, like the 'snow' and 'grass' quoted in the previous paragraph. Again, the victim of confidence tricksters in Elizabethan London was known as the 'cony', or poor foolish rabbit, while in the eighteenth and nineteenth centuries he had become a 'pigeon' to be 'plucked' (in Spanish too the victim was known as the *palomo*).[72] In the jargon of prisoners, in more than one language, to confess or inform is to 'sing', and the informer is a 'canary'. In the argot of the underworld in seventeenth-century France thieves were 'harvesters' (*vendangeurs*). In eighteenth-century London to hang was 'to dance the Paddington frisk', while Newgate Prison was described as 'Whittington's College', an analogy developed in the pamphlet *Hell on Earth* (1703) with its playful reference to 'those Collegians who are strictly examined at the Old Bailey and take their higher degrees near Hyde Park Corner'. In English, around 1800, a brothel and a prison could both be described as an 'academy', while a hundred years later prison was still known as the 'boarding-school', *lycée, studi* or *Seminar*.[73] Like crime, warfare generates a particularly rich vocabulary of euphemism. In the Royal Air Force slang of the Second World War, for instance, the sea was 'the drink'. The ultimate, or at least the penultimate, euphemism, before we all go up in smoke, is 'cheeseburger', currently in use in the USA to describe a particularly powerful bomb.

Pidgins and creoles

To turn from these argots to the forms of language known today as pidgins and creoles may seem like an abrupt change of subject, but there are some important connections between the two. To demonstrate this point one might begin with the observation that the French term *baragouin* was extended from the argot of criminals to the trade

language of the Caribbean, while the English word 'jargon' was used by
Daniel Defoe and Samuel Johnson to refer to the famous lingua franca
of the Mediterranean world, a language containing Venetian, Arabic
and Greek elements which facilitated trade and other forms of communication.[74] In the Baltic world, by contrast, it was German which
performed the functions of a lingua franca, in the Middle Ages and in
early modern times. In west Africa and the East Indies it was Portuguese. Other regions of the world developed special trading languages,
such as Swahili in east Africa, the Chinook 'trade jargon' in parts of
North America, from Oregon to Alaska, and 'Bazaar Malay' in parts of
south-east Asia.[75] Another function of lingua francas, in various
empires, has been to communicate between masters or mistresses and
their servants, as in kitchen Hindustani, though it should not be
forgotten that Anglo-Indian phrases were not confined to the kitchen or
the market, but were widely used in the army and the administration as
well.[76] A language of this kind might even be necessary at the centre of
power. In early modern times the language of the court of the sultan in
Istanbul was a mixture of Turkish, Arabic and Persian.

A lingua franca might well seem to be the opposite of a jargon, since it
is designed to allow two social groups to communicate with each other,
while jargons exclude outsiders. Nevertheless, there is something in
common between the two. Both are 'partial' or 'parasitic' languages,
supplementing the native vernaculars of the speakers. Both are 'marginal' languages, literally so in the case of a language which permits
trade across a cultural or political frontier.[77] Such a language is
developed by combining elements from vernaculars. A character in a
comedy by John Dryden indeed defined the lingua franca, 'as I have
heard the merchants call it', as 'a certain compound language made up
of all tongues, that passes through the Levant' (*Limberham*, 1678, Act 1
Scene 1). A famous example from another region is the 'general
language' (*lingua geral*) spoken in colonial Brazil, a mixture of the
language of the Tupi with that of other Indian tribes.[78]

Critics of jargon, as we have seen, often object to the special
languages precisely because they are compounds or mixtures, thus
contaminating what the critics consider to be the purity of the vernacular. Some occupational jargons do incorporate pidgin, or elements of
foreign languages. As discussed earlier, some of the jargons of beggars
and thieves drew on Romany and Yiddish. The fact that in France
occupational languages were much more common in some regions, such
as near the Alps, than in others has been attributed to the influence of
foreign languages.[79] The language of soldiers and sailors has long been a
semi-international one because regiments and crews were so often

composed of men from different places. Indeed, one theory of the origin of pidgin is that it developed out of nautical jargon. More recently, in the age of imperialism, the slang of French soldiers, many of whom had served in north Africa, drew on the Mediterranean lingua franca (using the Arabic word *baraka* for luck, for example), while the slang of their British colleagues drew on Hindustani, as Hindi was then called ('take a dekko', for instance, for take a look). Campaigns in Italy during the Second World War introduced Italian words into the vocabulary of the British army, from *niente* to *domani*.[80]

One of the most exciting discoveries made by linguists concerned with language contact and language change is the phenomenon they have christened 'creolization', derived from 'creole' in the sense of someone of European or African descent, born in the Americas. The term refers to the not uncommon process by which a partial language or pidgin becomes the only language of a particular speech community, and in the process develops the features of a complete vernacular.[81]

This is the case, for example, in Tok Pisin ('Talk Pidgin') in Papua New Guinea, in Urdu, originally the language of the Mughal bureaucracy (discussed by Javed Majeed, pp. 182–205), and in Swahili. In the seventeenth-century Swahili was a lingua franca employed for commercial reasons on the east African coast. Since then it has reached more and more people and taken on more and more functions. It was adopted by missionaries who wanted to convert people with different vernaculars. It was adopted by the British colonial administration, to communicate with the people. It was chosen as the language of the lower courts and the newspapers. It also developed into the language of the towns, especially Nairobi, in which immigrants speaking different vernaculars converged. In the Belgian Congo and Katanga it became the language of the army, at least for the training of recruits. More recently it has been adopted as the official language of Tanzania.[82]

There is something fascinating, exciting and inspiring about the process by which a pidgin becomes a vernacular, increasing its vocabulary and functions and turning from a mixture into a system. There are obvious parallels between this linguistic process and other cultural changes which have been taking place in the late twentieth-century world, parallels which have been drawn with skill by the Swedish anthropologist Ulf Hannerz.[83] To discuss them here, however, would go well beyond the bounds of my knowledge as well as those of the social history of language. It is time to hand over to the remaining contributors to this volume, to allow a variety of voices to be heard.

Notes

1 For more detailed discussion, see the introduction to P. Burke and R. Porter (eds), *The Social History of Language* (Cambridge: Cambridge University Press, 1987), 3.

2 M. A. K. Halliday, 'Antilanguages' (1976), repr. in his *Language as a Social Semiotic: The Social Interpretation of Language and Meaning* (London: Arnold, 1978); B. Geremek, 'Gergo', *Enciclopedia Einaudi*, 6 (Turin: Einaudi, 1979), 726.

3 B. Geremek, *Truands et misérables dans l'Europe moderne* (Paris: Julliard, 1980), 52–3.

4 R. Salillas, *El delincuente español*, 2 vols (Madrid: Suárez, 1896), 1: 207ff; F. A. Coelho, *Os ciganos de Portugal* (Lisbon: Imprensa nacional, 1892).

5 L. Sainéan, *L'Argot ancien* (Paris: Champion, 1907), 29–38; A. Dauzat, *Les Argots* (1929; rev. edn Paris: Delagrave, 1946), 5–12.

6 R. Cotgrave, *French–English Dictionary* (London: Whitaker, 1650).

7 M. van Beek, *An Enquiry into Puritan Vocabulary* (Groningen: Wolters-Noordhoff, 1969); H. Ormsby-Lennon, 'From Shibboleth to Apocalypse: Quaker Speechways during the Puritan Revolution', in P. Burke and R. Porter (eds), *Language, Self and Society* (Cambridge: Polity, 1991), 72–112.

8 J. Harris, *Lexicon technicum* (London: Brown et al., 1704).

9 H. Fielding, *Tom Jones* (1749; London: Methuen, 1905), bk 6, ch. 2.

10 F. Grose, *A Classical Dictionary of the Vulgar Tongue* (London: Hooper, 1785), s.v. 'cant'.

11 S. Johnson, *A Dictionary of the English Language* (London: Knapton et al., 1755); G. Hadley, *A Compendious Grammar of . . . the Jargon of Hindostan* (London: Sewell, 1801).

12 J. Hübner, *Reales Staats und Zeitungs Lexicon* (Leipzig: Gleditsch, 1704).

13 P. Guiraud, *Le Jargon de Villon* (Paris: Gallimard, 1968).

14 P. Camporesi (ed.), *Il libro dei vagabondi* (Turin: Einaudi, 1973), 183–4.

15 J. Knebel, 'Bericht über das Rotwelsch' (1479), in W. Vischer (ed.), *Basler Chroniken*, 3 (Leipzig, 1887), 556–7.

16 On Aretino, G. Aquilecchia, 'Pietro Aretino e la lingua zerga' (1967), repr. in his *Schede di italianistica* (Turin: Einaudi, 1976), 153–69. J. M. Moscherosch, *Geschichte Philanders von Sittewald* (1642–3; new edn Berlin, 1883), pt 2, sect. 6, 286–94.

17 C. Gesner, *Mithridates* (Zurich, 1555).

18 Camporesi (1973), 205; T. Harman, in G. Salgado (ed.), *Coney-catchers and Bawdy Baskets* (Harmondsworth: Penguin, 1972), 79–154; 'Le Jargon', in R. Chartier (ed.), *Figures de la Gueuserie* (Paris: Montalba, 1982), 133–80.

19 Dauzat (1929), 33.

20 A. Dauzat, *L'Argot de la guerre* (Paris: Colin, 1918), 48.

21 E. Vidocq, *Les Voleurs* (Paris: Vidocq, 1837); F. C. B. Avé-Lallemant, *Das deutsche Gaunertum*, 4 vols (Leipzig: Brockhaus, 1858–62), vol. 4.

22 Salillas (1896), vol. 1; Sainéan (1907); A. Niceforo, *Il gergo* (Turin: Bocca,

1897); A. Niceforo, *Le Génie de l'argot* (Paris: Mercure de France, 1912); A. Dauzat, *Les Argots de métiers franco-provençaux* (Paris: Champion, 1917); Dauzat (1929); L. Günther, *Die deutsche Gaunersprache* (Leipzig: Quelle und Meyer, 1919).

23 M. Cohen, 'Note sur l'argot' (1919), repr. in his *Cinquante années* (Paris: Klincksieck, 1955), 136–9.

24 J. Schrijnen, *Charakteristik des altchristlichen Latein* (Nijmegen: Dekker et al., 1932); C. Mohrmann, *Die altchristliche Sondersprache in den Sermons des hl. Augustin* (Nijmegen: Dekker et al., 1932).

25 O. Mausser, *Deutsche Soldatensprache* (Strasburg: Trübner, 1917); Dauzat (1918); J. Brophy and E. Partridge, *Songs and Slang of the British Soldier 1914–18* (London: Partridge, 1930).

26 F. Kluge, *Deutsche Studentensprache* (Strasburg: Trübner, 1895); M. Cohen, 'Le Langage de l'école polytechnique' (1909), repr. in Cohen (1955), 113–32.

27 J. Reinecke, 'Trade Jargons and Creole Dialects as Marginal Languages' (1938), repr. in D. Hymes, (ed.), *Language in Culture and Society* (New York: Harper, 1964), 534–46.

28 Moscherosch (1642–3), pt 2, sect. 6, 286–94; W. Coates, 'The German Pidgin-Italian of the Sixteenth-century *Lanzichenecchi*', *Papers from the 4th Annual Kansas Linguistics Conference* (1969), 66–74.

29 J. H. Parry, 'Sailor's English', *Cambridge Journal*, 2 (1948–9), 660–70; W. Granville, *A Dictionary of Sailor's Slang* (London: Deutsch, 1962); J. H. Roeding, *Allgemeines Wörterbuch der Marine*, 4 vols (Hamburg: Nemnich, 1794–8); F. Kluge, *Seemannsprache* (Halle: Waisenhaus, 1911).

30 F. Kluge, *Rotwelsch* (Strasburg: Trübner, 1901), 421–34.

31 N. Contat, *Anecdotes typographiques* (1762), ed. G. Barber (Oxford: Voltaire Foundation, 1980), 68ff; N. Z. Davis, 'A Trade Union in Sixteenth-century France', *Economic History Review*, 19 (1966), 48–69; A.F. Momoro, *Traité élémentaire de l'imprimerie* (Paris: Momoro, 1793).

32 Dauzat (1917), 130ff.

33 Günther (1919), 147ff.

34 M. Marples, *Public School Slang* (London: Constable, 1940); M. Marples, *University Slang* (London: Williams and Norgate, 1950); Cohen (1909); A. Peyrefitte, *Rue d'Ulm* (rev. edn Paris: Fayard, 1994), 613–24.

35 Kluge (1895); G. Objartel, 'Studentische Kommunikationsstile im späteren 18. Jht' (1985), in D. Kimpel (ed.), *Mehrsprachigkeit in der deutschen Aufklärung* (Hamburg, 1985), 28–41.

36 F. Rabelais, *Pantagruel* (1532 or 1533), in his *Oeuvres*, ed. J. Boulenger (Paris: Bibliothèque de la Pléiade, 1959), ch. 6.

37 R. Cambridge (1754), quoted in W. Nash, *Jargon, Its Uses and Abuses* (Oxford: Blackwell, 1993), 90.

38 G. Craig, *The Germans* (New York: Oxford University Press, 1982), Appendix; J. H. Melton, *Absolutism and the Eighteenth-century Origin of Compulsory Schooling* (Cambridge: Cambridge University Press, 1988), 86.

39 R. MacMullen, 'Roman Bureaucratese', *Traditio*, 18 (1962), 364–78, repr. in his *Changes in the Roman Empire* (Princeton: Princeton University Press, 1990), 67–77.

40 G. L. Beccaria, *Spagnolo e spagnoli in Italia* (Turin: Turin University Press, 1968); H. Yule and A. C. Burnell, *Hobson-Jobson* (1886; repr. London: Routledge, 1985).

41 H. G. Nicolson, *Diplomacy* (London: Butterworth, 1939), 226–50.

42 H. Hodgkinson, *Doubletalk: The Language of Communism* (London: Allen and Unwin, 1955); R. N. C. Hunt, *A Guide to Communist Jargon* (London: Bles, 1957).

43 Dauzat (1917).

44 Niceforo (1912), 131; cf. Geremek (1979), 726.

45 E. Goffman, *Asylums* (New York: Doubleday, 1961), 16.

46 J. Umiker-Sebeok and T. A. Sebeok (eds), *Monastic Sign Languages* (Berlin and New York: Mouton de Gruyter, 1987).

47 Salillas (1896), 1: 239ff; J. Kurczewski, 'Bluzg, Grypserka, Drugie Zycie', typescript (I should like to thank Jacek Kurczewski for sending me this text); W. K. Bentley and J. M. Corbett, *Prison Slang* (Jefferson, NC: McFarland, 1992).

48 *A Bang-up Dictionary* (London, 1812); P. Egan, *Boxiana*, 4 vols (London, 1812–14; repr. London: Folio Society, 1976); J. Badcock, *Slang* (London: T. Hughes, 1823).

49 Niceforo (1912), 32.

50 M. Roberts, *The Swedish Imperial Experience* (Cambridge: Cambridge University Press, 1979), 21.

51 M. L. Baeumer, 'Luther and the Rise of the German Literary Language: A Critical Reassessment', in A. Scaglione (ed.), *The Emergence of National Languages* (Ravenna: Longo, 1984), 95–117, at 104.

52 E. L. McAdam, jr, 'Inkhorn Words before Johnson', in *Eighteenth-century Studies in Honor of Donald F. Hyde* (New York: Grolier, 1970), 187–206.

53 H. L. Spencer, *English Preaching in the Late Middle Ages* (Oxford: Clarendon Press, 1993), 118.

54 S. Kolsky, *Mario Equicola* (Geneva, 1992), 104.

55 G. Miage, *A Dictionary of Barbarous French* (London: Basset, 1679).

56 G. Tory, *Champ Fleury* (Paris: G. Tory, 1529); J. Tahureau, *Les Dialogues* (Paris: Buon, 1565).

57 H. Estienne, *Deux dialogues* (1578), ed. P. M. Smith (Geneva: Droz, 1980), 19.

58 A. Baudeau, *Le Grand Dictionnaire des Précieuses*, 2nd edn (Paris: Loyson, 1660).

59 F. Poullain de la Barre, *De l'égalité des deux sexes* (1673), ed. and trans. A. D. Frankforter and P. J. Mormon (Lewiston: Mellen, 1989), 42.

60 Niceforo (1897), ch. 5; cf. Niceforo (1912), 137–40.

61 D. Erasmus, *Moriae Encomium*, ed. C. H. Miller (Amsterdam and Oxford: North Holland Publishing Company, 1979), 158.

62 P. Pellisson, *Oeuvres*, 3 vols (Paris: Coignard, 1735), 1:23.

63 Salillas (1896), 1: 9, 15: K. Hudson, *The Dictionary of Diseased English* (London: Macmillan, 1977).

64 J. Howell, Epistle dedicatory to Cotgrave (1650).

65 D. Boorstin, *The Americans: The National Experience* (New York: Random House, 1965), 277.

66 Niceforo (1912), 16.

67 B. Bernstein, *Class, Codes and Control* (London: Routledge, 1971), 76–8, 134–5.

68 Camporesi (1973), 359.

69 H. Rosen, *Language and Class* (1972; repr. Harmondsworth: Penguin, 1974), 6. Cf. Hudson (1977).

70 Nash (1993), 9–12.

71 Marples (1940); Halliday (1976), quoting an unpublished account by Podgórecki; cf. Kurczewski (above, n. 47).

72 Salillas (1896), 1: 153.

73 P. Linebaugh, *The London Hanged: Crime and Civil Society in the Eighteenth Century* (London: Allen Lane, 1991); Günther (1919), 107–8.

74 K. Whinnom, 'Lingua Franca: Historical Problems', in A. Valdman (ed.), *Pidgin and Creole Linguistics* (Bloomington: Indiana University Press, 1977), 295–310.

75 W. Whiteley, *Swahili: The Rise of a National Language* (Cambridge: Cambridge University Press, 1969); Reinecke (1938); M. Silverstein, 'Chinook Jargon', *Language*, 48 (1972), 378–406, 596–625; S. G. Thomason, 'Chinook Jargon in Context', *Language*, 59 (1983), 820–70.

76 Yule and Burnell (1886).

77 Reinecke (1938).

78 J. H. Rodrigues, 'The Victory of the Portuguese Language in Colonial Brazil', in A. Hower and R. Preto-Rodas (eds), *Empire in Transition* (Gainesville: University of Florida Press, 1985), 33–64.

79 Dauzat (1918), 6.

80 Dauzat (1929), 85ff; E. Partridge (ed.), *A Dictionary of Forces' Slang, 1939–45* (London: Secker and Warburg, 1948).

81 R. A. Hall, jr, *Pidgin and Creole Languages* (Ithaca: Cornell University Press, 1966); L. Todd, *Pidgins and Creoles* (London: Routledge and Kegan Paul, 1974); D. Hymes (ed.), *Pidginization and Creolization of Languages* (Cambridge: Cambridge University Press, 1971); Valdman (1977); J. A. Holm, *Pidgins and Creoles*, 2 vols (Cambridge: Cambridge University Press, 1988); S. Romaine, *Pidgin and Creole Languages* (London: Longman, 1988).

82 Whiteley (1969); J. Fabian, *Language and Colonial Power* (Cambridge: Cambridge University Press, 1986).

83 U. Hannerz, *Cultural Complexity* (New York: Columbia University Press, 1992).

1

The Jargon of the Schools

PETER BURKE

Today, university teachers, like the members of other professions, are often accused of speaking and writing jargon and ordered to stand in 'Pseuds' Corner'. The phenomenon of academic jargon – more exactly, the jargon of workers in particular 'fields' rather than of the profession as a whole – is sometimes explained by the over-specialization and competition of the modern academic world, the proliferation of new disciplines, journals and university departments and the consequent need for individuals and groups to mark out and defend their intellectual territory and to distinguish themselves from their competitors. Unintelligibility, we are told, is now at a premium.[1]

Such relatively new developments may encourage jargon, but the phenomenon – or the accusation anyway – goes back at least as far as the ancient world, as we shall see. What is more, despite changing circumstances and contexts, the essential criticisms have remained more or less constant, not to say repetitive, over the last two thousand years or so. This brief account of a form of discourse still virtually unexplored by historians, linguists and philosophers will concentrate on the sixteenth, seventeenth and eighteenth centuries. Needless to say, it will be selective rather than comprehensive, the primary aim being to place in context both the phrase 'jargon of the schools' and the wider debate in which it was coined.

So far as I have been able to discover, the exact English phrase was first used in 1688 by Matthew Prior, in an ode, written while he was at St John's College, Cambridge, exposing the vanity of learning as 'empty cant, all Jargon of the schools'.[2] Prior's example was followed almost immediately by John Locke, who asserted in *Concerning Human Understanding* (1690) that 'Modern philosophers . . . have endeavoured to throw off the Jargon of the Schools, and speak intelligibly.'[3]

Locke's point had, however, been made a generation earlier by Thomas Hobbes in his *Leviathan*, whose account of words which 'signify nothing' includes 'hypostatical, transubstantiate, consubstantiate, eternal-Now, and the like canting of Schoolmen' ('canting' being used here in the traditional sense of that term, to refer to slang rather than hypocrisy).[4] Elsewhere in his treatise Hobbes dismissed the terms 'Abstract Essences' and 'Substantial Forms' as 'Jargon'.[5]

Hobbes's purpose was, of course, to undermine (or, if late twentieth-century jargon be permissible, to 'delegitimate') the discourse of the 'School-Divines', as he called them – in other words, the theologians whose obscure political terminology, so Hobbes claimed, was respon-sible for the recent civil war.[6] To understand what Hobbes was doing it is necessary to place his book in context, or rather in multiple contexts, including both the political debates of his time and the seventeenth-century controversies over natural philosophy, topics to which we will return. It is equally necessary, however, to replace Hobbes's arguments, including his critique of academic jargon, in a long cultural tradition.

The classical tradition

Let us turn to this tradition, especially the tradition of the philosophers. I should have liked to have been able to show that their particular jargon came into existence at the time of the first professional teachers of philosophy, the sophists, thus illustrating the link between jargons and trades already discussed in the introduction to this volume.[7] The language of the sophists was indeed criticized by some of their con-temporaries, notably Plato, just as he criticized them (or made his protagonist Socrates criticize them) for 'merchandizing in knowledge'.[8] For example, the sophist Gorgias was described as one of those 'cunning artificers of speech' who 'make small things seem great and great things small by the power of their words', while the brothers Euthydemus and Dionysodorus were satirized for their disputatiousness and their dependence on quibbles and fallacies.[9] Plato's Socrates, by contrast, is presented as a plain man who speaks plain language, just as he chooses his analogies from ordinary life, from the work of midwives and shoemakers.

It should be noted, though, that Socrates' critique of 'sophistries' (*sophismata*) was directed against fallacies rather than jargon. For a precise technical vocabulary which might be condemned as jargon, or develop into jargon, we have to wait for Aristotle.

Aristotle, who defined science as 'right talking', was and is noted for the precision of his language and thought. His classification of types of argument or syllogisms encouraged self-consciousness and precision in others. Aristotle also coined a number of technical terms which passed into the common currency of Western philosophy, science and literary criticism, among them *aitia* (causes), *eidos* (form), *exis* (habit, disposition), *hyle* (matter), *idion* (property), *katharsis* (purging), *mimesis* (imitation, representation), *ousia* (being) and *symbebekos* (accident).[10]

Whether or not these technical terms provoked criticism in Greece in Aristotle's time is impossible to say, but the proper language of philosophy was certainly a subject of debate in the ancient world in the following centuries. Epicurus for example accused his colleagues of mouthing empty words. 'Vain is the word of a philosopher which does not heal any suffering of man.'[11] That he preferred ordinary to technical language is suggested by the discussion dramatized in Cicero's *Academica*. In this dialogue Varro defends the use of 'new words' (*verba nova*) by the academic school of philosophy, contrasting it with that of the followers of Epicurus, such as Amafinius and Rabirius, who discuss philosophical problems 'in ordinary language' (*vulgari sermone*) and 'in an amateur manner' (*nulla arte*), in other words, without definitions and distinctions.[12]

Echoes of this debate rumbled on in the later Roman world. Seneca argued, like Socrates and Epicurus, that the purpose of philosophy was to teach us how to live, and that over-subtle distinctions (*cavillationes*) and 'carping disputations' (*captiosae disputationes*) were an unwelcome distraction from important matters.[13] *Captio* had been a neutral term, translating the Greek *sophismata*, but in some mouths at least it was turning pejorative.

Speaking from the point of view of a specialist in the art of oratory in his textbook on the subject, the Roman writer Quintilian offered a complementary argument. According to him, it was breaking the rules of rhetoric to introduce syllogisms into a speech. Quintilian also warned orators against what he called 'that unhappy use of fine distinctions' (*infelix illa verborum cavillatio*) in their speeches. These technical procedures broke his fundamental rule, that oratory should follow linguistic usage (*consuetudo*), that is, the ordinary language of educated men.[14]

The Middle Ages

Despite Quintilian's advice, in the course of the Middle Ages Latin-speaking philosophers gradually created a set of technical terms, many of them translations from Aristotle's Greek. *Substantia* (substance) and *qualitas* (quality) go back to the sixth century, to Boethius (who adapted them from the Roman grammarian Priscianus). *Substantialis* goes back to the middle of the ninth century, together with *substantificus* (creative). So does *essentia* (essence), translating Aristotle's *ousia*, and bringing with it *essentialis* (essential) and *essentialitas*; *accidens* (what is not essential), translating Aristotle's *symbebekos*; *forma* (form), translating Aristotle's *eidos*; and *habitus*, translating Aristotle's *exis*. (One does not normally think of Pierre Bourdieu as an Aristotelian, but his concept of 'habitus' does indeed derive ultimately from Aristotle via the schoolmen and the art historian Erwin Panofsky.)

However, it was in the twelfth and thirteenth centuries, the great age of scholasticism, that these basic Aristotelian terms were elaborated into an intricate system of neologisms, a 'jargon of production', as Walter Nash calls it (see above, p. 14). The study of metaphysics, for instance, produced its own vocabulary, including *ens* (being, another version of Aristotle's *ousia*); *quidditas* (essence or, more literally, whatness); *quidditativus* and *substantivus* (both meaning essential; and *haecceitas* (thisness), a term coined by the fourteenth-century philosopher Duns Scotus to refer to what we might call the 'specificity' of things.

Again, the study of logic spawned such new nouns as *ampliationes* (extensions), *coniunctiones* (conjunctive propositions), *disiunctiones* (disjunctive propositions), *exponibilia* (propositions capable of exposition), *insolubilia* (problems without solutions), *instantia* (example or exception), *modalia* (modal statements, involving either necessity or possibility), *notiones* (concepts), *relationes* (logical relations), *restrictiones* (restrictive propositions), *supposita* or *suppositiones* (hypothetical propositions), *universales* (universals) and so on, some of them bringing in their train still more terms – adjectives such as *supposibilis* (hypothetical), adverbs such as *suppositialiter* (hypothetically) and set phrases such as *in modo et figura*.[15] The terms *categorema* (category) and *syncategorema* (something unable to be a subject by itself) were adopted in their original Greek forms and meanings, while the word *sophismata* was adapted to refer to puzzling sentences from which students could learn.

As so often happens in the history of slang, or jargon, the activities of a new institution, in this case the medieval university, generated a variety of new words. The students themselves, once they had passed their preliminary examinations, became known as *sophistae*, and their debates as *disputationes* or *obligationes* (compulsory exercises). To debate formally, in syllogisms, was 'to syllogize' (*syllogizare*). The place in which the debates were held was known as *scholae* (the schools), as in the Divinity Schools at Oxford and the Old Schools in Cambridge, names which have remained current to this day. The teachers became known as *scholastici* (the schoolmen). (The abstract noun 'scholasticism' is a much later coinage, which in English dates from the mid eighteenth century.)[16]

In an essay on language it is worth emphasizing that the Latin terminology described above was in oral as well as written currency. Indeed, the culture of scholasticism, and more generally that of the medieval university, was primarily oral, based on the lecture and the disputation, with reading and writing playing only a secondary role. The Latin of the schoolmen was a kind of lingua franca, like the English of scientists today, allowing students to move from one country to another yet continue to follow lectures or to engage in disputations.

The Renaissance: humanists versus schoolmen

During the Renaissance a group of scholars, writers and philosophers, known today as the 'humanists', came to reject the technical terminology of their academic colleagues in increasingly forthright terms.[17] Before attempting to explain why this should have been the case, it may be useful to examine exactly what it was that the humanists rejected, paying attention to the precise language of this critique of language.

Francesco Petrarcha (Petrarch), often described as the first humanist, seems to have been the first to denounce, in the middle of the fourteenth century, what he called 'the crazy and clamorous sect of scholastics', though more for the content – or lack of content – of their arguments than for their language. What he disliked in the scholastics, besides their 'insignificant little conclusions', was the way in which they supported these conclusions by means of fallacious arguments or 'caviling'.[18] Petrarch's follower Leonardo Bruni, who learned Greek and retranslated Aristotle's *Ethics* and *Politics* into Latin, was more concerned with the defects of the vocabulary of the schoolmen, witness the speeches he gave to his friend Nicolò Nicoli in his *Dialogues*.[19]

The most thorough and elaborate critique of this vocabulary is found in the work of Lorenzo Valla, a humanist with particularly strong views on language. Valla had had to leave the University of Pavia after denouncing what he considered to be the barbarous Latin of the lawyers there. His *Elegance of the Latin Language*, an introduction to classical Latin for the use of schools, claimed that Latin both rose and declined with the Roman Empire. His *Dialectical Disputations* (1439) was a diatribe against scholastic philosophy, essentially from the point of view of a rhetorician, one who admired Quintilian and shared his opinion that the ordinary usage of educated men should set linguistic norms.[20]

In his *Disputations* Valla tells his readers that whenever they are debating with a philosopher and he uses obscure terms, as such men commonly do, they should insist on clarity.[21] These men, who have replaced the traditional way of speaking (*veterum consuetudo loquendi*) by their new terms (*nova vocabula*) are like poisoners, and they must return to ordinary language (*naturalis sermo*).[22] He goes on to criticize specific neologisms, among them *quidditas* and *ens*. Whether or not Valla should be described as an 'ordinary language philosopher' in the late twentieth-century sense of that phrase is a controversial question (to which we must return). However, he certainly appealed to common usage on occasion. Whereof one cannot speak in Ciceronian Latin, he seems to be saying, thereof one should be silent.[23]

These criticisms of the language of the schoolmen were often repeated and occasionally elaborated by later humanists. Around 1480, for instance, the Netherlander Alexander Hegius wrote an invective against the *modistae*, a variety of scholastic philosopher characterized by their concern with the logical forms of the syllogism, charging them with writing barbarously (*barbare*) and of corrupting Latin with their 'vicious abuses of words' (*viciosae vocabulorum abusiones*).[24] For similar reasons, in a letter of 1485 to his fellow-humanist Giovanni Pico della Mirandola the Venetian Ermolao Barbaro describes the schoolmen as 'barbarians' using a new form of words (*genus verborum novum*) which is not only unintelligible to ordinary people, but so confused that even the 'initiates' do not understand one another.[25]

In the 1490s the French scholar Jacques Lefèvre d'Étaples singled out for criticism the terms '*suppositiones, ampliationes, restrictiones, appellationes, exponibilia, insolubilia, obligationes*', as well as rejecting the 'scholastic style' (*sophisticam expositionem*) more generally. Lefèvre identified the schoolmen of his day with the sophists of ancient Greece (an identification facilitated, as we have seen, by the coinage of the term *sophista*), and quoted Socrates' condemnation of the brothers Euthydemus and Dionysodorus (see above, p. 23).[26]

Such criticisms were to become increasingly common in the age of Erasmus. In his popular *Moriae Encomium* (*Praise of Folly*; 1511), for instance, Erasmus mocked the philosophers who claim to see 'universals, separate forms, prime matters, quiddities, ecceities', and the theologians with their 'newly-coined expressions and strange-sounding words'.[27] In a letter of 1518 he returned to the assault on the followers of Duns Scotus and William of Ockham and their 'prickly' and unintelligible language (literally *inextricabilis*, in other words, impossible to disentangle), selecting for condemnation such terms as *instantia, formalitates, quidditates* and *relationes*.[28]

The Valencian Juan Luis Vives, an admirer of Valla and a follower of Erasmus, launched a full-scale attack on the schoolmen of Paris in particular in his *In pseudodialecticos* (*Against the Pseudo-logicians*; 1520), summing up the criticisms of their philosophy and their language made by earlier humanists. They had, he claimed, invented 'a new language which only they themselves understand', a 'convoluted' language including terms like *suppositiones, ampliationes, restrictiones, coniunctiones, disiunctiones*. This language was barbarous, corrupt, 'depraved' (*depravata*) and 'unclean' (*immunda*). In the tradition of Quintilian and Valla, Vives stigmatized the linguistic practices of the logicians as an offence against 'common sense and ordinary language' (*communis hominum et sensus et sermo*) and 'the customs and usage of humankind' (*omnem hominum consuetudinem et usum*).[29] Pierre de la Ramée (Ramus) made a similar point in an oration against the separation of philosophy and rhetoric, picking out the same examples as Vives and Lefèvre before him – 'Suppositiones, Ampliationes, Restrictiones, Ascensiones, Descensiones, Exponibilia, Insolubilia, Obligationes'.[30]

Martin Luther, who had some sympathy for the humanist movement, put forward similar criticisms of Aristotle and his followers, more especially the contamination of the language of theology by their terminology. In similar fashion Beatus Rhenanus, who was both a Lutheran and a humanist, took exception to theologians who wrote of the Trinity, for instance, using such terms as *essentia, persona, supposita, notiones* and *relationes*. Beatus recommended a return to the usage of the early fathers of the Church such as Tertullian, whose work he edited in 1521.[31]

It was a brilliant comic writer, himself an admirer of Erasmus, who turned these criticisms into parody, caricature and fiction. In his *Gargantua* (1534) François Rabelais made the schoolman Janotus de Bragmardo deliver a speech in a Latinate French full of jargon-phrases like 'substantificque qualité' and 'nature quidditative'.[32] It only remained for someone to use the term 'jargon'. This term was extending its meaning, as we have seen (see above, p. 25), in the later sixteenth century. Geoffroy Tory and Jacques Tahureau applied the term to Latinized French, Henri Estienne applied it to the language of the court and Michel de Montaigne to the language of the college (*jargon de collège*), almost certainly a reference to scholastic philosophy.[33]

Throughout the later Renaissance the criticisms continue. They become so repetitive that it is virtually pointless to discuss them person by person, though a few comments on Italy, France and England, where the criticisms are particularly frequent, may be useful. In Italy the anti-scholastic tradition of Petrarch and Valla continued into the sixteenth century, witness the rise of a series of pejorative terms such as *cavillazioni, sofisterie, sofisticherie, sofisticaggine, scolasticherie, scolasticaggine* or *scolasticumi* (the Italian language has a genius for contemptuous word-endings).

In the French-speaking world we find Calvin rejecting *captions et vaines sophisteries*, the Calvinist nobleman Marnix de St-Aldegonde denouncing *syllogiseurs* and the neo-stoic philosopher Guillaume Du Vair remarking on the audacity of *subtils cavillateurs*.[34] As in the age of Seneca (see above, p. 24), technical terms were employed to criticize technical terms, or jargon to describe jargon. 'Captious' and 'cavilling' were the favourite adjectives to describe the practice of raising frivolous objections, a practice associated with lawyers and scholastic philosophers alike.

In England the reformer William Tyndale criticized scholastic interpreters of the Bible who 'rend and tear the scriptures with their distinctions', only to be criticized in his turn by Thomas More for his 'frivolous cavillations and sophisms'.[35] Quiddities were stigmatized with renewed vigour by Protestant writers such as Richard Taverner and William Fulke. Fulke also coined the phrase a 'distinction without a difference', while Thomas Nashe, whose linguistic inventiveness is notorious, contributed 'syllogistry' and 'syllogistical'.[36]

It is time to attempt to interpret the significance of these criticisms. It would not be difficult to make a case for the use of most of the technical terms which so irritated the humanists, above all the terms used in the study of logic. And yet, so far as I am aware, no supporter of scholastic philosophy has ever tried to make this case and so meet the critics on their own linguistic ground, emphasizing the contribution of technicalities to clarity. It is difficult to decide whether to explain this lack of response by the schoolmen by a lack of confidence on their part or by the exact opposite, for they may have been so sure of themselves – since they continued to dominate the universities – as to consider refutation unnecessary. For historians of language, on the other hand, the issue is not to justify these terms but to try to understand why it was that the humanists condemned them.[37]

The essential point to make here is that the attack on scholastic jargon was part of a more general criticism of the culture of the 'Middle Ages', the epoch from which the humanists believed they were emerging and against which they defined themselves. In a sense, it was they who constructed both the Middle Ages and the schoolmen in the process of rejecting them, since medieval people did not know that they were medieval, and scholastic philosophers did not see themselves as scholastic philosophers, but as members of rival groups such as realists, nominalists, Scotists and so on.

The humanists rejected the language of the schoolmen as a form of 'linguistic novelty' (*nova vocabula*, in Valla's phrase, or *novitas sermonis*, according to Vives), which was contrary to the return to classical antiquity of which they dreamed. They associated the Middle Ages with the barbarian invaders of the Roman Empire, especially the Goths (neatly eliding all that distinguished and separated the fifth century from the fifteenth). The revival of classical Latin, entailing the rejection of medieval neologisms, was part of a much wider movement to revive classical norms and forms.

The attack on scholastic logic was particularly fierce because the humanists were for the most part practitioners of the rival discipline, rhetoric. The conflict between logic and rhetoric – or, more generally, between philosophy and literature, a conflict which goes back at least as far as Plato – entered a particularly acute or at least a particularly self-conscious phase in the Renaissance.[38] The humanists were philologists, specialists in words, and they were very much concerned with literary grace, fluency and elegance. Some of their objections to scholastic philosophy were objections on aesthetic grounds, as the recurrent term 'barbarous' reveals. Like the schoolmen, the humanists were concerned with persuasion, but to achieve this goal they preferred the open hand of rhetoric to the closed fist of logic.[39]

Thus apparent trivialities, the term *suppositiones*, for instance, are best viewed as symbols of major differences in intellectual priorities, and even in world-views. Indeed, to humanists, for whom the reform of language was a necessary step to the reform of the world, these disputes did not even appear to be 'trivial' (a term which originally expressed humanist contempt for the *trivium*, the combined study of grammar, logic and rhetoric in which logic had been given the dominant place).

Words versus things

Despite the campaign mounted by the humanists, scholastic philosophy and theology did not disappear from European universities in their time.

Even in the seventeenth century the language of academic argument – like the organization and curriculum of the universities – retained many medieval elements.[40] Hence it should be no surprise to discover that the attack on the jargon of the schoolmen by seventeenth- and also eighteenth-century writers and thinkers often sounds like a continuation of the humanist tradition.

Hobbes, for example, criticized the 'strange and barbarous words' in 'the writings of School-Divines', 'the frivolous distinctions, barbarous terms and obscure language of the schoolmen'. Like Valla, he picked on the term *ens*, or, more generally, on 'Entity, Essence, Essential, Essentiality'. Thomas Sprat's uncomplimentary remarks on 'the philosophy of the schoolmen' also include a reference to 'the barbarousness of their style'.[41] Sir William Temple described the decline of classical Latin in the Middle Ages into 'a certain Jargon ... that passed among the Monks and Friars ... and among the students of the Several Universities'.[42] In similar fashion, in the middle of the eighteenth century the article on the schools ('École') in the *Encyclopédie* refers to their *termes barbares*.[43]

Other criticisms of the schoolmen were moral, condemning them for teaching 'how to dispute rather than how to live', as the preacher John Preston put it. They were often rebuked for 'wrangling' or 'jangling', in other words, quarrelling, their disputations being identified with disputes. Thus William Dell denounced 'wrangling, jangling, foolish and unprofitable philosophy', while his Cambridge colleague the Platonist Henry More charged the 'School-divines' with what he called 'fruitless disputacity'.[44] These charges too followed the tradition of humanists such as Erasmus; indeed, they went back much further, to the criticisms of the sophists made by Socrates, Epicurus and Seneca.

However, a closer reading of Hobbes and his contemporaries suggests that the humanist tradition had been reconstructed. Aesthetic terms such as 'barbarous' became relatively rare. The main point of the seventeenth-century criticisms was not that the language of the schools was clumsy, but that it was, as Hobbes puts it, 'senseless and insignificant' (that is, 'meaningless'). It serves only to mystify, to conceal the speaker's ignorance. It is not so much a 'jargon of production', to return to Walter Nash's useful distinction, as a 'jargon of pretension'. For example, Hobbes draws attention to the circularity of the statement that bodies rise because of their lightness or sink because of their heaviness, 'which is as much as to say, that bodies descend or ascend because they do'.[45] In similar fashion, Molière was soon to mock the physician who claimed that opium put people to sleep because it had the 'sleep-making virtue' (*virtus dormitiva*; cf. Roy Porter, p. 56 below).

In short, the debate was shifting from the aesthetic ground of elegance and barbarism to the philosophical ground of the relation between words and things. In Francis Bacon's famous image, often repeated by his followers, the schoolmen were like spiders, spinning webs of words from inside themselves rather than deriving them from the world around them.[46] Thus John Wilkins, putting forward his scheme for 'a Real Character and a Philosophical Language', or a universal language 'exactly suited to the nature of things', claimed that his invention would unmask 'many wild errors, that shelter themselves under the disguise of affected phrases', and 'pretended mysterious, profound notions, expressed in great swelling words'.[47]

For a vivid illustration of this concern with concrete things one might turn to John Webster's notorious attack on the English universities, *Academiarum examen* (1654). Mixing linguistic, moral and theological criticisms into a heady rhetorical brew, Webster described academic debate as a series of 'needless, frivolous, fruitless, trivial, vain, curious, impertinent [that is, irrelevant], knotty, ungodly, irreligious, thorny and hell-hatched disputes, altercations, doubts, questions and endless janglings'. Scholastic logic he rejected as 'a civil war of words' repeated parrot-fashion, 'vaporous and airy', without substance, pure show, the 'vainglory of syllogizing sophistry'. Aristotle he faulted as a philosopher who was 'merely verbal', full of 'affected obscurity', his 'words, terms, definitions, distinctions and limitations' having nothing to do with 'nature it self'.[48]

That final reference to nature reminds us that we have reached the age of what historians call the 'scientific revolution'. Webster and others like him wanted to reform the educational system and give more space to what they called 'natural philosophy', in other words, science. In the same way, in his essay *Of Education* (1644) John Milton criticized the universities as old-fashioned, 'not well recovered from the scholastic grossness of barbarous ages', since they 'present their novices at their first coming with the most intellective abstractions of logic and metaphysics'. Thirty years later he put forward similar criticisms in *Of True Religion* (1673), which argued that the Bible itself was 'plain and perspicuous', but that it had been obscured by 'Scholastic Notions' and 'Sophistic Subtleties'.[49] It may be tempting to dismiss Milton's objections as a case of the pot calling the kettle black, since his own vocabulary was full of unusual and difficult terms, like the adjective 'intellective' just quoted, but the general turn against scholastic language cannot be dismissed so easily.

A concern with nature, then, was coming to replace a concern with words. All the same, the natural philosophers did concern themselves with words, as a means if not as an end, precisely because they believed that words obscured the face of nature. Thus Thomas Sprat's *History of the Royal Society* (1667) called for an English academy, on the Italian and French model, in order to produce 'a great Reformation in the manner of our speaking and writing'. The point of the reform was to aid the study of nature by avoiding 'the colours of rhetoric', 'pomp of words', 'luxury and abundance of speech', 'vicious abundance of phrase' or, in Sprat's most famous sentence, by adopting 'a close, naked, natural way of speaking . . . bringing all things as near the mathematical plainness as they can'.[50] Wilkins's philosophical language had the same purpose. Thomas Burnet's *Theory of the Earth* (1684) offered concrete examples of what natural philosophers like Sprat were trying to root out. Burnet dismissed the traditional language of 'radical' and 'innate' heat and moisture as 'but a sort of cant'.[51]

Writers on religion made the same kind of point as writers on natural philosophy. The Cambridge Platonist Ralph Cudworth declared that 'When Religion and Theology . . . is made Philosophy, then is it all mere jargon and insignificant nonsense.'[52] In similar fashion a generation later, Jonathan Swift warned against the 'obscure terms' used by clerics, including the philosophical 'entity' and 'attribute' as well as the theological 'omniscience' or 'beatific vision'.[53]

These criticisms of the language of the schoolmen were summed up in a magisterial manner by John Locke (cf. Roy Porter, below, p. 51). In his analysis of human understanding Locke rejected such concepts as 'substantial forms', which were never 'thought on by any, but those who have in this one part of the world, learned the language of the Schools'.[54] They were abuses of language, 'insignificant terms', 'empty sounds' or 'affected obscurity', a form of 'learned gibberish' associated in particular with 'the Schoolmen and Metaphysicians'.[55]

Where the humanists were content to describe, denounce and reform barbaric language, seventeenth-century intellectuals also offered a theory of jargon, explaining it in terms of deceit (see above, p. 32). Locke called the language of the schoolmen a web 'to cover their ignorance', while Wilkins claimed that his philosophical language would expose 'the many impostures and cheats that are put upon men under the disguise of affected insignificant phrases', and the pseudo-profundities 'whereby some men set up for reputation'.[56]

These criticisms were not confined to England. The French writer Poullain de la Barre, for instance, in his plea for the equality of the sexes, criticized the obscurity and confusion of the language of the savants, adding that this was often the only reason for their intellectual dominance: 'ce n'est souvent que par cette qualité qu'ils dominent et qu'ils attirent la créance des personnes simples et crédules'.[57] In

Germany Christian Thomasius dismissed what he called *Scholastische Pedanterey*, while his colleague Ulrich Huber, in an oration of 1688 whose theme was also pedantry, took the terms *quidditas* and *haeceitas* – yet again – as 'vices which smell of the schools' (*vitii, quod scholas tantum redoleant*) and examples of 'the affectation of grand and sonorous words' (*affectatio grandium sonantiumque verborum*).[58]

In the next century David Hume would dismiss what he called 'mere scholastic quibbles' as 'unworthy of our attention', together with 'all that jargon which has so long taken possession of metaphysical reasonings and drawn disgrace upon them'. In a famous passage he urged the burning of works of 'school metaphysics', since they contained 'nothing but sophistry and illusion'.[59] The *Encyclopédie* of Diderot and d'Alembert summed up these criticisms of 'the language of the schools' (*langage de l'école*). Scholastic philosophers, it claimed, had 'substituted words for things, and frivolous or ridiculous questions for the great aims of true philosophy', the words condemned including 'universals, categories, predicaments, metaphysical degrees, second intentions, the abhorrence of a vacuum, etc.'. In a single damning phrase the schoolmen were accused of 'using empty words' (*ne dire que des mots*).[60]

British poets of the eighteenth century regularly attacked the language of scholastic philosophy. Matthew Prior has already been quoted (above, p. 22). His example was followed by John Pomfret's rhetorical question: 'What's all the noisy jargon of the schools / But idle nonsense of laborious fools?'[61] Pomfret was in turn followed by James Thomson, whose *Seasons* (1726–30) described Bacon as liberating 'true philosophy' from 'the gloom / Of cloister'd monks, and Jargon-teaching Schools'.[62] From a rather different point of view, that of a religious anti-intellectualism, the English poet William Cowper offered a similar-sounding criticism in his poem 'Truth' (1782). Cowper praised the peasants for their faith and humility: 'To them the sounding jargon of the schools / Seems what it is – a cap and bells for fools.'[63] Soon after Cowper, Robert Burns used the phrase in his 'Epistle to J. Lapraik' (1785), but in his case it was to contrast learning with 'parts' or inspiration: 'What's a' your jargon o' your schools, / Your Latin names for horns and stools; / If honest Nature made you fools?'[64] The appeal of the rhyme between 'schools' and 'fools' appears to have been irresistible.

Amateurs versus professionals

There were at least three main reasons for the rejection of the jargon of the schools in early modern Europe. Besides the humanist concern with elegance of language and the empiricist preference for things rather than words, there was also what might be described as a social motive, a distrust of or even a contempt for professionals on the part of cultivated amateurs of higher status.[65] This contempt is explicit in the linguistic standards formulated by French men of letters in the age of classicism, a purification of language which excluded 'low' words, whether they came from the lower classes, the provinces or the professions. It is implicit in the English phrase 'to talk shop', with its association between technical terms and tradespeople. Indeed, in a recent study of science and civility in the seventeenth century it has been argued that the rejection of pedantry by the Royal Society expressed, or at any rate appropriated, gentlemanly contempt for 'traditional scholarly modes of discourse'.[66]

For a relatively early and gentle example of this distrust of technical terms we may turn to count Baldassare Castiglione's famous *Cortegiano* (*Courtier*; 1528). At one point in the discussions of the perfect courtier two of the male participants in the dialogue begin to use Aristotelian concepts, evoking a protest from the *animatrice* of the group, Lady Emilia: 'For the love of God ... forget your matters and forms, and speak intelligibly.'[67] Since women were excluded from higher education, the use of these technical terms in mixed company was obviously an offence against the rules of good conversation. However, the dialogue often makes several points at once, and the author, who was himself educated at court and not at university, may well have intended to imply a more radical criticism of the unintelligibility of the jargon of the schools.

At all events, it was increasingly stigmatized as a form of pedantry. It seems to have been at this time that the term 'pedant', originally applied to a private tutor, acquired its current meaning. The pedant certainly appears as a figure of fun in a series of European comedies from F. Belo's *Il pedante* (1529) to J. F. Deshayes's *Le Pédant* (1748) and beyond. These tutors were accused of more than pedantry, and the symptoms of pedantry were not purely linguistic, but one of the characteristics for which these characters were mocked was their strange language, Latinate and smelling of the schools.[68]

As Montaigne's disciple Pierre Charron once put it, one should write intelligibly and directly and not 'scholastically or pedantically' (*scholastiquement ou pédantesquement*).[69] To be avoided was what Samuel Butler described in *Hudibras* (1663) as 'a Babylonish dialect / Which learned Pedants much affect'.[70] As we saw in the introduction, the Prince of Condé and the Duke of Orléans went so far as to fine members of their households for using terms that 'savoured . . . of the Schools'.

Similar warnings were issued in guides to good behaviour, success at court and polite conversation in the seventeenth and eighteenth centuries. Nicole Faret, in his *Honnête Homme* (1630), told his noble readers that they needed to study, but not 'to embroil themselves in all the disputes of philosophers'. In other words, no wrangling.[71] Obadiah Walker, writing *Of Education* (1673), warned young gentlemen against pedantry, defining a pedant as one who 'importunately, impertinently and with great formality, shows his learning in scraps of Latin and Greek' or discusses 'matters too subtle and curious' in ordinary company.[72]

If these warnings seem rather general or anodyne, let us turn to the stigmatization of syllogisms. One might have thought it otiose to warn readers against introducing syllogisms into conversation, but some seventeenth- and even eighteenth-century writers felt the need to do so. One criticized academics who want 'to prove everything by means of unanswerable arguments' and imagined one of them interrupting a conversation to complain that the participants were failing to employ syllogisms.[73] As late as the 1720s Adam Petrie, who was known as 'the Scottish Chesterfield', and J. C. Nemeitz, who was writing for noble visitors to Paris, felt that they needed to warn readers against the use of syllogisms in conversation, especially when ladies were present. Introducing 'the precepts of Aristotle and Descartes' will only give the impression of pedantry.[74]

It is difficult to fault this example, but it may be worth underlining the wider implications of this kind of recommendation. The jargon of the schools was considered inappropriate in polite conversation because ladies and gentlemen do not need to trouble their heads with philosophy, or any matters intellectual. It may be above their heads, but they are in turn above all that. This was not the point of Valla's criticisms, or those of Erasmus, or indeed of Diderot, who imagined dialogues set in high society in which the participants discussed the nature of the universe.

A submerged tradition

With the decline of scholastic philosophy in the eighteenth century, criticism of the language of the schoolmen obviously became superfluous. All the same, it is not unusual, even in our own century, to come across criticisms of the jargon of academics in general and philosophers in particular which seem to echo the keywords of the tradition whose history I have been trying to write. Whether the critics are aware of this history is difficult to say. If not, we may reasonably describe the tradition to which they belong not only as reconstructed, but also as submerged, below the level of consciousness. This idea of a submerged tradition may be illustrated by some examples from the recent history of philosophy.

In Britain the most distinctive philosophical movement of the century has been what is called 'linguistic philosophy'. The positive side of this movement is exemplified in the work of John Austin, who begged his colleagues to pay attention to ordinary language and 'the plain man' and avoid what he called 'the jargon of extinct theories'.[75] It was this aspect of the movement, a movement that 'abhors "shop"', which Ernest Gellner described with his usual irony as 'a philosophic form eminently suitable for gentlemen', the 'plain man' turning out in practice to be the academic resident in north Oxford.[76] From this point of view, Austin offers a late example of the cult of the amateur, the anti-professionalism discussed in the preceding section.

As for the negative side of the movement, it may be illustrated from R. G. Collingwood's critique of philosophers (presumably symbolic logicians) who employed what he dismissed as 'typographical jargon', or from Alfred Ayer's famous *Language, Truth and Logic* (1936), a little book devoted to what the author describes as 'the elimination of metaphysics'. The main objection to 'the metaphysician' (F. H. Bradley, for example, or Martin Heidegger) is that 'he produces sentences which fail to conform to the conditions under which alone a sentence can be literally significant'.[77] In plain language the charge is one of using words which are meaningless or, as Hobbes would say, 'insignificant'. Even the polemical tone of Ayer's essay is reminiscent of predecessors such as Hobbes and Valla. One of Ayer's examples has already occurred frequently in these pages: it is 'substance', stigmatized as a fictitious entity.[78] The parallel with the attack on the schoolmen will be obvious. Ayer is of course aware of the philosophical tradition running back through Russell to Hume, but he takes it no further than the eighteenth century.

Heidegger was also one of the targets of Theodor Adorno's essay *Der Jargon der Eigentlichkeit* (*The jargon of authenticity*; 1963), in which the author complained about the spread of terms, such as 'encounter', 'commitment', 'concern', 'genuine dialogue' and so on, 'from philosophy to theology – not only of Protestant academies – to pedagogy, evening schools and youth organizations, even to the elevated diction of the representatives of business and administration'. Like some of the seventeenth-century critics of the schoolmen quoted above, Adorno is interested in the employment of academic jargon 'as a means of power'.[79] In this case, however, the kind of jargon employed is rather different. It is the language of sincerity and authenticity which has become 'mechanical' as it has spread to 'the mass of the authentics', as Adorno cruelly describes them.[80] Adorno's complaint is part of a general critique of industrialization, the bourgeoisie and 'mass society'. For this reason, his work makes a good point at which to end – or to return to the contemporary criticisms of the jargon of academics with which this essay began.

Notes

1 Recent discussions include R. T. Lakoff, *Talking Power: The Politics of Language* (New York, 1990), ch. 8; W. Nash, *Jargon Its Uses and Abuses* (Oxford: Blackwell, 1993).

2 M. Prior, *Works*, 2nd edn (Oxford: Oxford University Press, 1971), 1: 68.

3 Locke, *Concerning Human Understanding* (London, 1690), 3.4.9.

4 T. Hobbes, *Leviathan* (1651), ed. A. D. Lindsay (London: Dent, 1914), 1.5, 4.46.

5 Hobbes (1651), 4.46.

6 Ibid., 2.18. Cf. T. Sprat, *History of the Royal Society* (London: J. Martyn and J. Allesby, 1667), 42.

7 On the 'professionalism' of the sophists, W. K. C. Guthrie, *A History of Greek Philosophy*, 5 vols (Cambridge: Cambridge University Press, 1962–81), 3: 35ff.

8 Plato, *Sophist*, 223–4. For all classical texts I have used the bilingual Loeb editions, but references are given to books and chapters rather than to pages. References to Plato are given in the traditional manner to the Estienne edition.

9 Plato, *Phaedrus*, 28; *Euthydemus*, 271–307.

10 There are helpful remarks on the language of Aristotle in J. H. Randall, *Aristotle* (New York: Columbia University Press, 1960), ch. 3, and a basic glossary in G. E. R. Lloyd, *Aristotle: The Growth and Structure of his Thought* (Cambridge: Cambridge University Press, 1968), 318.

11 C. Bailey (ed.), *Epicurus: The Extant Remains* (Oxford: Oxford University Press, 1926), 133.

12 Cicero, *Academica*, 1.2.

13 Seneca, *Epistolae*, 45.5.

14 Quintilian, *Institutio*, 5.14, 10.7.14, 1.6.43–5.

15 R. E. Latham (ed.), *Revised Medieval Latin Word-list* (London, 1965); cf. W. Kneale and M. Kneale, *The Development of Logic* (Oxford: Oxford University Press, 1962), 209, 222, 227–30, 254–60. I was unable to find any study of the language of the schoolmen.

16 N. Kretzmann et al. (eds), *The Cambridge History of Later Medieval Philosophy* (Cambridge: Cambridge University Press, 1982), esp B. H. Dod, 'Aristoteles latinus', 45–79.

17 B. P. Copenhaver and C. S. Schmitt, *Renaissance Philosophy* (Oxford: Oxford University Press, 1992).

18 F. Petrarch, 'On His Own Ignorance and That of Many Others', in E. Cassirer (ed.), *The Renaissance Philosophy of Man* (Chicago: Phoenix, 1948), 108, 135–6.

19 Cf. H. Baron, *The Crisis of the Early Italian Renaissance* (Princeton: Princeton University Press, 1955), 226–44.

20 L. Valla, *Opera Omnia* (1540; repr. Turin, 1962), 1: 643–761; on this work, S. Camporeale, *Lorenzo Valla: Umanesimo e Teologia* (Florence: Istituto nazionale di studi sul Rinascimento, 1972), 101–71; R. Waswo, *Language and Meaning in the Renaissance* (Princeton: Princeton University Press, 1987), 88–113; Copenhaver and Schmitt (1992), 214ff.

21 See the first version of the prologue to bk 3 in Camporeale (1972), 193.

22 The second version of the prologue, in Valla (1540), 731.

23 R. Waswo, 'Motives of Misreading', *Journal of the History of Ideas*, 50 (1989), 324–32; J. Monfasani, 'Was Lorenzo Valla an Ordinary Language Philosopher?', *Journal of the History of Ideas*, 50 (1989), 309–23; Waswo (1989); Copenhaver and Schmitt (1992), 214–27.

24 A. Hegius, 'Invectiva in modos significandi', ed. J. Ijsewijn, *Forum for Modern Language Studies*, 7 (1971), 306–18, esp. 308.

25 E. Barbaro, 'Epistola', in M. Crusius, *Elementa* (Basel: Oporinus, 1567), 593.

26 E. Rice (ed.), *The Prefatory Epistles of Jacques Lefèvre d'Étaples* (New York: Columbia University Press, 1972), 6, 39.

27 D. Erasmus, *Moriae Encomium* (1511), English trans. as *Praise of Folly* (Harmondsworth: Penguin, 1971), 152–5.

28 P. S. Allen (ed.), *Opus Epistolarum Erasmi* (Oxford: Oxford University Press, 1906–58), no. 858.

29 J. L. Vives, *In pseudodialecticos* (1520), ed. C. Fantazzi (Leiden: Brill, 1979), 27, 29, 35, 41, 49, 69, 77; cf. E. Garin, *La cultura filosofica del Rinascimento italiano* (Florence, 1961), 472–4; Waswo (1987), 113–33; Copenhaver and Schmitt (1992), 203–14.

30 P. Ramus, *Pro philosophica disciplina* (Paris: David, 1551), 91.

31 J. D'Amico, 'A Humanist's Critique of Scholasticism', *Archiv für Reformationsgeschichte*, 71 (1980), 37–62, 43.

32 F. Rabelais, *Gargantua* (1534), in his *Oeuvres*, ed. J. Boulenger (Paris: Bibliothèque de la Pléiade, 1959), ch. 19.

33 H. Estienne, *Deux dialogues* (1578), ed. P. M. Smith (Geneva: Droz, 1980); M. de Montaigne, *Essais*, 1 (1580), in his *Oeuvres*, ed. A. Thibaudet (Paris: Bibliothèque de la Pléiade, 1939), ch. 37.

34 J. Calvin, *Institution de la religion chrestienne* (1st French edn 1541), ed. J. D.

Benoît, 5 vols (Strasburg: Strasburg University Press, 1957–61), bk 6, sect. 431.

35 W. Tyndale, *Works* (London: J. Day, 1572–3), 1.46; T. More, *Works* (New Haven: Yale University Press, 1961–), 8: 425.

36 R. Taverner, *The Garden of Wisdom* (London: W. Teletson, *c*.1540): W. Fulke, *D. Heskins . . . Overthrown* (London: G. Bishop, 1579); T. Nashe, *Works*, ed. R. B. McKerrow, 5 vols (London: Sidgwick and Jackson, 1910).

37 Garin (1961).

38 P. O. Kristeller, *Renaissance Thought and Its Sources*, ed. M. Mooney (New York: Columbia University Press, 1979), pt 5.

39 W. S. Howell, *Logic and Rhetoric in England, 1500–1700* (Princeton: Princeton University Press, 1956).

40 W. T. Costello, *The Scholastic Curriculum at Early Seventeenth-century Cambridge* (Cambridge, Masso: Harvard University Press, 1958).

41 Sprat (1667), 16.

42 W. Temple, 'Essay on Ancient and Modern Learning' (1690), repr. in his *Essays*, ed. J. E. Spingarn (Oxford: Clarendon Press, 1909), 24.

43 D. Diderot (ed.), *Encyclopédie* (1751–80; repr. in 5 vols, New York: Readex Microprint Corporation, 1969), s.v. 'École'.

44 Preston (1628); W. Dell, *Testimony against Divinity Degrees* (London: G. Calvert, 1653), 29; More (1660), 69, 472.

45 Hobbes (1651), 4.46–7.

46 F. Bacon, *The New Organon* (1620), ed. F. Anderson (Indianapolis: Bobs-Merrill, 1960), no. xcv; J. Webster, *Academiarum examen* (London: G. Calvert, 1654), 15, 33, 84; Sprat (1667), 18; Locke (1690), 3.10.8.

47 J. Wilkins, *An Essay Towards a Real Character and a Philosophical Language* (1668; repr. Menston: Scolar Press, 1968), dedication. Cf. T. Davies, 'The Ark in Flames: Science, Language and Education in Seventeenth-century England', in A. E. Benjamin et al. (eds), *The Figural and the Literal* (Manchester: Manchester University Press, 1987), 83–102.

48 Webster (1654), 15, 33, 38, 40, 63, 67.

49 J. Milton, *Complete Prose Works*, 8 vols (New Haven: Yale University Press, 1953–82), 2: 374, 8: 425.

50 Sprat (1667), 39, 41, 62, 111–13.

51 T. Burnet, *The Theory of the Earth* (London: W. Kettilby, 1684), 1: 214.

52 R. Cudworth, *The True Intellectual System of the Universe* (London, 1678), 1.5.651.

53 J. Swift, 'Letter to a Young Gentleman', in *Works*, 13 vols (Oxford: Blackwell, 1939–59), 9: 63–81, at 66.

54 Locke (1690), 3.6.24.

55 Ibid., 3.10.2, 3.10.6, 3.10.9.

56 Ibid., 3.10.8.; Wilkins (1668), dedication.

57 F. Poullain de la Barre, *De l'égalité des deux sexes* (1673), ed. and trans. A. D. Frankforter and P. J. Mormon (Lewiston: Mellen, 1989), 42.

58 U. Huber, in C. Thomasius, *Introductio ad philosophicam aulicam* (Halle: Renger, 1702), 277–8.

59 D. Hume, *Treatise on Human Nature* (1739), ed. L. A. Selby-Bigge (Oxford: Oxford University Press, 1888), 1.2.2; D. Hume, *Enquiries* (1777), ed. L. A. Selby-Bigge (Oxford: Oxford University Press, 1894), 2. 17, 12.3.

60 Diderot, (1751–80), s.v. 'École', 'Aristotélisme'.

61 J. Pomfret, *Remains* (London, 1724), 3.

62 J. Thomson, 'Summer' (1727), in his *Seasons*, ed. J. Sambrook (Oxford: Oxford University Press, 1981), 130, line 1544.

63 W. Cowper, 'Truth' (1782), in his *Poetical Works*, ed. H. S. Milsford, 4th edn (London: Oxford University Press, 1967), 38.

64 R. Burns, 'Epistle to J. Lapraik' (1785), in his *Poems and Songs*, ed. J. Kinsley (Oxford: Oxford University Press, 1969), 67.

65 Cf. N. Elias, *The Civilizing Process* (1939), English trans, 2 vols (Oxford: Blackwell, 1981–2), 1, 36–7.

66 S. Shapin, *The Social History of Truth* (Chicago: Chicago University Press, 1994), 124.

67 B. Castiglione, *Il cortegiano* (1528), ed. B. Maier (Turin, 1964), 3.17.

68 Cf. M. Lazard, *La Comédie humaniste* (Paris: PUF, 1978), 252–5.

69 P. Charron, *De la sagesse* (Bordeaux: Millanges, 1601), Preface.

70 S. Butler, *Hudibras* (1663), ed. J. Wilders (Oxford: Oxford University Press, 1967), pt 1, canto 1, lines 93–4.

71 N. Faret, *L'Honnête Homme* (1630), ed. M. Magendie (Paris, 1925), 40.

72 O. Walker, *Of Education* (1673; repr. Menston: Scolar Press, 1970), 249–50.

73 Chalesme (1671), 198–9.

74 A. Petrie, *Rules of Good Deportment* (1720), repr. in his *Works* (Edinburgh, 1877), 5–136, at 58; J. C. Nemeitz, *Séjour de Paris* (Leiden, 1727), 134.

75 J. L. Austin, *How to Do Things with Words* (Oxford: Oxford University Press, 1961), 35, 37, 130.

76 E. Gellner, *Words and Things* (London: Gollancz, 1959), 238–40.

77 R. G. Collingwood, *Autobiography* (1939: Oxford: Oxford University Press, 1970); A. J. Ayer, *Language, Truth and Logic* (1936), 2nd edn (London, 1946), 35; on Bradley and Heidegger, 36, 43.

78 Ayer (1936), 42.

79 T. W. Adorno, *Der Jargon der Eigentlichkeit* (1963), English trans as *The Jargon of Authenticity* (Evanston, 1973), 5–6.

80 Adorno (1963), 49.

2

'Perplex't with Tough Names': The Uses of Medical Jargon

ROY PORTER

Beware of language, for it is often a great cheat.
Peter Mere Latham, *Lectures on Subjects Connected with Clinical
Medicine, Comprising Diseases of the Heart*

The professional ideal requires that practitioners of the liberal vocations should use their privileges responsibly, dealing fairly with clients and upholding ethical standards amongst peers.[1] Exploitation or aggrandizement through individual or collective malpractice spells abuse of that trust; precisely because professionals enjoy arcane knowledge, however, they are particularly well placed to blind their clients with jargon.[2] Involving an admixture of what Walter Nash has dubbed 'show talk' and 'shop talk',[3] jargon doubtless has its legitimate uses as a trade shorthand; but willy-nilly it also generates mystifying verbiage opaque to the public. Professional soils are well prepared for its luxuriant growth and, as pointed out throughout this volume, jargon has flourished in many fields, not least the law and the Church, where the Protestant Reformation sought to cleanse the faith of the quiddities of scholastic theology while also abjuring the magical aura assumed by mere words (hocus-pocus) in the Roman Catholic liturgy.[4]

Medicine has been no exception to such linguistic miasmatism. 'The sociologist and financial experts have a jargon that is all their own and it keeps them from being found out,' James Murphy once pointed out; 'the majesty of the law is upheld in like manner and the medical craft could not survive if it prescribed its medicines and described its diseases in the vernacular.'[5] Resort to extravagant or enigmatic expressions to blind with science has long been the target of medical satire. In Thomas Middleton's early seventeenth-century play *A Faire Quarrell* the Colonel, wounded in a duel, is discovered prostrate on a couch. Intercepting the attending surgeon, his sister asks, 'What hope is there?'

SURGEON: Hope, *Chillis* was scapt miraculously lady.

SISTER: Whats that sir.

SURGEON: *Cava Vena*: I care but little for his wound 'ith *orsophag*, not thus much trust mee, but when they come to *diaphragma* once, the small *intestines*, or the *Spynall medull*, or i' th rootes of the *emunctories* of the noble parts, then straight I feare a *syncope*; the flankes retyring towards the backe, the urine bloody, the excrements *purulent*, and the colour pricking or pungent.

SISTER: Alasse, I'me neer the better for this answer.

SURGEON: Now I must tell you his principal *Dolour* lies i' th region of the liver, and theres both inflamation and *turmefaction* fear'd marry, I made him a *quadrangular plumation*, where I used *sanguis draconis*, by my faith, with powders *incarnative*, which I temperd with oyle of *Hypericon*, and other liquors mundificative.

SISTER: Pox a your mundies figatives, I would they were all fired.

SURGEON: But I purpose lady to make an other experiment at next dressing with a *sarcotrike, medicament*, made of *Iris* of Florence. Thus, *(masticke,) calaphena, apoponax, sacrocalla.*

SISTER: Sacro-halter, what comfort is i' this to a poore gentlewoman: pray tell me in plaine tearmes what you thinke of him.

SURGEON: Marry in plaine tearmes I know not what to say to him, the wound I can assure you inclines to *paralisme*, and I find his body *cacochymicke*: being then in fear of fever and inflamation, I nourish him altogether with *viands refrigeratives* and give for potion the juyce of Savicola, dissolv'd with water *corefolium*: I could doe noe more lady, if his best *guiguimos* were dissevered.[6]

Exchanges of this kind between pompous, prating practitioners and uncomprehending auditors formed a comic stock-in-trade. Around the same time Thomas Dekker coined the phrase 'a gibberish surgion', while the playwright John Wilson has a character recount of an injured man, 'as far as I conjecture, the greatest danger of his wound, lies in the chirurgeon's hard words'.[7] Drawing on the same conceit, one of Ben Jonson's characters, Peni-Boy, describes a doctor as a 'canter' – that is, one who indulges in canting or recondite jargon:

> When he discourseth of dissection,
> Or any point of anatomy: that hee tells you,
> Of *vena cava*, and of *vena porta*,
> The *meseraicke*, and the *mesenterium*,
> What does he else but cant? Or if he runne
> To his judiciall astrologie,
> And trowle the Trine, the Quartile, and the Sextile,
> Platicks aspect, and Partile, with his Hylef
> Or Alchcochoden, Cuspes, and Horroscope.
> Does he not cant? Who here does understand him?[8]

Long open to attack from wits accusing it of using empty or enigmatic language, the profession has occasionally launched campaigns to purge its nomenclature. But so long as one man's otiose jargon is another's serviceable technical terminology, critiques of vacuous verbiage in the name of sober science will continue to produce (to many eyes) only new crops of obfuscation.

The proper language of medicine has ever been a matter of fierce debate. For some, the upholding of traditional terms has been paramount; for others, such as seventeenth-century populist reformers challenging the tyranny of Greek and Galen, medical writing must be in the vernacular; for others, medical progress inevitably involves neologisms;[9] for still others, the value of certain arcane terms and formulae has consisted in their distinctive magico-psychological healing power, though once again, satirists have mocked such descent into medical magic.[10] Ben Jonson's Compasse declares,

> The doctor is an asse then, if hee say so,
> And cannot with his conjuring names, Hippocrates,
> Galen, or Rasis, Avicen, Averroes,
> Cure a poore wenches falling in a swoune:
> Which a poore farthing chang'd in rosa solis,
> Or cynnamon water would.[11]

It is debates between these different positions that this essay will chart.

All trades spawn insider talk, and medicine is no exception. Subtle recommends in Ben Jonson's *Alchemist*:

Infuse vinegar,
To draw his volatile substance and his tincture:
And let the water in glass E be filt'red,
And put into the gripe's egg. Lute him well;
And leave him closed in balneo.

FACE: I will, sir.

SURLY: What a brave language here is! next to canting.[12]

Shop talk wears a double face. 'One of the constant butts of ridicule, both in the old comedies and novels, is the professional jargon of the medical tribe,' remarked that avid observer of trade mysteries, William Hazlitt, but he came to its defence:

> Yet it cannot be denied that this jargon, however affected it may seem, is the natural language of apothecaries and physicians, the mother-tongue of pharmacy! It is that by which their knowledge first comes to them, that with which they have the most obstinate associations, that in which they can express themselves the most readily and with the best effect upon their hearers; and though there may be some assumption of superiority in all this, yet it is only by an effort of circumlocution that they could condescend to explain themselves in ordinary language.[13]

Yet what is natural, spontaneous and inoffensive from within is likely to appear bombastic and crafty to outsiders. No friend of the medical tribe in general, Pliny the Elder was particularly trenchant in his criticisms of physicians' neologisms. 'There is no doubt,' he declared in his *Natural History*,

> that all these, in their hunt for popularity by means of some new gimmick, trafficked for it with our lives. This is the cause of those wretched, quarrelsome consultations at the bedside of patients, when no doctor agrees with another, in case he may appear to acknowledge a superior. This is also the case of that unfortunate epitaph on a tomb: 'He died from an overdose of doctors'. Medicine changes every day, again and again it is revamped, and we are swept along on the puffings of the best brains of Greece. It is obvious that anyone among them, who acquires the power of speaking, immediately assumes supreme control over our life and death, just as if thousands of people do not in fact live without doctors, though not without medicine, as the Roman people have done for more than six hundred years.[14]

The Roman natural historian was especially hostile to medical half-truths and linguistic evasions, precisely because physicians had quite unjustifiably arrogated to themselves a character for professional honesty. 'Whosoever professeth himself a physician,' he noted,

> is straightwise believed, say what he will: and yet to speak a truth, there
> are no lies dearer sold or more dangerous than those which proceed out of
> a Physician's mouth. Howbeit, we never once regard to look at that, so
> blind we are in our deepe persuasion of them, and feed ourselves each one
> in a sweet hope and plausible conceit of our health by them.[15]

Over the centuries it was inevitably quacks who were most relent-
lessly accused of spellbinding rodomontades: indeed, verbal pyrotech-
nics, involving elaborate claptrap with a technical ring and a foreign air,
were *ipso facto* taken as symptoms of quackery. Quack jargon came in
two guises. It was either *sui generis*, unique to the individual patterer, or
it might have degenerate echoes of regular scholarly terminology.[16] The
eighteenth-century travelling oculist John (Chevalier) Taylor exploited
the prestige of another mode of trade talk – Latin – by constructing an
original English prose style combining high-flown terms with a Latinate
syntax and an inverted word order ('Of the eye on the wonders lecture
will I'), maintaining he held forth in 'the true Ciceronian, prodigiously
difficult and never attempted in our language before'.[17]

Taylor could make capital in this way because Latinate vocabulary
continued to dominate anatomy, physiology and pharmacy, being
supposedly precise and pristine. Latinisms also carried authority in
other departments of medicine. Like fellow academics and divines,
medical men Latinized their personal names. Hence the Italian
Gabriello Falloppio became Fallopius, the Fleming Andreas van
Wesele, Vesalius and the Frenchman François de le Boë, Sylvius.

Within orthodox medicine, jargon has operated in various ways. It
may be salesmanship designed to impress; it may serve to inflate
authority and create awe; or it may function as a smokescreen, especially
when involving formulaic utterances meaning something other than
meets the ear. At the end of the Second World War Franklin D. Roosevelt's health, as his inner circle of advisers knew all too well, was
deteriorating rapidly. Dr Ross McIntire, his personal physician published a book, *White House Physician* (1946), to allay reports that the
President was more gravely ill than McIntire had admitted and to
counter the suggestion that Roosevelt's senior physicians had withheld
this information from the American public. McIntire's campaign of
disinformation about the presidential health was conducted through
selective use of statements that were essentially true but incomplete. 'To
his credit,' it has been said in exoneration of the physician, 'McIntire
never lied about Roosevelt's condition. He told the truth, but in

language that could easily be misleading.' Medical jargon has become an essential ingredient of media management.[18]

'Show talk' jargon – medicalese designed to dazzle or obfuscate – has naturally hinged upon its impact on its hearers. The great cartoonist Thomas Rowlandson dramatized the possibility of its backfiring by presenting in his print *JACK, Hove Down – With a Grog Blossom Fever* a confrontation between a sick sailor and his physician, each trapped within his characteristic trade. In the engraving a thin, elderly doctor crouches by a cannon before a drunk and pocky seaman lying sick in his hammock. Both figures typify their occupations, with their peculiarities of dress and their (to a layman) incomprehensible speech. The old-fashioned doctor wears a powdered wig, spectacles and a cocked hat. In his left hand he carries a box of pills, in his right a bottle labelled 'a Sweat', and a gold-headed cane is tucked under his arm. His pocket bulges with a bottle labelled 'Jollop' and a clyster, while beside him is a pestle and mortar and two cannonballs (popularly dubbed 'pills'). 'Hold – I must stop your Grog Jack,' he exclaims: 'it excites those impulses, and concussions of the Thorax, which a company [*sic*] sternutation by which means you are in a sort of a kind of a Situation – that your head must be Shaved – I shall take from you only – 20 ozs of Blood – then swallow this Draught and Box of Pills, and I shall administer to you a Clyster.' Wearing a seafarer's striped shirt and neckerchief, the sailor responds, 'Stop my Grog. – Belay there Doctor – Shiver my timbers but your lingo bothers me – You May batter my Hull as long as you like, but I'll be d– 'nd if ever you board me with your Glyster pipe.'[19] The joke here is of the *de te fabula narratur* kind: the jargoneer gets a taste of his own medicine – and both parties appear equally absurd.

Over the centuries medicine has been able to enhance its authority thanks to its claim to unique power to name and explain the hidden parts and interior processes of the human frame.[20] Well into the eighteenth century, clinicians perforce worked largely with the expressions for the body and its maladies that their patients tendered: they had little alternative. This can be seen from a remarkable study by the medical historian, Barbara Duden, of nearly two thousand women from Eisenach in Saxony, whose illnesses were logged in the casebooks of their physician, Johann Storch. Storch's early eighteenth-century patients experienced their insides as sites of astonishing changeability. Patients might claim, for example, that the disappearance of freckles caused their breath to stink; their sweat sometimes smelled of urine; if they failed to menstruate, they developed diarrhoea, they said, or the delayed discharge came out as bloody sputum. Almost any bodily process could turn into any other. The interior was thus a magic mixer, a

source of limitless metamorphosis. Bodies had to flow to be healthy. In
an agrarian society preoccupied with changes in the weather, soil and
seasons, the system beneath the skin was viewed as equally fluid, a
succession of transactions: digestion, fertilization, evacuation, parturi-
tion. What counted was not structures but processes.

Aware of the processes going on out of sight in their insides, the
Saxon women gave Dr Storch very 'subjective' and vernacular accounts
of their illnesses. They complained, Duden notes, of the following
ailments:

> Slight headache, darkness of the eyes, a feeling that their hair was falling
> out or sight was fading or hearing was disappearing, a tearing in the jaw, a
> dizzy and dull headache, heavy tongue and speech, toothache, nosebleed,
> a flux in the ear, hiccups, a sore throat, a rising in the throat and
> constriction of the same, contraction of the throat, withdrawing of the
> gum, bilious vomiting, choking, hoarseness and coughing, phlegm drip-
> ping from the head onto the throat, neck pains, tightness of throat,
> sweating of the head, gloominess of thoughts, sadness. Searing pain in the
> limbs, numbness in the arm, trembling, tingling in the limbs, numb hands,
> cramped hands, crushed limbs, heaviness in the arm, stirring in the arm,
> apoplexy in the right arm, tearing fluxes in the limbs, fright in the limbs,
> painful gout. A rising of the blood toward the breast, shortness of breath,
> a tight shortness of breath, choking in the breast, stinging pains around the
> breast, anxiety, fearfulness, a wooden stake in the heart, squeezing in the
> pit of the heart, heart anxiety, a pain in the breast that felt as though
> something was eating inside, anxiousness, throbbing of the heart, burning
> under the breastbone. Painful womb colic, womb fear, womb anxiety,
> womb trouble, cramps, a cold womb that was open too wide, a knot in the
> womb, a closed-in wind turning toward the womb, a womb cramp
> manifesting itself mostly in the mouth and in the tongue and rendering the
> latter useless for speaking. A swollen body, thick belly and rumbling,
> upward rising wind, downward moving wind, stagnating wind, stomach
> cramps, a rising from the stomach, rattling in the body, griping in the
> body, a feeling as if everything was turning about in the body, a fluttering
> sensation in the lower body, a body full of wind and water, burning the
> stomach, constipation, burning pain in the side, pain around the area of
> the liver, pleurisy, spleen fear, pain in the soft part of the belly like a cold
> stone, fits of the evil thing, stone colic, raging pain in the hip, urge to
> urinate, knots on the buttocks, lameness in the back, sensitive pains in the
> back, loins, and hips, stoppage of urine, pressing of feces. Feet and knees
> that are stiff and lame, sensitive pain in the shin, heat in the feet, swollen
> legs, swollen varicose veins, pains in the foot as though the blood itself was
> trying to force its way out, cold feet, a bad foot.[21]

It is an exhausting catalogue, and that is the point. These women experienced practically no discrete 'diseases' of the kind unambiguously identifiable by the diagnostic tests that modern medicine runs. Rather they noted, *in lay terms*, highly personal changes that they could feel and which, being strange and painful, incommoded and frightened them. They suffered 'diseases' but not 'disease', and their physician accepted their disease terms *in their language* – he had no preferable alternative.

This situation was to change, and in this process the adoption of formal physical examination by the medical profession was an important factor and marker, permitting the consolidation of disease taxonomies independent of the terms traditionally used by sufferers. Physical examination, which crystallized during the nineteenth century, revolved round a sequence of highly stylized acts performed by the doctor – feeling the pulse, sounding the chest, taking blood pressure, inspecting the throat, taking the temperature and so forth – all of which bypassed the sick person's tale of his or her condition and so facilitated the entrenchment of an independent professional jargon. Medical shop talk thereby overprinted the language of the patients, in a development contributing to and illustrating the more general withdrawal of elite from popular culture during the eighteenth and early nineteenth centuries.[22] On the basis of a study of the Bristol region Mary Fissell has pointed out that practitioners were content, around 1750, to use vernacular terms like 'chill', 'feverish' and 'hoarse' in writing case records; by 1820, however, their successors had gone over to professional jargon terms like 'cynanche' or 'peripneumonia'. At the Bristol Infirmary in the 1770s, she has noted, 70 per cent of diagnoses were in English; by 1800, however, 79 per cent were in Latin. Growing use of a more Latinate medical jargon marked the fact that a rising percentage of the physicians involved were graduates, resulting in a more academic *esprit de corps*.[23]

To say this is not to imply that the old medical language died out. Rather it was relegated to the status of a lay idiom – one, in practitioners' eyes, based largely on folk medicine and superstition and on misunderstanding of human anatomy, physiology, pathology and pharmacology. Of course, many lay expressions utterly excluded from the speech of physicians are still in circulation: the patients may say that they feel a 'stitch' in their side or a 'crick' in their neck or 'heartburn'. If these terms get into medical records at all, they are put in quotation marks.[24]

The turn of the nineteenth century thus saw medical jargon becoming separated from lay idiom, paralleling the widening gulf between elite and popular culture at large. An American author noted for his perspicacity with words commented upon this process. 'There is no counting the names', wrote Herman Melville,

> that surgeons and anatomists give to the various parts of the human body ... I wonder whether mankind could not get along without all those names, which keep increasing every day, and hour, and moment; till at last the very air will be full of them; and even in a great plain men will be breathing each other's breath, owing to the vast multitude of words they use that consume all the air ... But people seem to have a great love for names; for to know a great many names seems to look like knowing a good many things.[25]

To Melville, multiplication of nebulous words was the sin of the sciolist, for science proper lay in material realities. 'A man of true science', he argued, 'uses but few hard words, and those only when none other will answer his purpose; whereas the smatterer in science ... thinks, that by mouthing hard words, he proves that he understands hard things.'[26]

But Melville's desideratum – a science of simplicity – could not easily be accomplished, as the needs and wants of both sides of the medical encounter, public and practitioners alike, began to diverge in striking ways. The new sensibility, with its related bowdlerizing tendencies, spurred the progress of medical euphemism amongst the polite and the propertied. 'People of wealth and rank', wrily observed the Revd Sydney Smith, 'never use ugly names for ugly things. Apoplexy is an affection of the head; paralysis is nervousness; gangrene is pain and inconvenience in the extremities.'[27] Euphemisms were useful to bedside doctors. Certain canny old physicians, commented the late nineteenth-century American physician Oliver Wendell Holmes,

> have a few phrases always on hand for patients that will insist on knowing the pathology of their complaints without the slightest capacity of understanding the scientific explanation. I have known the term 'spinal irritation' serve well on such occasions, but I think nothing on the whole has covered so much ground, and meant so little, and given such profound satisfaction to all parties, as the magnificent phrase 'congestion of the portal system'.[28]

The phenomenon Holmes identified has, of course, mushroomed. The medical profession has often been guilty of evading unpleasant issues by using euphemisms like 'growth' for cancer or 'problem' for alcoholism; indeed, a recent writer on medical language has maintained that 'it is only common decency to avoid, when possible, such emotionally charged words as *cancer, epilepsy, underdeveloped,* and *senile*'.[29]

Over the years, many physicians have striven to create a technical language, free from the taints of the popular tongue and possessing the virtue of precision. 'Clear and precise definition of disease,' argued the great eighteenth-century surgeon Percivall Pott, 'and the application of such names to them as are expressive of their true and real nature, are of more consequence than they are generally imagined to be: Untrue or imperfect ones occasion false ideas; and false ideas are generally followed by erroneous practice.'[30]

All the while, the profession has attempted to police its linguistic style.[31] Seventeenth-century medicine vehemently rejected scholastic jargon, and such leading reformers as Robert Boyle attempted to weed and prune medical lingo.[32] Physician no less than philosopher, John Locke was enthusiastic for purifying professional language of what he dubbed '*learned Gibberish*', complaining of the 'several *wilful Faults and Neglects*, which Men are guilty of, in this way of Communication, whereby they render these signs less clear and distinct in their signification, than naturally they need to be'. In particular he rejected the tendency of philosophers and men of science to '*coin* new Words' as substitutes for precise thought.[33]

Locke's attempts to cleanse language, and to tie words down to things, became a battle-cry of the Enlightenment. The *philosophe* Condillac and the physician Cabanis both followed Locke and, on empiricist grounds, urged a purge of terminological excrescences, so as to raise medico-scientific idiom to something akin to the precise language of mathematics or chemistry.[34]

The same purifying spirit fired an attempt early in the twentieth century to purify medical language of infelicities. Sir Clifford Allbutt, Regius Professor of Physic at Cambridge University, produced *Notes on the Composition of Scientific Papers*, which denounced creeping medical jargon.[35] Warning against extravagant formalism, foreign importations and 'gaudiness' – even the term 'foreword' was culpable, he judged – Allbutt denounced jargon for encouraging muddled or woolly thinking.[36] A little earlier 'appendicitis' had been omitted from the *Oxford English Dictionary* because the Regius Professor of Physic at Oxford advised its editor, James Murray, that it was pure jargon that would not last. (Eleven years later the word won universal acceptance when Edward VII's coronation had to be postponed because of the removal of his appendix.)[37]

The great American medical editor Morris Fishbein also attempted a campaign of linguistic cleansing. In *Medical Writing, the Technic and the Art* (1938) Fishbein lambasted jargon, sloppy speech, slang and 'solecisms'.[38] In a section headed 'Medical Jargon' he complained:

Many words have found their way into medical vocabularies with unusual meanings that are not recognized even by medical dictionaries. Such writings may be characterized as medical jargon or medical slang. When these words appear in medical manuscripts or in medical conversation, they are unintelligible to other scientists, particularly those of foreign countries; they are not translatable and are the mark of the careless and uncultured person.[39]

Fishbein hounded jargon. It was unacceptable that slovenly interns should write of 'acute abdomen': the correct expression was 'acute condition with the abdomen'. Likewise the noun 'alcoholic' would not do: proper was 'alcoholic addict' or 'person with alcoholism'; 'cardiac patient' had to yield to 'patient with cardiac disease', and similarly 'diabetic' to 'person with diabetes' and 'epileptic' to 'person with epilepsy'. 'Flu' was unacceptable in medical writing – 'influenza' was the correct form. Nor was a doctor to write of a 'postmortem', but rather of 'autopsy' or 'necropsy'. 'Right heart' was to give way to 'right side of the heart', just as 'upper respiratory infection' must be abandoned for 'infection of the upper part of the respiratory tract'. Because 'biopsy is an examination of tissue,' noted the schoolmasterly Fishbein, 'it therefore is not correct to speak of "taking a biopsy"': rather one was to speak of 'taking a specimen for biopsy'.[40] Many other tricks of jargon riled him. 'It is incorrect', he insisted, 'to say that a patient had "no temperature." "No fever" or "no elevation of temperature" may be used, although it is perhaps better to say that the temperature is "normal" or "higher than normal" or "subnormal".'[41]

Crusading against jargon, Fishbein even objected – it may surprise us nowadays – to the use of the term 'case' as in 'the case had a fever' or 'thirty cases were admitted to the hospital'. These were not 'cases' but 'patients', a 'case' being 'an instance of disease, the totality of the symptoms and of the pathologic and other conditions'. Pulling rank as a medical editor, Fishbein warned: 'In the publications of the American Medical Association such usages are banned.'[42] Here hostility to jargon went beyond linguistic fastidiousness, having implications for medicine as a humanistic enterprise.

In place of such solecisms Fishbein proffered his 'Preferred Usages'. 'Humans' should make way for 'human beings' or 'man' (an intriguing reversal of today's political correctness), 'insanity' should yield to 'mental disease', 'individual' to 'person'.[43] Fishbein sought to root out medicalese, slang and lay terms in favour of correctness, but in retrospect it is clear that his recommendations would in turn have created a different form of jargon: a lifeless, stilted prose with the hollow ring of scientific gravity.

Fishbein also condemned the supposedly deplorable trend towards eponyms. 'On one page of an article on tabes,' he noted,

> appeared the following terms to indicate tests or reactions: Cheyne-Stokes, Babinski, Strümpell, Marie-Foix and Klippel-Weil. While it is historically interesting to have a sign, test, reaction or disease known by the name of its discoverer, it is in the interest of scientific medicine to use a descriptive term. Certainly, 'reflex rigidity of the pupil' is better then 'the Argyll Robertson pupil'; 'great toe reflex' is preferable to 'the Babinski sign'; 'exophthalmic goiter' is better then 'Basedow's disease.' When a discovery is credited to several writers, the matter becomes complicated by the fact that national pride may assign a different name to the disease in several different countries. What is known in England as Graves's disease is called Basedow's disease on the Continent except in Italy, where it is known as Flanjani's disease.[44]

In Fishbein's day another medical author grumbled at the existence of around six hundred such eponyms.[45] Sixty years later, their proliferation would, one expects, have left Fishbein apoplectic. The latest *Dictionary of Medical Eponyms*, which ranges from 'Abadie Sign', 'Aberhalden-Kauffman-Lignac Syndrome' and 'Achard-Thiers Syndrome' all the way through to 'Zuckerkandl Bodies', is 591 pages long. The compilers note that although 'over the years many people have condemned the use of eponyms in medical practice . . . eponyms are with us to stay whether the more fastidious like it or not'.[46]

Modern analysts of medical prose, perhaps bowing to the inevitable, tend to be more flexible about jargon than Fishbein. Like slang J. H. Dirckx has maintained technical argot cannot be stopped; it is a natural growth, with regional peculiarities and shifting conventions. The succinctness of many unconventional phrases lends them so strong an appeal that, in defiance of purists and pedants, they become legitimized by long usage. Such terms as 'Leukocytosis with a left shift', 'a high index of suspicion' and 'sick sinus syndrome' are all irregular in formation or eccentric in tone, Dirckx notes, but they have won acceptance because they are apt and vivid.[47]

So entrenched is medical argot that the physician has ceased to be aware how far it diverges from lay English. It is full of conventional words that have assumed unconventional meanings: for instance, a peptic ulcer 'refractory' to conservative management, an 'episode' of hypoglycemia, 'documented' pancreatitis, a pulmonary 'cripple' and 'classical' migraine. Lymphocytes are 'elevated', aspirin was 'incriminated' and we speak of 'heroic' doses and 'elderly' primigravida.[48]

Alongside such peculiarities of usage, medicine resounds with oro-
tund phraseology. Pithy English words are scrapped in favour of long-
winded and often nebulous phrases, so that neck becomes 'cervical
region' and bones are called 'osseous structures'. Some inflated terms
have been adopted as euphemisms, such as 'purulent material' for pus
and 'inguinal area' for groin.[49]

Dirckx has suggested reasons for such shop talk. Speaking in con-
clave, doctors must make complex ideas intelligible; talking amongst
themselves in front of patients, they will seek to make simple ideas
opaque. Most clinical teaching is done in the patient's presence, hence
physicians veil disagreeable subjects in cryptic double-talk. For instance,
before the patient doctors do not speak of a diagnosis of syphilis; they
use the archaic 'lues'. If the patient's heart is weak, they have spoken of
the 'cor'; if something is wrong with the liver, the 'hepar' is discussed. A
malignancy may be called a 'neoplasm', 'hemoglobin' or 'erythorcytes'
may be used to refer to blood; 'motor disorder' or 'dysrhythmic
episodes' to epilepsy; 'ketogenic disturbance of carbohydrate metabo-
lism' is diabetes mellitus.[50] The manufacture of new technical terms is at
its worst within psychiatry, resulting in psychobabble, especially the
endless lists of -*manias* and -*phobias*. Psychology and psychiatry are
especially vulnerable to jargon-creep, because the entities so labelled
have no visible, tangible reality, but are labels for processes, tendencies
and hypothetical entities – or, as many would say, mere fictions.[51]

There have always been medical iconoclasts, who insist on simple
language. 'I would never use a long word', announced Oliver Wendell
Holmes, 'where a short one would answer the purpose. I know there are
professors in this country who "ligate" arteries. Other surgeons only tie
them, and it stops the bleeding just as well.'[52] In all centuries there have
been many medical critics of the 'jargon of the schools'. In the 1730s the
Yorkshire physician William Hillary insisted that medicine must follow
the 'Method of reasoning from Data, founded upon Observations and
real facts',

> for if we once quit our Reason for Mystery, and abandon a just Method of
> Mechanical and Geometrical Reasoning, for the unintelligible terms of
> Occult Faculties and Qualities, with all such like Metaphysical and
> Chymical Jargon and Nonsense, heretofore too much used in the Schools;
> we must wander through endless Mazes, and dark Labyrinths, playing at
> Hazard with Men's Lives, and suffer ourselves to ramble wherever
> conceited Imagination, or whymsical Hypothesis will lead us.[53]

'Such vague terms, as hidden seizures, sympathies, irritations, revulsions, crises, antiphlogistics, nervous exhaustions, and others familiar to our mouths – what do they mean?' demanded Benjamin Ward Richardson towards the end of the nineteenth century, 'What are they worth? Where are the two men who shall give to them the same definition? What other science would foster or even permit, such ragged phraseologies?'[54] But the real deflation of medical jargon has come not from doctors, but from writers and satirists. In festive mood Rabelais – himself, admittedly, a medical man – disclaims as follows on his aspirations to bring solace to the afflicted through the manipulation of words:

> Sometimes I make a long speech to them, explaining what Hippocrates in a number of passages, but especially in the sixth book of his *Epidemics*, has to say concerning the profession of the physician, his remarks being addressed to his disciple; also what Soranus the Ephesian, Oribasius, Dr Galen, Hali Abbas and other later authors have to say on the same subject, regarding the patient's gestures, bearing, glance, touch, countenance, manners, personal appearance, facial cleanliness, clothing, beard, hair, hands, mouth – even going so far as to specify the care he should take of his nails, just as though he were about to play some amorous role or other ... or as though he were about to enter the martial lists to combat some powerful enemy. And to tell the truth, the practice of medicine has been very aptly compared by Hippocrates to a battle, or to a face with three characters; the patient, the physicians and the disease...
>
> Above all, the aforementioned authors have had special advice to give the physician concerning the words, remarks, discourses and conversations that should take place between him and the patients by whom he is summoned, the object being that all should tend to one end, namely, the cheering of the patient (without any offense to God) and the avoidance of anything that may in the least serve to make him sad.[55]

The classic debunking of traditional medicine as pure gammon came from Molière. In *Le Médecin malgré lui* Sganarelle, masquerading as a physician, is called to treat a girl who has supposedly been struck dumb. The girl's father has great faith in doctors, and Sganarelle offers a long harangue purporting to explain how the patient lost her speech:

> These vapours of which I was speaking, passing from the left side, where the liver is situated, to the right side where the heart is, finds that the lung, which we call armyan in Latin, communicating with the brain, which we call nasmus in Greek, by means of the vena cava, which we call cubile in Hebrew, meets in its path the abovementioned vapours, which fill the ventricles of the omoplate.[56]

Her father, Géronte, is impressed, but timidly questions the positions of the liver and heart. 'It seems to me that you place them opposite to where they are, that the heart is on the left side and the liver on the right.' 'Oh yes,' Sganarelle airily replies, 'it used to be that way, but we have changed all that and now we practise medicine according to quite a new method.'[57]

In *Monsieur de Pourceaugnac* long medical diatribes occur, and the physicians – real members of the faculty this time – express themselves in periphrasis. The two doctors lob long-winded compliments at each other, while establishing their different points of view. After being subjected to their interminable opinions, the bewildered 'patient', Monsieur de Pourceaugnac, asks, 'What a Devil wou'd ye be at, with your Gallymaufry and Blockheadisms?'[58]

Le Malade imaginaire was first produced in 1673. In the third intermezzo a medical examination and the conferring of a medical degree are burlesqued. The faculty subjects the candidate to rigorous questioning. One examiner asks:

> Demandabo causam et rationem quare
> Opium facit dormire.

To which the bachelor candidate replies:

> Mihi a docto doctore
> Demandatur causam et rationem quare
> Opium facit dormire.
>
> A quoi respondeo,
> Quia est in eo
> Virtus dormativa,
> Cujus est natura
> Sensus assoupire.

For this dazzling answer the candidate received the plaudits of the audience:

> Dignus, dignus est intrare
> In nostro docto corpore.
> Bene, bene, respondere.

Asked why rhubarb and senna purge and drive out bile, the candidate declares,

Quia est in illis
Virtus purgativa
Cujus est natura
Istas duas biles evacuare.[59]

Molière directed his medical satire against two different aspects of medicine. One concerned the physician as a person – his vanity, pride, ignorance and pomposity – while the other condemned the medical doctrines of the times. To some extent, of course, these two coincide.

Molière's parodic consultations found an English counterpart in Aphra Behn's *Sir Patient Fancy*. In Act 5 Sir Patient, the hypochondriac, has summoned a handful of physicians in an attempt to guide him back to health. There are Monsieur Turboon, a Fat Doctor, doctors from Amsterdam, Leyden and Brunswick, and Sir Credulous Easy disguised as a physician – six sons of Hippocrates, any one of whom could single-handedly slay his man. The sick man greets them all:

SIR PATIENT: You're welcome, sir, – Pray sit; ah. – Well sire, you are come to visit a very crazy sickly person, sir.

BRUNSWICK: Pray let me feel your pulse, Sir; – what think you gentlemen, is he not very far gone? –

AMSTERDAM: Every morning a dose of my pills Merda queor-usticon, or the amicable pill.

SIR CREDULOUS: Fasting?

LEYDEN: Every hour sixscore drops of adminicula vitae.

SIR CREDULOUS: Fasting too?

(Sir Credulous writes still.)

FAT DOCTOR: At night twelve cordial pills, gallimofriticus.

TURBOON: Let blood once a week, a glister once a day.

BRUNSWICK: Cry mercy, sir, you're a French man. – After his first sleep, threescore restorative pills, call'd cheatus redivivus.

SIR CREDULOUS: And lastly, fifteen spoonfuls of my aqua tetra-chymagogon, as often as 'tis necessary; little or no breakfast, less dinner, and go supperless to bed.

FAT DOCTOR: Hum, your aqua tetrachymagogon?

SIR CREDULOUS: Yes, sir, my tetrachymagogon; for look ye do ye see sir, I cur'd the Arch-Duke of Strumbolo of a gondileero, of which he dy'd, with this very aqua tetrachymagogon.

(Enter Sir Patient.)

SIR PATIENT: Well, gentlemen, am I not an intruder?
FAT DOCTOR: Sir, we have duly consider'd the state of your body;
                    and are now about the order and method you are to
                    observe.
BRUNSWICK: Ay, this distemper will be the occasion of his
                    death.
SIR CREDULOUS: Hold, brothers, I do not say the occasion of his
                    death; but the occasional cause of his death.[60]

Molière and others mocked old-fashioned jargon. The newfangled
jargon, especially the new language of the Royal Society, was also
ridiculed, notably in Thomas Shadwell's *Virtuoso*. 'Sit, I beseech you,'
Longvil tells Sir Nicholas Gimcrack, 'what new curiosities have you
found out in physick?'

SIR NICHOLAS: Why, I have found out the use of respiration, or
                    breathing, which is a motion of the thorax and lungs,
                    whereby the air is impell'd by the nose, mouth, and
                    wind-pipe, into the lungs, and thence expell'd farther
                    to elaborate the blood, by refrigerating it, and sepa-
                    rating its fulaginous steams.
BRUCE: What a secret the rogue has found out.
SIR NICHOLAS: I have found too, that an animal may be preserved
                    without respiration, when the wind-pipe's cut in two,
                    by follicular impulsion of air; to wit, by blowing wind
                    with a pair of bellows into the lungs.[61]

In *The Humourists* Shadwell similarly derided pseudo-medical mumbo-
jumbo:

CRAZY: Did not I put my self into your hands when it was first a
                    gonorrhea virulenta? Did not you by your damn'd French
                    tricks, your styptick-injections, and your turpentine-
                    clysters, suffer me to be chorde, to come to caruncles, to
                    the phymasii, caries, pubii, bubones, herniae.
RAYMUND: Nay, have you not driven his enemy out of the open field,
                    where he might have been easily conquer'd, into his
                    strong holds and garisons.
PULLIN: Ver vel, ver vel.
CRAZY: Is there any one symptome which I have not had? – Oh –
                    have I not had your carbuncula, acbrocordones, mer-

mecii, thymi, all sorts of ulcers superficial and profound, callus, cancerous, fistilous.

RAYMUND: Hey-brave Crazy! Thou has terms enough to set up two reasonable mountebanks.

CRAZY: Have I not had your pustulae, crustatae, and sine crustic verucae, cristae, tophi, ossis, caries, chyronya, telephia, phagaenia, disepulotica.

RAYMUND: What art thou going to raise the devil with these hard words?

PULLIN: Vel! and have I no cure all dese? Have I no given you de sweate, not in a damned English tub or hot-house, but I have taught you to sweat in de cradle, and vid spirit of vine in de Pape lanthorn, a la Francois, and taught you de use de Baine d'Alexandre.

CRAZY: And has all this done any thing but driven him to his winter quarters, where he domineers as much as ever? Oh I have him here.[62]

In the end, medicine must have a language. Jargon will not disappear, for in medicine as with other professions, it is demanded by a double impulse: the need for a technical terminology, and the taboos that the body and its diseases require. Nevertheless, the last word should be with Sir Ernest Gowers. Gowers, who died in 1966, became known as the great English advocate of the use of plain words. 'Some seventy years ago,' he wrote,

a promising young neurologist made a discovery that necessitated the addition of a new word to the English vocabulary. He insisted that this should be *knee-jerk*, and *knee-jerk* it has remained, in spite of efforts of *patellar reflex* to dislodge it. He was my father; so perhaps I have inherited a prejudice in favour of home-made words.[63]

The link from Sir William Richard Gowers to Sir Ernest Gowers captures the dialectic of medical jargon in a nutshell.

Notes

The quotation in the title is from James Shirley, *The Brothers*, Act 4.

1 For a traditional idealization, see A. Carr-Saunders, *The Professions* (Oxford: Clarendon Press, 1933); for a less rosy account, see Terence James Johnson, *Professions and Power* (London: Macmillan, 1972), and specifically for medicine, see Eliot Freidson, *Professional Dominance: The Social Structure of Medical Care* (Chicago: Aldine and New York: Atherton Press,

1970), and Jeffrey L. Berlant, *Profession and Monopoly: A Study of Medicine in the United States and Great Britain* (Berkeley: University of California Press, 1975).

2 Walter Nash, *Jargon, Its Uses and Abuses* (Oxford: Blackwell, 1993).

3 'Any study of this subject needs to take some account of the interplay of *shop talk* and *show talk*; jargon links the callings people follow with the impressions they try to create. Of the two, the phraseology of pursuits, invites the more sympathetic consideration, because even if we are sometimes baffled and irritated by technical terms – "terms of art", our ancestors would have called them – we can nevertheless understand that over the centuries mere shop talk has usefully and even pleasurably enlarged the general vocabulary of English' (Nash, *Jargon*, 7).

4 Keith Thomas, *Religion and the Decline of Magic: Studies in Popular Beliefs in Sixteenth- and Seventeenth-century England* (London: Weidenfeld and Nicolson, 1971).

5 James Murphy, Epilogue to Max Planck, *Where is Science Going?* (London: Allen and Unwin, 1933), 208.

6 Thomas Middleton, *A Faire Quarrell*, Act 4, quoted in Herbert Silvette, *The Doctor on Stage: Medicine and Medical Men in Seventeenth-century England*, ed. F. Butler (Knoxville: University of Tennessee Press, 1967), 269.

7 Thomas Dekker, *Wonder of a Kingdome*, Act 4; John Wilson, *Belphagor*, Act 4, quoted in Silvette, *The Doctor on Stage*, 269; see also Thomas Spaulding Willard, 'John Wilson's Satire of Hermetic Medicine', in Marie Mulvey Roberts and Roy Porter (eds), *Literature and Medicine During the Eighteenth Century* (London and New York: Routledge, 1993), 136–50.

8 Ben Jonson, *Staple of Newes*, Act 4, quoted in Silvette, *The Doctor on Stage*, 269.

9 Richard Asher called the 'disease' of coining new medical terms 'neologopoiesis': see Bernard J. Freedman, *Just a Word Doctor: A Light-hearted Guide to Medical Terms* (Oxford: Oxford University Press, 1987), 30. See also Kenneth Hudson, *The Dictionary of Diseased English* (New York: Harper and Row, 1977).

10 On medical magic, see W. G. Black, *Folk Medicine: A Chapter in the History of Culture* (London: Folklore Society, 1883); on hostility to dead tongues, see Andrew Wear, 'The Popularization of Medicine in Early Modern England', in Roy Porter (ed.), *The Popularization of Medicine, 1650–1850* (London: Routledge, 1992), 17–41; Andrew Wear, 'The Foundations of Cartesian Natural Philosophy', *Seventeenth-century French Studies*, xii (1990), 224–30.

11 Ben Jonson, *The Magnetic Lady*, Act 3 Scene 3 Lines 17–22, in *The Complete Plays of Ben Jonson*, ed. G. A. Wilkes (Oxford: Clarendon Press, 1982), iv: 523.

12 Ben Jonson, *The Alchemist*, Act 2 Scene 3 Lines 37–42, in *The Complete Plays of Ben Jonson*, iii: 263.

13 William Hazlitt, 'Old Pedantry', in *The Round Table* (London: Dent, 1936), 81.

14 Pliny the Elder, *Natural History*, bk xxix. See Vivian Nutton, 'Murders and Miracles: Lay Attitudes Towards Medicine in Classical Antiquity', in Roy Porter (ed.), *Patients and Practitioners: Lay Perceptions of Medicine in Pre-industrial Society* (Cambridge: Cambridge University Press, 1985), 23–54.

15 Pliny, *Natural History*, bk xxix.

16 This is documented in Roy Porter, 'The Language of Quackery in England, 1660–1800', in P. Burke and R. Porter (eds), *The Social History of Language* (Cambridge: Cambridge University Press, 1987), 73–103.

17 John Taylor, *History of the Travels and Adventures* (London: J. Williams, 1761), 22. For these themes, see Roy Porter, *Health for Sale: Quackery in England 1650–1850* (Manchester: Manchester University Press, 1989), ch. iv, esp. 67.

18 Jerold M. Post and Robert S. Robins, *When Illness Strikes the Leader: The Dilemma of the Captive King* (New Haven: Yale University Press, 1993), 90.

19 Reproduced in Kate Arnold-Forster and Nigel Tallis (comps), *The Bruising Apothecary: Images of Pharmacy and Medicine in Caricature* (London: Pharmaceutical Press, 1989), 68, pl. 66: *JACK, Hove Down – With a Grog Blossom Fever.*

20 On the question of matching names to interior organs and functions, see Drew Leder, *The Absent Body* (Chicago and London: University of Chicago Press, 1990).

21 Barbara Duden, *The Woman Beneath the Skin: A Doctor's Patients in Eighteenth-century Germany*, trans. Thomas Dunlap (Cambridge, Mass., and London: Harvard University Press, 1991), 89–90.

22 See for this process, Peter Burke, *Popular Culture in Early Modern Europe* (London: Temple Smith, 1978).

23 Mary E. Fissell, *Patients, Power, and the Poor in Eighteenth-century Bristol* (Cambridge: Cambridge University Press, 1991); and in particular her 'Disappearance of the Patient's Narrative and the Invention of Hospital Medicine', in Roger French and Andrew Wear (eds), *British Medicine in an Age of Reform* (London and New York: Routledge, 1992), 92–109, esp. 103.

24 J. H. Dirckx, *The Language of Medicine: Its Evolution, Structure, and Dynamics* (New York: Praeger, 1983), 107.

25 Herman Melville, *Redburn* (London: R. Bentley, 1849), ch. xiii.

26 Herman Melville, *White Jacket* (London: R. Bentley, 1850), ch. lxiii.

27 Sydney Smith, letter to Mrs Holland, January 1844, in Lady Holland (ed.), *A Memoir of the Reverend Sydney Smith*, 2 vols (London: Longman, Brown, Green and Longmans, 1855), ii: 517, letter 534.

28 Quoted in Dirckx, *The Language of Medicine*, 128–9.

29 Dirckx, *The Language of Medicine*, 135.

30 Percivall Pott, 'A Treatise on the Fistula in Ano', in *Chirurgical Works*, 3rd edn (London: printed for L. Hawes, W. Clarke and R. Collins, 1771), ii: 11. See Dirckx, *The Language of Medicine.*

31 Dirckx, *The Language of Medicine*, 119–31.

32 Barbara Beigun Kaplan, *'Divulging of Useful Truths in Physick': The*

Medical Agenda of Robert Boyle (Baltimore: Johns Hopkins University Press, 1993); Roger French and Andrew Wear (eds), *The Medical Revolution of the Seventeenth Century* (Cambridge: Cambridge University Press, 1989); on the idea that the reform of science depended on the reform of language, see R. F. Jones, *Ancients and Moderns: A Study of the Background of the Battle of the Books* (St Louis: Washington University Press, 1936); Charles Webster, *The Great Instauration: Science, Medicine, and Reform 1626–1660* (London: Duckworth, 1975), 266–75.

33 John Locke, *An Essay Concerning Human Understanding*, ed. Peter H. Nidditch (Oxford: Clarendon Press, 1975), 490–1. See also C. G. Caffentzis, *Clipped Coins, Abused Words, and Civil Government: John Locke's Philosophy of Money* (New York: Autonomedia, 1989); Andrew E. Benjamin, Geoffrey N. Cantor and John R. R. Christie (eds), *The Figural and the Literal: Problems of Language in the History of Science and Philosophy, 1630–1800* (Manchester: Manchester University Press, 1987); Hans Aarsleff, *From Locke to Saussure: Essays on the Study of Language and Intellectual History* (Minneapolis: University of Minnesota Press, 1982).

34 See M. Staum, *Cabanis: Enlightenment and Medical Philosophy in the French Revolution* (Princeton: Princeton University Press, 1980); Isabel Knight, *The Geometric Spirit: The Abbé de Condillac and the French Enlightenment* (New Haven: Yale University Press, 1968); for the parallel with chemistry, see M. P. Crosland, *Historical Studies in the Language of Chemistry* (New York: Dover Publications and London: Heinemann, 1962).

35 Sir Clifford Allbutt, *Notes on the Composition of Scientific Papers* (London: Macmillan, 1904).

36 Ibid. 33.

37 Philip Howard, *Weasel Words* (London: Hamish Hamilton, 1978), 12.

38 Morris Fishbein, *Medical Writing, the Technic and the Art* (Chicago: Press of American Medical Association, 1938).

39 Ibid., 47.

40 Ibid., 54.

41 Ibid., 47.

42 Ibid., 49, 54.

43 Ibid., 59.

44 Ibid., 60.

45 Sir Humphry Rolleston, 'Medical Eponyms', *Annals of Medical History*, ix (1937), 1–12.

46 B. G. Firkin and J. A. Whitworth, *Dictionary of Medical Eponyms* (Carnforth: Parthenon Publishing Group, 1989), v. See also Stanley Jablonski, *Illustrated Dictionary of Eponymic Syndromes and Diseases and their Symptoms* (Philadelphia: W. B. Saunders, 1969): that volume is a mere 330 pages.

47 Dirckx, *The Language of Medicine*, 121.

48 Ibid., 123.

49 Ibid., 128.

50 Ibid., 132–3.
51 For the necessarily metaphorical nature of the language of the mind, see Graham Richards, *On Psychological Language* (London: Routledge, 1989); Graham Richards, *Mental Machinery*, pt i: *The Origins and Consequences of Psychological Ideas from 1600 to 1850* (London: Athlone Press, 1992). For psychobabble as abuse, see Thomas S. Szasz, *The Myth of Mental Illness: Foundations of a Theory of Personal Conduct* (New York: Paladin, 1961; London: Granada, 1972; rev. edn New York: Harper and Row, 1974); Anthony Clare and Sally Thompson, *Now Let's Talk About Me: A Critical Examination of New Psychotherapies* (London: BBC, 1981).
52 Oliver Wendell Holmes, 'Scholastic and Bedside Teaching', *Medical Essays*, 5th edn (Boston: Houghton, Mifflin, 1888), 273–311.
53 William Hillary, *A Rational and Mechanical Essay on the Small Pox* (London: printed for G. Strahan, 1735), discussed in Christopher Booth, *Doctors in Science and Society: Essays of a Clinical Scientist* (London: British Medical Journal, 1987), 60.
54 Benjamin Ward Richardson, 'The Vocation of Being a Scholar, being the 83rd Anniversary Oration Delivered Before the Medical Society of London', *Glasgow Medical Journal*, iv (1856), 80.
55 Rabelais, Epistle dedicatory to Prince Odet, *Gargantua and Pantagruel* (Harmondsworth: Penguin, 1978), bk 4.
56 Molière, *Le Médecin malgré lui*, in *The Misanthrope and Other Plays* (Harmondsworth: Penguin, 1959), 186. See M. Raynaud, *Les Médecins au temps de Molière* (Paris: Didier, 1863); David Jaymes, 'Parasitology in Molière: Satire of Doctors and Praise of Paramedics', *Literature and Medicine*, xii (1993), 1–18.
57 Molière, *Le Médecin malgré lui*, 187.
58 Molière, *Monsieur de Pourceaugnac*, in *The Works of Molière*, 6 vols (New York: Benjamin Bloom, 1967), 4: 194.
59 Molière, *Le Malade imaginaire*, in *Molière: Oeuvres Complètes*, 2 (Paris: Éditions Garnier Frères, 1962), 848–9. See the excellent discussion in Lester King, *The Philosophy of Medicine: The Early Eighteenth century* (Cambridge, Mass.: Harvard University Press, 1978).
60 Aphra Behn, *Sir Patient Fancy*, quoted in Silvette, *The Doctor on Stage*, 255.
61 Thomas Shadwell, *The Virtuoso*, quoted in Silvette, *The Doctor on Stage*, 165.
62 Thomas Shadwell, *The Humourists*, quoted in Silvette, *The Doctor on Stage*, 189.
63 Sir Ernest Gowers, *Plain Words* (London: HMSO, 1948), ch. 5, 30n. Sir William Gowers (1845–1915) did distinguished work at the National Hospital in Queen Square on many aspects of nervous diseases and diseases of the brain. A brilliant observer, he was dogmatic as a teacher and impatient of criticism.

3

Anti-language or Jargon? Canting in the English Underworld in the Sixteenth and Seventeenth Centuries

LEE BEIER

The study of underworld slang – cant or canting in English – is a well-travelled field of enquiry. From the fifteenth century to the present the subject has fascinated poets, pamphleteers, lexicographers, sociologists, linguists and historians. The literature on criminal argot is sufficiently voluminous that someone with the requisite linguistic, bibliographical and historiographical skills might write a history of it. This is not the subject of this chapter, which is intended to be a modest contribution to the social history of English underworld slang in the sixteenth and seventeenth centuries. Nor will the paper consider the etymology and semiology of canting, subjects that are beyond the scope of a single chapter. Instead, it sets out to examine three questions. The first concerns the semantics of the argot: what were those who allegedly used canting actually saying? What were they talking about? Secondly, how did canting change over time, again in its semantics? Did it incorporate new words and new meanings? Were there any significant new developments in the period? Thirdly, what is the importance of the argot? Is it the key to a subculture, to an anti-language of an anti-society, to a criminal underworld? Or is it simply another instance of a jargon, a specialized vocabulary, such as the others studied in this volume?

Consideration of these three topics directs attention to some central issues in the study of underworld slang. Despite numerous works on canting and the criminals who are supposed to have used it, there is no serious examination of its semantics. This is not wholly surprising, given the interest in semiology in the past few decades. The study of language as symbol, as sign or code, has flourished since the 1970s unaccompanied, where cant is concerned, by a parallel growth in interest in the meanings of its vocabularies. Without taking anything from semiology, the result has been a tendency to assume that canting represented such a code before seriously considering the evidence. For instance, a recently published sociological study of London's underworld between 1550 and 1700 posited that the argot was 'a private code of identification and a social passport into hidden worlds and practices' even while noting that there were 'few rules that decode the intended significance of authors and audience' and 'no codes for assessing how meanings were carried and projected'. The upshot was a study that a priori treated canting as an underworld language and failed to analyse it in any depth.[1]

Recent research on canting has given limited attention to its development over time. The reason is that some students of the slang, following one line of linguistic thought, have adopted a static approach to its study.[2] One historian has observed that it is typical of post-Saussurean linguistics to emphasize structure versus change, or sychronicity as opposed to diachronicity. Similarly, structuralism, which greatly affected anthropology, linguistics and sociology from the 1960s, focuses on the inner structure of a text or *parole*, seeing the past as 'a series of successive synchronic states, each in itself static, rather than as a long-span diachronic process, whether of change or of continuity'.[3] This approach to language has influenced recent sociological studies of canting. The sociologist cited above stated that his approach 'does not imply that temporality must be abandoned for decontextualization'. Yet in the previous breath he affirmed a commitment to 'delineating continuities within discourses, to demonstrating that the things accomplished through the medium of argot express a congruence over time'.[4] Another sociologist of crime takes a similar line, citing the 'remarkable continuity of cant'.[5] Such assumptions – and often they are no more than that – naturally lead their proponents to eschew questions about changes in canting. Yet it is possible to trace the development over time of canting and to relate it to a larger social and cultural context, as a later section of this chapter attempts to do.

The third issue examined here is whether canting was an 'anti-language' generated by an 'anti-society', representing the 'acting out of a distinct social structure . . . the bearer of an alternative social reality' and a set of values opposed to the dominant social and linguistic order. This is the position taken by M. A. K. Halliday in an important article published in 1976. Halliday concluded that underworld slang constituted a social dialect, which could be used for defensive purposes to sustain an alternative reality, or for offensive ones to protest against the prevailing order.[6] Does English canting vocabulary of the sixteenth and seventeenth centuries support the view that it was an anti-language of an anti-society? This question is addressed in the final section of the chapter.

Canting: genesis and evidence

The recorded history of canting in Europe begins, not surprisingly, with the growth of lay literacy in the late Middle Ages.[7] This was also a period of labour shortage and high wages, when civil authorities first began to legislate against and to prosecute vagabondage.[8] The German variant, or *Rotwelsch*, apparently originated in the thirteenth century; there are recorded instances of its usage in Augsburg municipal records of 1342–3 and in trial records of the city of Basle in the first half of the fifteenth century. The Basle records included not just examples of vocabulary, but also the categorizations of beggars and thieves that became so popular in the literature of roguery. In 1510 there was published a thorough compilation of the *Rotwelsch* material entitled the *Liber vagatorum*, which went through many editions, including one in 1528 to which Martin Luther wrote a famous preface. The most recent study of the German argot adopts a sociolinguistic approach that is close to that of Halliday. The book examines the content and the structures of *Rotwelsch*, its linguistic origins and its processes of word-formation. Using judicial records, it shows that German canting was not just a literary creation. In 1487 one Hans of Strasbourg, described as a Jew, confessed to the Nördlingen authorities that he knew eight confidence tricks that were later listed in the *Liber*. The author also relates *Rotwelsch* to its speakers' social positions, concluding that it provides evidence of the mental world of the marginal population in Germany. More recently, the same authority accepted that canting did not represent an alternative ideology, nor did it indicate a full-blown language of a counter-culture. Rather it was a vocabulary of survival, whether by fair or foul means. It did, however, possess semiological significance. It was 'more than just a special vocabulary typical of certain highly specialized professions'; it was 'a kind of watchword which signalled that somebody was part of a vagrant community with its own codes of honour and its various, often illegal, strategies of survival'.[9]

The use of and interest in criminal argot were pan-European phenomena. In France underworld argot appears in the mid fifteenth century. François Villon – 'poet of the vagabonds', a convicted murderer and thief and thus possibly the first recorded 'participant-observer' in the history of crime – used thieves' jargon in his ballads. The *Coquillard* gang active in Burgundy in the 1450s and cited by Peter Burke in the introduction to this volume had its own vocabulary for specialized crimes and criminal roles.[10] In the Spanish-speaking world canting was called *germanía* and concerned much the same ilk as elsewhere, above all prostitutes and thieves. The study by Hernandez also employed a semiological approach. While engaging in limited social analysis of the material, the author gave a detailed examination of the argot's vocabulary. Prostitutes were divided into those living inside and outside brothels, the first group including five sub-categories – for example, economic aspects, pejorative citations, references to advertising – and the second group nine terms for apprentice prostitutes, those of low quality and their clients. Likewise, thieves were categorized as those robbing houses, shops, churches and on the highway, stealing from purses and taking money and jewels. As in German and English underworld slang, *germanía* reportedly had a hierarchy of 'valentones' – rogues or bully-boys. Unlike the recent study of *Rotwelsch*, however, Hernandez's work made little effort to document the argot in judicial records. When, moreover, his linguistic analysis dealt with changes in *germanía*, the concern was with signifiers and signified and developments in figures of speech, such as metaphors, metonymy and synecdoche.[11] Italy too had a vagabonds' slang, which began to flourish in the fifteenth century and contained references to confidence, begging and thieving ploys and descriptions of the specialized gangs that allegedly perpetrated the crimes. The *Speculum cerretanorum* (1484/6) of Teseo Pini listed about forty orders of vagabond. There exists some later judicial evidence from Rome in the 1590s, which mentions the names of gangs and uses the jargon they employed to describe themselves.[12] After the publication of the *Speculum* and *Liber vagatorum* the literature of roguery flourished. Most examples found a place for descriptions of the argot that their subjects were supposed to speak.

In England no examples of canting have thus far been discovered in late medieval evidence; the earliest recorded instance of its usage occurs in the literature of roguery of the late sixteenth century.[13] The first apparent literary use was in *The Highway to the Spital-house* by Robert Copland (1535 or 1536), who quoted seven lines in verse form. In *A Manifest Detection of the Most Vile and Detestable Use of Dice-play*

(1552) reference was made to the special criminal vocabulary of 'sacking law' (prostitution), 'high law' (robbery) and 'figging law' (cutting purses). From the 1560s England began to see the type of literary production that Germany had seen in the *Liber vagatorum*; that is, the typologies of beggars and thieves, usually in underworld jargon, together with examples of the vocabulary. In 1561 John Awdeley's *Fraternity of Vagabonds* listed 19 types of vagrant and a further 3 members of 'the company of coseners and shifters'. Thomas Harman's *Caveat for Common Cursitors* (1566 and later editions) gave 23 categories of beggar and thief and 114 words and phrases in cant, as well as a lengthy dialogue between 2 vagabonds, complete with translation. Harman has traditionally been the most credible of observers of the canting underworld. He claimed to have interviewed some of its members who passed his home in Kent, cited his own and the experiences of acquaintances in dealings with them and listed what he said were the actual names of 75 of them.[14]

There were numerous later additions to this first phase of literary versions of canting. After Harman, most of the pamphleteers writing about vagabonds, thieves and card-sharps included some reference to canting or the various forms of criminal vocabulary, or 'law'. In the case of Thomas Dekker's *Lantern and Candlelight* (1608) the author's first chapter was entitled 'Of Canting', but it was almost entirely plagiarized from Harman.[15] The author of *Martin Markall, Beadle of Bridewell* (1610) not only noted Dekker's theft, but produced his own 'Canters' Dictionary', claiming to give credit to Harman where it was due, and producing further examples of canting in verse form. In lexicographic terms the pamphlet's greatest achievement was to alphabetize canting words for the first time. By 1626, when the first wave of the literature of roguery was ending, the list of English cant words had increased to at least 363.[16]

In the second half of the seventeenth century there was regression and then recovery in the lexicography of canting. The first major publication was Richard Head's *The English Rogue* (1665), which, like the works of Robert Greene and Dekker before it, largely comprised amusing, picaresque stories of Meriton Latroon, 'a witty extravagant'. The book included the by now requisite snatch of verse in argot and a 'Canting Vocabulary'. The latter is a disappointing effort, hardly advancing upon Harman with its 187 entries and regressing from the conflated total of 363 produced by 1626. In truth, most of the vocabulary would have been familiar to Harman.[17] But as was so typical of this genre and its authors – like Greene and Dekker, Head was usually only a few steps ahead of his creditors – the matter did not end there. In 1673 Head produced *The*

Canting Academy, which, as well as much extraneous material, contained an enlarged dictionary with some new wrinkles. It included, as usual, translations of cant to English, but also of English words to cant ones, the net total being 275 phrases or words, and thus rather fewer than had appeared between 1535 and 1626. In the manner of Harman, Head claimed to have played the role of cant-ethnographer, in this case by interviewing prisoners. '[T]he greatest assistance I had in this discovery,' he stated, 'was from *Newgate*; which with much difficulty I screw'd out of the sullen rogues.'[18]

Later lexicographers of cant would be hard put to match Head's grandiloquence, but they tended to do a better job. From the late seventeenth century canting began to be incorporated in standard dictionaries – a subject discussed in the final section of this chapter – and, most importantly for us, to be the subject of special lexicons of popular speech. About 1700 there was published the first such book, *A New Dictionary of the Terms Ancient and Modern of the Canting Crew* . . ., by B.E., Gent.[19] This volume is the progenitor of a distinguished line of dictionaries of popular speech, which in the next century includes Francis Grose's *Classical Dictionary of the Vulgar Tongue* (1st edition, 1785), in the nineteenth century John S. Farmer's *Slang and Its Analogues, Past and Present* (1st edition, 1890) and in the twentieth Eric Partridge's *Dictionary of Slang and Unconventional English* (1st edition, 1937). The *New Dictionary* was unlike anything produced before in English. For one thing, it was wholly devoted to popular speech – to the old and new sayings of those who canted, including 'Several Tribes, of Gypsies, Beggers, Thieves, Cheats, etc.' – and also contained 'proverbs, phrases, figurative speeches, etc.' The total number of pages, not counting a preface, was 166, the total entries approximately 2,500. As Grose was later to do, the author specified which words and phrases were cant ones. In all, he catalogued 855 of them, a considerably larger number than previous lists. For this reason, the dictionary by B.E. is used extensively in the rest of the chapter.[20]

Before examining the evidence of canting vocabulary, however, something needs to be said about source materials and methodology. A cautionary word is especially needed concerning the literary records of underworld slang, of which dictionaries must be considered exemplars. Until 1985 no student of canting had ever established from sources other than literary ones that it was in fact spoken by anyone in early modern England.[21] Yet for centuries the writers of the literature of roguery, lexicographers, linguists, historians and sociologists accepted that it was. In 1984 a sociologist of early modern criminal organization admitted that 'although compilers explain argot terms, we have no way of assessing their actual use within historical criminal populations', and then went on to ignore his warning by treating the compilers' words as true to life.[22]

This is not to say that the literary sources are inherently of less value than others; just that some corroborating evidence would give them greater credibility. Prima facie, the literary record is suspect. The fictional evidence was the work of professional writers penning a product for a market, and their anecdotes, plots and characters were often stereotyped, exaggerated and plagiarized. If the authors' stories lack verisimilitude, why should one accept as accurate their efforts at lexicography? Early dictionaries were often pirated and were not compiled on historical lines; indeed, it is frequently difficult to ascertain any *modus operandi* in these publications. Unlike Farmer and Partridge, seventeenth- and eighteenth-century lexicographers did not cite their sources and borrowed mercilessly and without attribution from earlier listings. Their main purpose was to sell books, which a section of canting words apparently promoted, giving an air of authenticity and producing some titillation. Of secondary importance was producing an accurately researched product; many compilers were quite honest about their opportunism.[23]

Other than the claims of Harman and Head to be cant-ethnographers, which can be neither confirmed nor denied, what evidence besides literary sources have we that canting was practised? There is not a great deal of it, it is largely anecdotal and it still comes second-hand, from judicial records. But it is the sort of evidence that historians of Continental criminal slangs have discovered and cited as 'control' instances to confirm statements in the literary sources, though this has not been done for England.[24] As elsewhere in Europe, in England judicial records include depositions or examinations taken by justices from persons suspected of crimes. These documents often give detailed and revealing information about the lives of itinerant folk, sometimes for periods of several years, even decades. The examinees were themselves surprisingly frank, even to the point of incriminating themselves through telling justices about a host of personal matters: sexual and marital relations; family and job histories; movements, haunts and confederates. Despite the abundance and availability of these records, those who have studied canting have not consulted them.[25]

Yet occasionally justices' examinations confirm that canting was spoken in the Elizabethan underworld. Not only do they give confirmation, they also cite actual examples of argot terminology. Admittedly the evidence is not abundant, and nor is it usually very detailed. This is not entirely surprising, since canting was supposed to be a secret vocabulary.

In fact, we will see that some of those overheard using it then denied it. Nevertheless, there is probably sufficient documentation to support the view of literary sources that canting existed and was spoken.

The earliest known references to the use of an underworld slang in early modern judicial records mentioned it somewhat obliquely. The first case appears in Essex quarter sessions examinations taken from four itinerants arrested in Ilford in 1580. The group comprised two couples, one of whom carried a false marriage licence and a forged passport, good indicators that they were living outside the law. A further piece of evidence cited was that the two women 'were heard to speak "Pedlar's French" [a contemporary term for canting], but they both deny the same'. Knowledge and use of canting vocabulary was not illegal, but it might well tip off justices that all was not right with someone's story.[26]

There were other such passing references in judicial records. In an examination before Warwick magistrates in 1581 Michael Hedge, recently come from Ireland, was drunk, disorderly and without papers. He admitted to having wandered about for the last eighteen months and claimed he had a back injury 'and could cant'.[27] Yet another terse reference to canting occurred in Essex in 1590. Once again, a group of transients was arrested, accused of stealing three hens. They included one Thomas Jackson, who, the interviewing justice recorded, told him 'concerning his Pedlar's French he will not make to me any account where he learned the same'. Jackson, like the women ten years earlier, was secretive about canting. But what was perhaps most remarkable was that Jackson claimed to have served in two aristocratic households, including that of Edward, third Lord Stafford. Since both Jackson and Stafford had Gloucestershire addresses, the story may have been true, but what was a transient suspected of theft doing in the household of a great lord? Is this possibly an early instance of cant cutting across social boundaries?[28] The final instance of brief allusions to canting concerns Stephen Christen, whose age is unknown but who was probably of Oliver Twist vintage and size, since he crawled through windows for a pair of female housebreakers named Black Jane, or Jane Williams, and Grace Smith. Christen described several such crimes to Kent justices in 1606, implicating a number of others, among them the receivers of the stolen goods. At the end of his statement he was asked 'whether he can cant and how long it was since he learned it'. The boy replied that he could and had 'learned it about some three years since'.[29]

The most extensive use of canting to appear in official records before the seventeenth century occurs in a well-known document of 1585. It was included in a letter from the Recorder of London, William

Fleetwood, to William Cecil, the Lord Treasurer, concerning (among other things) 'a school house set up to learn young boys to cut purses'. The alleged proto-Fagin was one Wotton, a gentleman born and formerly a prosperous merchant who, facing financial ruin, hit upon the idea of a cutpurses' academy, which he established near Billingsgate. Fleetwood's account of Wotton's school for thieves is interesting because it includes several canting words, which the magistrate translated for Burghley. He cited the cases of 'a public foister' (pickpocket) and 'a judicial nipper' (cutpurse), and described their training by Wotton. Both 'nip' and 'foist' were canting words, according to the literary sources, though they were usually used as verbs. 'Public' and 'judicial' were not cant and were possibly added by Fleetwood for rhetorical effect; certainly they were part of his jargon. He also told Burghley of poetry in cant that was discovered 'written in a table' in Wotton's house. The lines read:

Si spie sporte, si no spie, tunc steale

and

Si spie, si no spie, foist, nip, shave and spare not.

'Si spie' and 'sporte' he did not translate and do not appear in early canting lexicons; 'tunc', of course, is Latin. After repeating his own translations of 'foist' and 'nip', Fleetwood added that 'lift' was to rob a shop and 'shave' to steal a cloak, sword or silver spoon. The former was a cant word for theft, while the latter meant to defraud and, Judges claims, was not canting. Finally, Fleetwood noted that 'mylken ken' meant to commit a robbery or burglary in the night, which is a corruption of 'to mill a ken'.[30]

The best case thus far discovered of a transient using cant is that of Mary Roberts, who was arrested in November 1613. The case is remarkable because of its considerable use of underworld slang and because Roberts and her husband were themselves part of the world they described. They were itinerant beggars and for many years had rambled round south-west England collecting alms using false papers. When arrested, the couple were found to have three sets of counterfeit papers on them. In her examination, included in the appendix to this chapter, Mary Roberts described an extensive web of counterfeiters of false papers in south-west England. Using these licences and passes, itinerants pretended to be disabled soldiers, dumb beggars and collectors for fire losses. These kinds of allegations are not rare in judicial records of the period, but it is exceptional to have the alleged offenders described with canting vocabulary. To identify the writers of false papers Roberts used the cant word 'feaker'; the false dumb beggar was a 'counterfeit dumb maunder', fraudulent fire victims were 'glimmer maunderers' and a card-sharp a 'cheater at all plays'. She also referred to a 'counterfeit madman', though without calling him by the appropriate cant term, 'Abram-man'. A month later the woman's husband, Anthony, appeared before the same justice in the role of informer. Had the couple plea-bargained a deal, which might explain their candour in revealing cant terms? We shall never know definitively, but it is worth noting that Anthony too used canting words in referring to 'priggers' (thieves). The Roberts interviews are important in showing that their evidence is not a case of nature imitating art; that is, there is no possibility that the legal documents simply reflected the influence of the literature of roguery. The justice of the peace who examined the Robertses specified that the slang words were theirs. He states that 'counterfeit dumb maunder' is *'her'* term' and 'feakers' is *'their'* canting word for their passmakers'.[31]

The judicial records show that canting was used in the underworld and offer some general observations about its usage. They suggest that the argot was a learned vocabulary and a tool of the trades of thieving and begging. Stephen Christen seems to have learned it as part of his career in burglary. Wotton's alleged school for thieves proves that canting was not only spoken, but could be written by the alleged crooks themselves, as well as by hack-writers and justices. The purpose in the Wotton case was evidently to teach thieves. This material is especially tantalizing. Was canting being taught to the apprentices? Were the words 'written in a table' possibly the teacher's notes, some lessons being copied or students' notes scratched on a table in a moment of boredom? The sloppy mixing of English, Latin and cant, particularly in the first line of poetry, suggests poor note-taking might be the answer. The judicial evidence also confirms the view that canting was meant by its users to be a covert vocabulary. Members of both groups of Essex itinerants denied speaking it or knowing it. The cases occurred ten years apart, pointing to consistent attempts to keep it secret. It is noteworthy that this detailed judicial evidence of canting comes in cases where its users were acting as informers – the Robertses.

More speculatively, even where people denied speaking cant words or where the details are sketchy, their alleged behaviour could have been well described by the (quite limited) lexicon of canting, lending credibility to the probability that they were using it. The two couples seized in Essex in 1580 had evidently consulted a 'bene-faker of gybes' or 'jarkman' (false passport maker), as well as a 'patriarch co' or 'patriarco' (a minister who made false marriages). If the foursome were begging with a false passport, they were 'fakers of loges'.[32] As for Jackson and the others arrested in the county ten years on, if they had stolen the hens, there was a multitude of canting words to describe the act: 'to cloy' was the most generic. The objects of their alleged crime were 'margery-praters'.[33] As for Christen and his housebreaking companions, Harman used the term 'to mill a ken' for robbing a house, while a 'stalling-ken' was a receiver's or fence's home. There were also cant words for many of the items the group took, such as 'duds' for clothing generally, 'caster' for a cloak, 'slate' for a sheet, 'muffling-cheat' for a napkin and 'commission' for a shirt. We have no evidence that these particular suspects used the words cited, but it would not seem to be 'fictionalizing the archives' unduly to think that they might have, since canting provided them with the requisite vocabulary.[34]

Of course, the discovery of canting words in judicial records is informative only up to a point. It does not signify that authors' compilations of cant were accurate; just that a few words crop up in both literary and court records. A dictionary such as B.E.'s lists several hundred words, but we have no way of knowing how often each was used. Apart from verses and occasional snatches of canting, which were probably the work of the hack-writers, we have virtually nothing that tells us about its syntax. Harman said it was 'half mingled with English when it is familiarly talked', which makes sense given the limited canting vocabulary.[35] But the excerpt provided by Harman reads more like a Dickensian version of popular speech, written for the literate and comfortable classes, rather than the genuine article. Even the judicial records, with the possible exception of the Wotton poetry, do not contain direct quotations from those who canted.

We are equally at a loss about diction, in the sense of word-choice as well as enunciation. As to the first, we know that canting words increased in number over time, a point discussed below. But we know little about when and why words went in and out of fashion. Harman observed that canters 'have begun of late to devise some new terms for certain things, so will they in time alter this, and devise as evil or worse'. Likewise, Head reported that his Newgate exertions told him 'that the mode of canting alter'd very often'. This was because rogues 'were forced to change frequently those material words which chiefly dis-covered their mysterious practices and villanies, least growing too common their own words should betray them'. His *Canting Academy* was therefore a compilation of old words and 'many new never published in print, and but very lately minted'.[36] On the second element in diction, there is evidence that canters whined when they spoke, at least when begging from people, but obviously if such intonation were used in ordinary speech, it might prove counter-productive. Certainly it seems unlikely that card-sharps, who were supposed to employ canting a good deal, would have made whining noises during a game.[37]

A few words now about the evidence and methods deployed in the rest of the chapter. The materials used to document the semantics of canting consist of two main blocks. The first includes 363 words from eighteen examples of the literature of roguery published between 1535 and 1626, and edited in *The Elizabethan Underworld* by A. V. Judges. About half of these words are from two of the pamphlets, *A Caveat for Common Cursitors* (1566) by Thomas Harman and *Martin Markall, Beadle of Bridewell* (1610) possibly by Samuel Rid, both of which included the lengthiest glossaries. The second half is from the sixteen other pamphlets and is based upon Judges' own composite glossary, but with Harman's and Rid's contributions excluded.[38] The second body of evidence is derived from B.E.'s *New Dictionary of the Canting Crew*, which contains 855 canting terms. Together, these sources yield 1,218 words, which is very likely the bulk of recorded sixteenth- and seventeenth-century canting.

The methodology employed is to analyse the words in eighteen categories encompassing the multitude of nouns (used for activities, types of person, objects, parts of the body, animals, institutions and places) and the smaller numbers of verbs and adjectives. This taxonomy was derived in part from valuable studies of German *Rotwelsch* and Spanish *germanía*,[39] but ultimately it was the contents of the texts themselves that dictated the categories. Unlike those projects, however, the present study eschews etymology, syntax and semiology, because of lack of space. Instead the emphasis is upon discovering what the semantics might tell us about the reality – or, in Halliday's lexicon, the 'counter-reality' – of canting.[40]

Categorizing cant

Table 3.1 summarizes the contents of canting vocabulary between around 1535 and 1700. This section will focus upon those categories of the argot that changed relatively little over the period. All categories, of course, grew considerably, but the mean average growth rate of 2.4 times (855 entries from 363) between the first and third compilations is taken as the base line. Categories surpassing that rate will be discussed at greater length in the following section. Head's material from 1673,

Table 3.1 The semantics of English cant, c.1535–c.1700

	1535–1626		Head, 1673		B.E., c.1700		E Absolute growth[a]	F Relative growth[b]
Canting words	A No.	C %	No.	%	B No.	D %		
1 Types of vagrant/criminal	109	30.0	34	12.4	187	21.9	1.7	−27.0
2 Verbs: non-criminal acts	33	9.1	31	11.3	65	7.6	2.0	−16.5
3 Legal, penal system	17	4.7	22	8.0	64	7.5	3.8	+59.6
4 Social classes	2	0.6	2	0.7	5	0.6	2.5	no change
5 Units of time, measurement	3	0.8	2	0.7	4	0.5	1.3	−37.5
6 Verbs: criminal acts	20	5.5	8	2.9	57	6.7	2.9	+21.8
7 Places/features in landscape	15	4.1	7	2.6	12	1.4	0.8	−65.9
8 Buildings/businesses	11	3.0	10	3.6	19	2.2	1.7	−26.7
9 Reading/writing	3	0.8	4	1.4	8	0.9	2.7	+12.5
10 Religion/church	5	1.4	3	1.1	7	0.8	1.4	−42.9
11 Animals	9	2.5	12	4.4	21	2.5	2.3	no change
12 Adjectives	6	1.7	15	5.5	22	2.6	3.7	+52.9
13 Food/drink	17	4.7	15	5.5	30	3.5	1.8	−25.5
14 Money/precious metals	12	3.3	15	5.5	80	9.4	6.7	+184.8
15 Clothing/objects worn or carried	19	5.2	18	6.5	85	9.9	4.5	+90.4
16 Household goods/furnishings	4	1.1	18	6.5	15	1.7	3.8	+54.5
17 Parts of body	14	3.9	18	6.5	29	3.4	2.1	−12.8
18 Other nouns	64	17.6	41	14.9	145	16.9	2.3	−3.9
Total	363	100.0	275	100.0	855	100.0		100.0

[a] Column E results from dividing B by A, and expresses a rate of increase. For example, 9 Reading/writing increased from 3 references to 8, or 2.7 times.

[b] Column F is the result of comparing C and D, with the difference expressed in percentages. For example, 1 Types of vagrant/criminal: 30.0 − 21.9 = 8.1; 8.1/30.0 = −27.0%. Column F therefore represents the change in percentages.

Sources: A. V. Judges (ed.), *The Elizabethan Underworld: A Collection of Tudor and Early Stuart Tracts and Ballads* (1930); Richard Head, *The Canting Academy; or, the Devils Cabinet Opened* (1673); B.E., *A New Dictionary of the Terms Ancient and Modern of the Canting Crew, in Its Several Tribes, of Gypsies, Beggers, Thieves, Cheats, etc.* (n.d.)

though of less interest, is included for comparative purposes. The smallest and least changeable categories are still interesting, because they can reveal something about the mental furniture of the slang. Overall, the distribution of cant terms shows that it was a specialized jargon with limited horizons. References to social classes (category 4: 0.6 per cent of the total vocabulary), the Church and religion (category 10: 0.8 to 1.4 per cent of the total) were both exiguous in number and static over time. With the exception of allusions to legal and penal systems, discussed below, the mental world of canters largely excluded the respectable world of State and Church. In the literature up to 1626 there were references to gentlemen ('gentry cove') and women ('gentry mort'), to the Queen ('rum cove'), the Church ('autem'), to priests ('patricos'), the mass ('Salomon') and the Devil ('Ruffin'). Even B.E.'s lengthy dictionary added only a few words to the existing stock: 'oak' for a rich man, 'queer-duke' for a decayed gentleman and 'tercel-gentle' for a knight or gentleman of good estate (also, for any rich man).[41]

Time (category 5: 0.5 to 0.8 per cent) was virtually insignificant in the canting lexicon. When B.E. wrote his *New Dictionary* about 1700, England was in the throes of a commercial revolution, but the 'time–work discipline' was foreign to those who allegedly canted. The hours of the day were reduced to night and day: 'darkmans' for night, 'lightmans' for day (or, occasionally, daybreak). There was no awareness of the month, the year, the reigns of monarchs, sittings of parliament, dates of civil wars or revolutions. Transient criminals regularly frequented hundreds of fairs and market days held on specific days during the year, as well as the village 'wakes' and 'revels' celebrated every year, yet these dates do not show up in the canting calendar.[42] Their world, it seems, was almost timeless.

Places and the landscape (category 7: 1.4 to 4.1 per cent) figured a little more in the argot, without looming very large. This was apparently a population divorced from any roots in rural society. The main references were urban. Apart from prisons, considered below, the only place to figure noticeably was London, or 'Rome-vill' (also used generically for large towns), and its neighbourhoods: 'Gracemans' for Gracechurch Street market, 'Numans' for Newgate market and 'Chepe-mans' for Cheapside market. The allusions to the countryside were generic: highway ('high-pad'), ditches ('jagues'), forests ('ruffmans'), gardens ('smellers' or 'smelling-cheats'), hedges ('crackmans') and fields ('Greenmans'). The term for the country, 'dewse-a-vill', had a distinctly pejorative ring to it.

References to buildings and businesses were relatively infrequent (category 8: 2.2 to 3.6 per cent) and indicate a homeless population that frequented alehouses, brothels and others' homes; in the last case, not always with the best of intentions. 'Ken' was the root for house, but was rarely used on its own. Instead it was combined with other words to describe various establishments: 'bousing-ken' (alehouse), 'stalling-ken' (receiver of stolen goods), 'libken' (house to sleep in), 'croppin-ken' (privy), 'queer-ken' (shabby lodgings), 'gentle cove's ken' (gentleman's house) and 'touting-ken' (alehouse or tavern). Attention was also given to shops ('swags'), brothels ('Academy'; 'School of Venus'; 'vaulting' or 'cavaulting school') and barns ('skippers'). Mentions of the appurtenances of buildings highlighted such areas as might interest criminals: windows ('glazes'), stairs ('dancers'), doors ('jiggers') and gates and casements ('wickets').

If time and place were relatively insignificant in cant, so were other basic features of everyday life. Animals (category 11: 2.5 to 4.4 per cent) figure in the lists, to be sure, but canting zoology would not impress a schoolchild. There were 'bufes' (dogs), 'mowers' (cows), 'battners' (oxen), 'bleating-cheats' (sheep), 'cackling-cheats' (chickens), 'margery-praters' (hens), 'cobble-colters' (turkeys), 'grunting-cheats' (pigs), 'grunters' (sucking pigs), 'panters' (harts), 'prancers' (horses), 'red-shanks' (ducks) and 'tibs of the buttery' (geese). This was a period when animal husbandry was beginning to flourish, a development that eventually helped produce an agricultural revolution after 1650 and the super-bovine and super-equine worlds, respectively, of Bakewell and Stubbs.[43] Entomology was non-existent, with the exception of a telling allusion to lice, or 'chatts'.

The vocabulary for food and drink (category 13: 3.5 to 5.5 per cent) included a basic meat, grain and dairy diet, but with heavy doses of intoxicants. Among the comestibles were 'pannam' (bread), 'cassam' (cheese), 'cackling farts' (eggs), 'lap' (pottage), 'peck' or 'peckridge' (meat), 'grunting peck' (pork), 'ruff-peck' (bacon), 'scruff' (scraps of meat), 'grannam' (corn) and 'yarum' (milk). Peas ('trundlers') were the only vegetable, while fruit was cited twice: as 'crassing cheats' (apples, pears) and 'rum boozing welts' (grapes). References to intoxicants were as numerous as ones to food in B.E.'s lexicon (fifteen citations each). Beer was not mentioned, even though it was a staple among the poor; it was probably covered by the generic term 'bowse'.[44] The allusions to alcohol concern wine and other strong drink ('rum-booze'; 'suck'; 'bene-booze'), more specifically canary wine ('rum-gutlers') and French brandy ('rum-nantz'). Although tea and coffee consumption was increasing, the canting population did not have a special term for them. Tobacco, on the other hand, was recorded. It cropped up in Head as 'fogus'; by B.E.'s time it was also called 'cloud' and 'funk'.

Citations of parts of the body (category 17: 3.4 to 6.5 per cent) suggest a basic awareness of human anatomy, with special interests in sight, evacuation and genitalia. B.E. listed three versions of the eyes – 'glaziers', 'ogles' and 'peepers' – which were obviously important to anyone involved in crime. There were fewer versions of the hands – 'fambles' and 'famms'. The arse was variously described as 'cracker' and 'fun', the buttocks as 'pratts'. The male sexual member was 'jockum', and the female organs were 'bite' and 'gig'. But most references to bodies simply cite such common parts as teeth ('crashing cheats'), the mouth ('gan'), ears ('hearing cheats'), the nose ('gigg'; 'smeller'; 'smelling-cheat'), the head ('nab'; 'nob'), arms ('smitters') and legs ('stamps').

Among the absolutely largest categories of cant were nouns describing various types of criminal and vagrant (category 1: 12.4 to 30.0 per cent). We should be a little sceptical about this tendency, which could simply reflect the passion for taxonomy that certainly existed in the literature of roguery. The *Liber vagatorum*, Awdeley and Harman all classified crooks in some detail.[45] But there was more to it than a penchant for listing. As shown by the testimonies of the Robertses, transient criminals themselves used canting categories to describe their world. Moreover, their behaviour squares well enough with that portrayed by glossary writers. There were real thieves who stole clothing with long staffs like the hookers or anglers described by Harman; the horse-thieves, or 'priggers of prancers', listed in cant glossaries; and card-sharps, or 'cony-catchers', who figure so prominently in the pamphlets. They were not necessarily typical of all the transient poor, nor even of all thieves and frauds, but they did exist.[46]

A multitude of types of thief, beggar and fraud is catalogued in canting vocabulary: 109 from 1535 to 1626 and 187 in B.E.'s *Dictionary*. The main categories of pilferers were pickpockets ('divers'; 'shoulder shams'; 'bulks and files'), cutpurses ('bung-nippers'), shoplifters ('shop-lifts'; also 'bobs', 'blosses'), burglars (many cant names), horse-thieves ('prig-nappers' and 'priggers of prancers') and highwaymen ('padders'; also 'bully-ruffins', 'rank-riders'). Beggars were pretend ex-soldiers ('rufflers'), ex-seamen ('whip-jacks'; 'freshwater mariners'), gatherers for hospitals ('fraters'), cripples ('washmen'), epileptics ('counterfeit cranks'), the dumb ('dummerers') and those claiming losses by fire ('demanders for glimmer'; 'glimmer maunderers'). Card-sharps were 'cony-catchers', but also 'sheep-shearers', 'captain-sharp', the 'eagle' and 'nickum'. There were further, specialized roles and hierarchies assigned within each of these activities. The numbers of references to the various lines of crime expanded and contracted in the period.

The category of verbs for non-criminal acts (category 2: 7.6 to 11.3 per cent) requires scrutiny. Some actions were innocent-sounding enough – to go ('bing'; 'rattle'), to go to bed ('couch a hogshead'), to eat ('peck') and to speak gently ('cut'). But as to their propriety or legality, many other expressions were borderline. A number referred to rapid departures: 'budge a beak', 'brush', 'pike' and 'scowre'. Others possibly concerned violent assaults, including 'flick' for cutting, 'fag', 'fib' and 'sock' for beating and 'smash' for kicking downstairs. Others implied potentially incriminating situations: 'cut me bene whids' (to tell the truth); 'couch' or 'cut queer whids' (to lie); 'stow your whids' (be wary); 'it's all bob' (all is safe); 'tout' (to look out sharp); 'whiddle' (to tell or discover); 'the culi cackles' (a rogue tells all); and 'squeek' (to discover or impeach).

B.E. listed more and more verbs concerned with having sex. Harman had provided 'niggle', and Head added 'wap' or 'jockum cloy'. B.E. supplemented the list with 'dock', 'jock', 'prigging' (as in riding), 'straping' and 'tiffing'. He also cited 'velvet' as cant for 'to tongue a woman' and 'buttered bun' for 'lying with a woman that has just lain with another man'. This expansion of the canting sexual lexicon may simply reflect the growth of this vocabulary in the language generally.[47] References to prostitutes and their associates proliferated in the English argot.

Nouns tended to dominate canting, just as they do the English language as a whole, including the speech of late twentieth-century gangs. It is estimated that nominals accounted for 77 per cent of new words coming into American English from 1963 to 1972, and that 68 per cent of gang terminology in Midwestern towns in the early 1990s were nouns.[48] The proportion in early modern canting was even higher. If the non-nominal categories (2, 6 and 12) in table 3.1 are subtracted, the results show 84 per cent nouns in the literature between 1535 and 1626, 80 per cent in Head's glossary of 1673 and 83 per cent in B.E.'s. Category 18 is a catch-all of nouns that did not readily fit into any other slot. This was a substantial residual group (14.9 to 17.6 per cent) with a number of components. These included a host of gaming terms, among them at least eleven kinds of false dice cited in the literature up to 1626. 'Bat-fowling' was card-sharping; 'lime-twigs' were playing cards; a 'bird', 'bleater', 'bub' or 'bubble' and 'gull' all referred to victims; a 'slur' was a cheater at dice; a 'cross-lay' a wager designed to deceive; 'jugging-law' was a dishonest game; 'termage' the gains of the cheaters; a 'vincent' the victim of bowling-alley cheats; a 'forlorn hope' a losing gamester; a 'woodpecker' a bystander who bets. There were numerous references to devices for thieving. A 'bess' was a tool to break open doors; a 'ginny' or 'jenny' was for lifting grates to steal from shop windows; a 'tricker' was for forcing windows or cutting metal; a 'filch' was a staff for stealing clothing; a 'cuttle-bung' a cutpurse's knife; and a 'wrester' or 'dub' a lock-pick key.

The vocabulary of nouns describing potential victims was large and covered more than the prey of cony-catchers. Already in the Elizabethan pamphlets there was the stereotype of innocent newcomers to town and of criminals waiting to fleece them. Indeed, this was frequently used as justification for the publication of yet another cony-catching pamphlet. This position was still taken in B.E.'s book at the end of the period, which sold itself as being 'useful for all sorts of people, (especially foreigners) to secure their money and preserve their lives'.[49] Certainly canting argot suggests that those using it were on the lookout for the unsuspecting but well-heeled bumpkin. A 'nizie' was a fool or coxcomb, a 'rumcully' a rich coxcomb. A 'buzzard' was a fool, easily robbed, and a 'chub' someone inexperienced in the art of gaming. A 'hick' was a 'silly country fellow' and 'Jason's fleece' someone readily cheated of his gold. 'Nocky' meant a 'silly, dull fellow'; someone who was 'noddy' was a simpleton. A 'queer cull' was a fop, a 'rum cul' a rich fool who was easily defrauded and 'reversed' meant setting a man on his head to empty his breeches of his money.

Where do we stand? Eleven of the eighteen categories have been analysed (numbers 1, 2, 4, 5, 7, 8, 10, 11, 13, 17 and 18). They make up the bulk of the canting lexicon, that is 61.3 per cent of the total around 1700; 63.7 per cent in Head's book of 1673; 77.7 per cent of the words in the tracts published between 1535 and 1626. Having examined this evidence, there is little doubt that canting was a jargon. It was not only a thieves' argot, as in the days of Villon. The number of cant words expanded considerably during the period, from 363 to 855. Its purview extended to day-to-day matters of the body, eating and drinking, sexual relations, lodgings, places of hospitality. It included references to Church and State, to the rural world as well as the urban. Yet there can be little question that most cant words concerned the worlds of thieves, beggars, prostitutes and frauds. By 1700 there was a large category of words, numbering nearly 200, to describe the various members of these groups. Some of their designations may have sprung from the imaginations of the rogue writers, but we know from judicial records that some were used by canters. In addition, there was a host of words for the victims of thieves and cony-catchers, for tools for theft, for gaming techniques. Many of the supposedly 'non-criminal' verbs were suspect in the activities they described: escapes, fear of detection and betrayal, illicit sex. There can be little question that most topics of canting were outside the law.

Changeable canting

Contrary to the diagrams of linguists, which suggest immutable languages, canting evolved during the sixteenth and seventeenth centuries. Some of these changes involved small numbers of words. The jump of 2.7 times in words relating to reading and writing was above the average of 2.4, but the total number was just three between 1535 and 1626 and eight around 1700, hardly suggesting a sharp rise in literacy. Similarly, references to household goods and furnishing rose 3.8 times over the period, but in reality the absolute increase was from four to fifteen citations, with the peak coming in 1673 with eighteen in Head. Adjectives rose in number 3.7 times, from six to fifteen, and on to twenty-two, but again the absolute numbers remained small. Many of the words, moreover, had old nominal roots: 'crackish' for whorish; 'bowsy' for drunk; 'priggish' for thievish. The most striking developments in canting occurred in four categories: references to the legal and penal systems; verbs depicting criminal actions; allusions to money and precious metals; and words for clothes or other items carried on the person.

Seventeenth-century England saw the evolution of an increasingly rich vocabulary to describe the authorities and institutions appointed to suppress crime. As shown in tables 3.1 (category 3) and 3.2 this lexicon increased 3.8 times in the period, from seventeen words in the pamphlets published between 1535 and 1626, to twenty-two in Head and sixty-four in B.E.'s dictionary. Although the absolute numbers of references are not huge, it is worth breaking them down to see what they tell us about the perception of crime and punishment in canting (see table 3.2). When this is done, the results are interesting. It seems the number of words relating to hanging rose, from just two between 1535 and 1626 to seven in Head's list and to fourteen in B.E.'s. By the time Head wrote, almost one in three (31.8 per cent) references to the judicial system mentioned hanging. This increase is not entirely surprising. Hanging was a dramatic event – for a criminal, of course, one of the most dramatic he or she would ever experience. In the seventeenth century the 'last dying speeches' of the hanged were published in chapbooks. In the eighteenth century the chaplain or 'Ordinary of Newgate' produced *Accounts* of their lives and crimes, which over time expanded from a few broadsheet folios to twenty-eight quarto pages.[50] Clearly, hanging was good copy.

Table 3.2 References to the criminal justice system in English cant, c.1535–c.1700

	1535–1626		Head, 1673		B.E., c.1700	
	No.	%	No.	%	No.	%
Total references to criminal justice	17	100.0	22	100.0	64	100.0
Hanging	2	11.8	7	31.8	14	21.9
Imprisonment	2	11.8	5	22.7	17	26.9
Public punishment	2	11.8	2	9.1	7	10.9
Judicial system	2	11.8	2	9.1	7	10.9
Police	1	5.9	3	13.6	11	17.2

Sources: A. V. Judges (ed.), *The Elizabethan Underworld: A Collection of Tudor and Early Stuart Tracts and Ballads* (1930); Richard Head, *The Canting Academy, or, the Devils Cabinet Opened* (1673); B.E., *A New Dictionary of the Terms Ancient and Modern of the Canting Crew, in Its Several Tribes, of Gypsies, Beggers, Thieves, Cheats, etc.* (n.d.)

But the historian of canting should be wary of assuming that the increased vocabulary reflected a greater use of capital punishment. In fact, we know the trend was in the opposite direction; capital punishments declined rapidly in England from about the mid seventeenth century, until by the mid eighteenth century they had fallen to a tenth or less of their previous levels. In this light, it is worth noting that the share of hanging references in cant references to criminal justice fell between 1673 and around 1700, from about a third in Head to just over a fifth (21.9 per cent) in B.E. So the canting lexicons were not wholly out of touch with the judicial system. In yet another respect both Head and B.E. showed themselves up to date with penal practices by referring to being 'marinated', or transported to a foreign plantation, a punishment that was used more and more in this period.[51]

Allusions to other parts of the state apparatus are rather more straightforward in their interpretation. The increase in references to imprisonment may reflect the growth of sentencing and the expansion of such facilities in the period. We do not know whether more people were being sentenced to incarceration in traditional gaols. Complaints about imprisonment for debt, so prominent from the mid-seventeenth century, might suggest they were. Little seems to be known about the size of gaols before the eighteenth century, but the frequent rebuilding of shire halls in the late seventeenth century might well have included an expansion of the gaols that were often attached.[52]

It is known, however, that sentencing convicts to spells in bridewells or houses of correction grew, as did the numbers of lock-ups themselves.

These institutions were virtually brand-new in the period and incarcerated a variety of petty offenders for spells of days or weeks. Between 1600 and 1630 about one a year was created, though thereafter, until 1690, numbers were just maintained. Then between 1690 and 1720, another seventeen were set up. The numbers locked up in these places could be significant: between 1620 and 1680 Chelmsford's house of correction received 846 offenders, and this was only one of three such institutions in Essex.[53] The London bridewells appeared in cant. In B.E.'s lexicon they were called 'boarding schools'; the whipper or beadle there was the 'flogging-cove'; the inmates were 'bridewell birds' or 'boarding scholars'. The original Bridewell, founded in 1553, was the 'old Nask'; the Clerkenwell institution was the 'new Nask'; and the Westminster one in Tothill Street was called 'Bridewell in Turtle Fields'.

Although canting words concerned with public punishments are few in number in table 3.2, that they hardly increased in the period is consistent with the evidence of sentencing. Not all whippings were public and so the generic expression to 'cly the jerk' (be whipped) has not been included here. In south-east England, at least, the authorities continued to prescribe public whippings and the pillory well into the eighteenth century. Whipping increased towards the end of the seventeenth century as petty larceny charges were substituted for grand larceny ones. References to imprisonment might have been growing, but they were not wholly supplanting public humiliations as a form of punishment in the canting lexicon.[54] B.E. produced three versions of the pillory – 'wooden-ruff', 'nut-crackers' and 'penance board'. He also listed two different versions of being whipped at a cart's tail: 'flogged at the tumbler' and 'to shove the tumbler'.

References to the worlds of magistrates and police were also few, though in the case of the latter on the increase. Words relating to judges, justices of the peace and their courts show little consciousness of the legal system. Until the end of the period canting vocabulary included no more than the occasional reference to a justice, or 'queer cuffin'. Only in B.E.'s glossary was there any detailed awareness of officialdom and the judiciary. He cited the term 'fortune-tellers' for judges of life and death, 'fur-men' for aldermen and 'lamb-skin men' for the judges of the several courts. There was, however, a growing vocabulary to describe the various kinds of police. 'Harman beck', 'beck' and 'flogging-cove' were used for beadles, 'nightwalker' and 'child of darkmans' for bellmen, 'hamlet' for high constable, 'harman' for constable and 'myrmidons' for the men of the watch.

The foregoing suggests a canting world that was more and more conscious of certain features of the criminal justice system, above all of the gallows, imprisonment and the police. Far less attention was given to public punishments and the judiciary. The rise in references to the police and the gallows are difficult to connect with actual developments. There is no obvious reason to believe that policing increased, and we know that hanging did not. Rather, what these changes in canting seem to represent is a world in which crime was at the forefront. To criminals the gallows, the police and imprisonment were matters of survival, involving detection, capture and loss of freedom and possibly life. Public humiliation associated with flogging or the pillory was of secondary importance, as were the judges.

As was seen in table 3.1 (category 6), the number of verbs describing criminal acts grew faster than the general rate of increase in cant words – by 2.9 times as compared with 2.4. What is more, verbs involving illegal activities rose faster than those that did not, which increased 2.0 times. While the enlarged vocabulary did not include wholly new kinds of crime, it involved new techniques and greater violence. Housebreaking, picking pockets and defrauding people, often in card games, continued to be the main crimes throughout the period. Head cited a more sophisticated method of picking pockets, the 'bulk and file', which meant that one thief jostled the victim while the other did the dirty work. The partner was called the 'shoulder sham'. Another development in theft from the person was the virtual disappearance of allusions to cutting purses, which may reflect a growing fashion for pockets.

When nouns are examined, they too indicate new techniques and specialities of thieving. The vocabulary of shoplifting appears for the first time. Harman mentioned the phrase to 'heave a bough', which meant to rob or rifle a booth, an allusion to the market stalls that characterized retail trade in sixteenth-century fairs and markets. Seventeenth-century cant described how thieves pestered shops: 'shoplifter' appeared in Head's list of canting words in 1673.[55] B.E. added 'bob' and 'bubber' for the accomplices. The same author cited other cant words for specialized theft. The 'buffenapper' stole pedigree dogs, including setters, hounds, spaniels and lapdogs; the 'clank-napper' had a line in silver tankards; the 'biter of peeters' lifted boxes and trunks from horses, coaches and wagons; 'water-pads' stole from ships on the Thames; and the 'wiper drawer' took handkerchiefs.

Mentions of violence increased. The main shift was towards more terminal and gruesome forms of mayhem. Before 1626 the vocabulary was limited to beating people – 'filching' and 'fibbing'. The later seventeenth century augmented this lexicon by adding homicide and new techniques of assault and robbery. B.E. added 'crashing' and 'milling' for murder (Head limited 'milling' to robbery), 'kimbaw' for beating severely and 'dinging' for knocking down. Robbery with violence was expressed in two new forms: 'reversing', already mentioned as a noun, and 'gagging', or putting iron pins into victims' mouths to stop them crying out. Nouns also heighten the impression of greater violence in the taxonomy. Before B.E.'s dictionary there were few mentions at all of assaults and murders in canting. His listings, however, included several terms for criminals who committed assaults: for a murderer, a 'miller'; for bullies, 'bouncer', 'bully rock', 'captain hackum', 'ding boy', 'hackum' and 'knight of the blade'.

It is probable that the appearance of these names reflected real changes in patterns of crime. In seventeenth-century Essex assault was the third most commonly indicted crime after grand larceny and illegal alehouse-keeping. What is more, indictments for the crime rose 'steadily although gently' between 1620 and 1680. At Surrey quarter sessions and assizes between 1660 and 1800 assault cases ran a close second to non-capital property offences – 4,493 compared with 5,211.[56] There is good reason to believe that indictments in these courts understate the situation. Church, leet and borough courts also heard assault cases, but the indictments rarely survive. Even at quarter sessions such offences were often treated as civil disputes, which justices attempted to settle out of court. Further, eighteenth-century grand juries showed a clear preference for indicting property crimes rather than assaults, because they were terrified of robbers and thieves. But if, homicide excepted, interpersonal violence was common and on the increase, it is hard to accept the statement that assaults tell us little about the society in which they were committed.[57] At the very least, their persistence suggests that it is premature to conclude from declining murder rates that England was experiencing a 'civilizing process' that was improving social relations.[58]

The final changes to notice in canting semantics concern categories 14 (money/precious metals) and 15 (clothing/objects worn or carried), which grew more than any other group. References to cash and precious metals increased 6.7 times, and those to clothing and so on 4.5 times. These rises suggest that canting became more and more attuned to the essentials of life – money and goods – in a commercializing, consumer society. They also reflect, of course, the barely concealed assumption that those who canted wished to relieve the possessors of their property. Before B.E.'s dictionary there were just one or two canting words for the nominal money. 'Lour' was in common usage from Harman onwards, and by 1627 'shells' was added to describe stolen money. Head added no further nominals, but B.E. listed a bunch of them – 'balsom', 'chink', 'cly', 'cole', 'coliander seed', 'crap', 'gelt', 'King's pictures', 'lurries', 'prey', 'quidds' and 'ribbin'. There were now typologies of different kinds of cash. Ready money was 'darby', 'ready' and 'rhino'. A goodly sum of cash was 'caravan', 'cargo', 'well equipt', 'flush in the pocket' and 'rum cod'. 'Mint' was gold (and had been since *Martin Markall*), and 'gorce' was mainly gold coin. 'Old Mr Gory' or 'yellow' was a piece of gold. 'Recruits' was money that one expected to receive, and 'rum cole' and 'rum gelt' were new money, possibly meaning newly minted.

There was also a remarkable expansion in canting words for coin-clipping. Before B.E. wrote, no argot terms for clipping have been discovered. The bulk of the vocabulary referring to money cited denominations of coin, as table 3.3 indicates. But in B.E.'s lists there are eleven citations of the crime. They have been 'round the Tower with it' referred to money that had been clipped. The crime was also called 'nigging'; clippings were described as 'shavings', 'nig', 'parings' and 'curle'; clippers were 'niglers' and 'queer cole makers'; receivers 'queer cole fencers'; clipped money 'queer cole'; and the tools 'nipps'. Coinclipping was a capital offence, and groups of clippers were periodically prosecuted from the 1640s to the 1780s. North-west England experienced an especially virulent outbreak of clipping and counterfeiting in the reign of Charles II. The subject of the currency was being widely aired around the time that B.E. published his dictionary, because the Great Recoinage was carried out in 1696–8.[59]

Canting terms for denominations of the coinage became highly elaborate in the period. As table 3.3 shows, the pamphlets up to 1626 listed just five kinds of coin, whereas Head included ten, among them five new ones, and B.E. had thirty-three of which twenty-three were not previously cited. Some of the words were just new names for old coins, such as 'croaker' for a groat, 'half a hog', 'pig', 'sice' and 'simon' for 6d and 'twelver' for a shilling. But there were also terms for denominations not previously cited: 'husky-lour', 'job' and 'meggs' for the guinea, first minted in 1663; 'half a job', 'half a piece', 'half Angel' and 'smelt' for half a guinea; 'decus' for a crown; 'george', 'slate' and 'trooper' for half-crowns; 'grig', 'mopus' and 'rag' for a farthing; and 'ill-fortune' for 9d. The proliferation of cant words for money reflects the growing commercialization of English life. Canters, like everyone else, needed a larger vocabulary to describe the process. The preoccupation with cash even enveloped the lives of the hanged. According to B.E., 'six and eight pence' was the canting term for 'the usual fee given, to carry back the body of the executed malefactor, to give it Christian burial'.

The category 'clothing/objects carried on the person' (number 15,

Table 3.3 Denominations of coins in canting vocabulary, c.1535–c.1700

	1535–1626	Head, 1673	B.E., c.1700
bord (shilling)	x	x	x
bulls eye (5s)			x
croaker (groat)			x
dace (2d)			x
decus (5s)			x
dewswins (2d)		x	x
flag (groat)	x	x	x
george (2s 6d)			x
grig (farthing)			x
half bord (6d)	x	x	x
half a hog (6d)			x
half a job (half-guinea)			x
hog (shilling)		x	x
husky-lour (guinea)		x	x
Jack (farthing)			x
job (guinea)		x	x
ill-fortune (9d)			x
loon-slatt (13½d)			x
make (halfpenny)	x	x	x
meggs (guineas)			x
mopus (farthing)			x
pig (6d)			x
rag (farthing)			x
sice (6d)			x
simon (6d)			x
slate (2s 6d)			x
smelt (half-guinea)			x
threpps (3d)			x
thrumms (3d)			x
tres wins (3d)		x	x
trooper (2s 6d)			x
twelver (shilling)			x
win (penny)	x	x	x

Sources: A. V. Judges (ed.), *The Elizabethan Underworld: A Collection of Tudor and Early Stuart Tracts and Ballads* (1930); Richard Head, *The Canting Academy, or, the Devils Cabinet Opened* (1673); B.E., *A New Dictionary of the Terms Ancient and Modern of the Canting Crew, in Its Several Tribes, of Gypsies, Beggers, Thieves, Cheats, etc.* (n.d.)

table 3.1) rose from nineteen words in the pamphlets before 1626 to eighty-five in B.E.'s listings, or by 4.5 times. As a share of the total canting vocabulary of the respective periods, the increase was from 5.2 per cent to 9.9 per cent. One reason was that the taxonomy of apparel became richer: for stockings, 'drawers' or 'stock-drawers', added by Head; for breeches, 'farting crackers', by B.E.; for a wig, 'flash', 'scandalous' and 'strum', by the same. Foreign words added to the variety. B.E. included 'accoutrements' for fine dress: 'camesa' for shirt, 'kilkenny' for a poor frieze-coat and 'shappeau' for hat.

The vocabulary was also expanding because canting paid greater attention to the quality of goods, another sign of consumerism. 'Tackle' and 'rum rigging' specified fine clothes. 'Rum' was high quality, as opposed to 'queer', or poor quality. According to B.E., 'blackmuns' were hoods and scarves that were 'alamode' and made of 'lustrings', a glossy silk. A 'queer degen' was a sword with a brass, steel or iron hilt, a 'rum degen' a silver-hilted or inlaid one. A 'queer nab' was a felt, Carolina or cloth hat 'not worth whipping off a man's head', while a 'rum' one was a beaver or other fine hat. 'Queer peepers' were 'old-fashioned, ordinary, black-framed, or common looking-glasses'; 'rum' ones were silver. And so on. By 1700 the canting vocabulary, like the rest of English society, was in the midst of commercial and consumer revolutions.

Canting: anti-language or jargon?

Sixteenth- and seventeenth-century cant described a criminal world cut off from respectable society that was urban rather than rural in its habitats; its people were homeless and commonly resorted to alehouses and brothels. Those who canted were portrayed as under the influence of intoxicants, since their vocabulary referred to alcohol and tobacco as frequently as to food. The most common words were nouns referring to types of criminal, crooked gaming, tools for thefts and varieties of victim. As the period progressed, the argot increased its references to the penal system, to prisons, hanging and the police. Both verbs and nouns cited new methods of theft and a widening range of terms to describe violence against persons. The lexicon covering money and articles of clothing increased considerably, suggesting a criminal vocabulary attuned to a commercializing, consumer society.

It remains to be seen whether English canting of this period constituted an anti-language in the sense used by Halliday. Certainly the notion finds support from recent studies of slang. Its employment in

Oliver Twist (1837–8), it is said, allows the criminals in the story to 'communicate with one another by employing signifiers whose connection with the signified objects of criminal ideology evade the understanding of outsiders ... As linguistic perimeters, these signifiers not only keep the dominant propertied and mercantile ideology on the outside; they also call attention to an inside, where criminal subjects have chosen to identify with the criminal life.'[60]

Similarly, a study of the argot of gangs in Midwestern cities in the 1990s finds that, however great the animosity between rival gangs, they share a common slang and ultimately their greatest hatred is reserved for the dominant culture.[61] Even non-criminal uses of jargon can express alienation from a hegemonic order. A recent study of slang among (mainly white) South African secondary school students cites 'its widespread use within a social group to defy linguistic or social convention'.[62] Whether used by seventeenth-century vagabonds, the Artful Dodger or middle-class South African teenagers, there seems to be a consensus that an argot was part of an intended rebellion. In Halliday's view the break involves conscious intent by the protesters. An anti-language, he writes, '*creates* . . . an alternative reality, one that is *constructed* precisely in order to function in alternation. It is the language of the antisociety.'[63]

Attitudes towards slang were formed not only by protesters, but also by the protested. One of the strengths of Halliday's paper is its attention to the transactional character of social relationships and dialects that go with them. Language, like social relations, is a two-way street, where travellers meet and interact. His insight that the statement 'I don't like their vowels' really signifies 'I don't like their values' is especially pungent. Equally useful is his typology of a sociolinguistic order in which the anti-language is at the bottom.[64]

But how was the hierarchy defined, and where was cant's place in it? As Peter Burke shows in the introduction to this volume (pp. 1–21), disapproval of many forms of jargon was pervasive in the early modern era. This resulted partly from official attempts to purify national languages, and also from hostility to the perceived affectation and obfuscation of jargon. Canting was held to be an ungrammatical and improper way of speaking. Robert Copland called it 'babbling French'; Harman castigated it as 'peevish [meaning foolish; but also possibly spiteful] speech'; Dekker described it simply as 'gibberish'. *The English Rogue* (1665) also called it 'a confused invention of words; for its dialect I cannot find to be founded on any certain rules'.[65]

In the case of canting, there were reasons besides intelligibility, including social and political ones, to attack it, since it was linked with moral failings, crime and threats to the established religious and political order. Harman brought up its criminal links in referring to it as 'the lewd, lousy languages of these loitering lusks [sluggards] and lazy lorels [rogues, blackguards]'. According to *The English Rogue*, the chaos of cant was consistent with its origins. It was irreligious, 'that language of the Devil's imps'; it was also a challenge to the status quo: that it was gibberish was 'no wonder since the founders and practicers thereof are the chief fathers and nourishers of disorder'.[66]

The earliest lexicographers of English were uneasy about including cant words. The first five dictionaries published between 1604 and 1658 included no criminal slang.[67] When specialized lexicons of the 'vulgar tongue' began to appear from the late seventeenth century, they were often prefaced with apologies for any possible offence to readers. Francis Grose's compilation of 1785 included a bowdlerized reference to the word 'F–K, to copulate'.[68] Underworld argot continued to signify social and moral divisions in the nineteenth century. In *Oliver Twist* Dickens is said to have used the canting language as a code to demarcate boundaries of class and morality: a 'confrontation between the denizens of the underworld and the dominant ideology of law, order, and respectability'.[69] In France the period saw the middle classes writing argot 'in the construction of an image that showed the people as a foreign, threatening, distant entity'.[70]

There is no doubt that the literature of roguery and its lists of cant vocabulary fostered the belief that an anti-society of criminals stood ready to destroy good order in sixteenth- and seventeenth-century England. But the terms 'create', 'demarcate' and 'construct' impart a degree of teleology that is perhaps unwarranted. The idea that canting developed because it served a purpose is partly true. But above all it assisted the canting elements to disguise their speech and crimes. A well-known statement in *A Manifest Detection of the Most Vile and Detestable Use of Dice-play* (1552) said that cheaters used canting 'to the intent that ever in all companies they may talk familiarly in all appearance, and so covertly indeed that their purpose may not be espied'.[71] In the process boundaries were demarcated, but we should be wary of reifying the experience of criminality, just as we should that of class.[72] From the vantage point of the criminal, the boundaries were the result of a complex process, originating, first, in the lived experience of engaging in crime and, secondly, in various needs arising from that activity: pre-eminently, to conceal criminal identities and acts, and to have familiar terms with which to conduct crimes. In this sense canting would be more accurately described as a counter-experience rather than a counter-reality. In fact, as noted, cant words were attuned to mainstream social realities in the seventeenth century, above all the growing influence of commerce and consumerism.

The lines of demarcation were blurred in other areas, making it simplistic to talk about an anti-language serving an anti-society. The oppositional and protest elements in canting can be exaggerated. There were few words to suggest frontal attacks on the social, political or religious systems. Like Midwestern gangs of the 1990s, there was hostility to the authorities. B.E. quoted the following menacing piece of canting: 'As the ruffin nab the cuffin queer, and let the harman beck trine with his kinchins about his colquarron', which meant 'Let the Devil take [the] justice, and let the constable hang with his children about his neck.' Yet the same author gave an example of canting that indicated social contact between a gentleman and criminals, citing an incident when 'The gentry cove tipt us rum peck and rum gutlers, till we were all bowsy, and snapt all the flickers', which he translated as 'The gentleman gave us so much good victuals, and canary, that we were all damned drunk, and broke all the drinking glasses.'[73] If the boundaries were so sharply demarcated, what was a gentleman doing giving hospitality to a bunch of rogues?

The same tendency towards boundary-crossing is seen in the development of English lexicography. As stated, none of the earliest dictionaries published up to 1658 included canting words. But this situation changed in 1676 with the publication of Elisha Coles's *English Dictionary*, which included numerous examples. Although most were taken from Head's lists of 1673, it is interesting to note the compiler's justification for their inclusion: ''Tis no disparagement to understand the canting terms: it may chance to save your throat from being cut, or (at least) your pocket from being pick'd.'[74] Here, then, was a deliberate crossing of boundaries with a similar purpose to that of the canters: survival. Other such crossovers occurred more and more frequently, as canting began to enjoy 'widespread vogue'. In 1694 the printer John Dunton brought out *The Ladies Dictionary*; it offered cant words describing the various types of female vagrant. The Coles and Dunton dictionaries began a wave of publication that included B.E.'s *New Dictionary*, which was wholly devoted to popular language. B.E.'s book was widely imitated in the eighteenth century, and the fascination with canting has persisted right down to the twentieth century and Partridge's productions.[75] The crossing of boundaries was not, of course, limited to dictionaries. Henry Fielding's *Tom Jones* and Dickens's *Oliver Twist* are just two examples of a tradition in which the innocent entered the dangerous underworld territory of criminals.

It goes without saying that the reception of canting vocabulary was never wholly complete, nor positive. *Cocker's English Dictionary* of 1704, while drawing upon Coles, excluded the argot. When it gave examples in later editions, it disparagingly cited Coles's practical justification: 'as if these miscreants would be kinder to any one for speaking or understanding a little of their gibberish'. The compiler sardonically added of cant words, 'I have inserted some few, but omitted a multitude.'[76] Other standard dictionaries began to include cant in their compilations; one or two contained special sections for the argot. Others, however, notably Dr Johnson's of 1755, largely purged the words, except where they were cited by respectable authors, and he usually referred to them as being in bad taste.[77] Nevertheless, it is worth concluding this essay by quoting Johnson's definition of cant, which was far more neutral than might be expected from 'a strenuous opponent of corruption in speech':

> TO CANT. *v. n.* [from the noun] To talk in the jargon of particular professions, or in any kind of formal affected language, or with a peculiar and studied tone of voice.

Here was no frontal assault upon canting. Rather Johnson's definition suggests that cant was entering the mainstream of the language, albeit as an instance of jargon.[78]

Appendix

The Examination of Mary Roberts, the wife of Anthony Roberts, taken the 28th day of November 1613 before Christopher [Anketill?], justice of peace within the town and borough of Shaston.

Who says that she has been married unto Anthony Roberts about eight and thirty years and that he stole her from her friends in Gloucestershire when she was but fourteen years of age and that they lived in London together until it was about nineteen years since, at which time her said husband left her and remained from her about fifteen years, until she hearing at St James Tide last was two years that her said husband was hanged at Chard within the county of Somerset. She repaired into that country to know the certainty thereof, when and where she met him living at a place called Burrow [?] in the county aforesaid, with whom she continued, where they remained but two days from whence this examinant and her husband travelled into Herefordshire and Gloucestershire, where they spent some six months amongst their friends. And further says that her said husband would often bring her to town where he would leave her sometimes fourteen days together and then would return unto her.

And said further that about Christmas last they were in Worcestershire at Henley upon Thames [*sic*; *recte* Oxfordshire], where they remained all the holidays. From thence they wandered begging the country not all known unto her. Says they came into Dorsetshire, which as this examinant thinks was near about St Lawrence Day last. Being further examined where her husband had those few passes that were taken about him, saith that one of them he had at Wimborne Minster within the county of Dorset, made by one Oliver Oake, petty chapman, with the names of Sir John Windham, knight, George Lutterell and John Francis, Esqs. Being further examined who made the other two passes with the names of Thomas Bishop and George Goring, knights, and Anthony Shertey, Esquire, says it was made by one William Martyne, a shoemaker dwelling in Axbridge near Wells within the county of Somerset. And further says that there is one [Fr?] Day, minister dwelling in Pilton, who makes passes for travellers, as namely for one John Munday, William Jeavell, and Thomas Gardner, all wandering travellers and for one John Maunder, who has been twice burnt in the shoulder and for one [?] Picke, both which have had passes made by the aforesaid William Martyn.

And further says that the minister of [Up Osborne?] within the county of Somerset is a common pass maker for all these wanderers, and further says, that there is one Barnes Baker, who is a notable housebreaker, who has in his company a woman named Winnie Ernste, who has had already three pardons and also says that one [?] Picke and Ned Cable, both Somersetshire men, are notorious housebreakers. And there is one Parker and her daughter, who travel with Ned Cable and he keeps them and lies with them at [Buppaies?] in Shaston. And further says that one John Marten and John Picke are dangerous rogues. Being further examined, who made the pass that Sir Thomas Vavasor's name is fixed unto, says that it was made by Sir Thomas Vavasor's clerk, in Salisbury at the King's Arms last being there.

Being further examined what others she knew that were of these travelling rogues, says that she knows one John Carlyle that begs by a pass that he has from Denmark as a servitor there, who walks with two women, the one named Edith Balhacheth and the other Joan Butt, what more she knows not, but says that they are both cutpurses and have been in Ilchester gaol. She says further that there is one John Tucker that travels with these [?] passes and hath them from William Martin at Axbridge.

She says further that there is one Hugh Hyde, a Somersetshire man dwelling in Martock, who wanders with his wife up and down all the country begging, who has made himself a lame leg and under colour of that wanders without a pass, but his [purpose?] is to filch and steal in the market towns all manner of small things as shoes, knives, gloves, or the like. And further says that there is one Philip Harris, dwelling in Wareham [Dorset], who is a petty chapman, and with his use of false passes he has gotten three pensions, besides a part of a seal, to gather [in?] Hampshire. Being further examined who else she knew of this wandering trade, says that she knows one John Gibb, a counterfeit dumb *maunder, as her term is,* who wanders with the privy signet counterfeited by one Cable who is a *feaker,* that is a pass maker, that teaches children in Marshfield [Gloucestershire] within the county of Wiltshire [*sic*]. And withall she says that there is one Philip Skoole dwelling in Reading, who is a partner with the aforesaid Harris in all his passes; and says that they did gather four shires, as Sussex, Hampshire, Wiltshire, and Dorset, and that there is another called George Williams and as this examinant thinks he lives in or near about Reading, who rides up and down the country begging. She says that he is to be known by one of his legs is shorter than the other and travels with false passes as the rest and is a great director of those *feakers* and *maunderers*, and says that withall that there is one dwelling at the Flying Horse in Catteren Street in Salisbury who is a *feaker*.

And further says that she knows one Thomas Paule who [?] to Salisbury that is a *feaker* and a beggar and sometimes plays the butcher in stealing sheep and sells them; he has in his company a woman that is not his wife, whose name they call Rebecca Paule.

And being further examined what other she knew of this cursed crew, says she knows one Thomas Jones, who travels with false passes and counterfeit letters as from Sir William Wake, Sir Daniel Donne, and Sir Thomas Vavasor, and hath three pensions, one in Monmouthshire and another in Herefordshire, but the other shires she knows not, unless it be in Somersethshire.

Upon further examination, she confesses that there is one Tobieth Hooke that is a [lame?] soldier, a notable rogue and dwells in Roudge Lane, who is a *feaker* exceeding all the rest. And further says that he is a *cheater* at all plays whatsoever and she does describe him to be a handsome tall man with a yellow bushy beard, of a fair complexion with a little scar in his face, wearing a laced jerkin and his rapier in a belt hanging about his neck. And says that he is a nimble dancer and wears a pair of green say garters that were of a wench's apron, and goes with a pass for the service of Denmark. She says his companions are one Thomas Evans, who dwells in Southwark and is married to a midwife there, and one Thomas Jones, dwelling in Southwark. All those are *cheaters* and are of one consort.

And she says further that she knows one John [Zeager?] that is a *feaker*, a Londoner who travels with these [?] passes. He is a Kent Street man in Southwark, as is this Tobieth Hooke and his companions. And says that this [Zeager?] has a lame arm made by his villainy and keeps it so filthy that it smells very contagiously. He *is termed a glimmer maunderer* and so are all the rest that say were burnt with fire.

She says further that she knows one Thomas Philips, a glassman who lately had his abode in [Ramsbury?] beyond the bridge as you come from Mr Douce's house southward, who travels with a counterfeit pass, but is [?] carries it who is a dangerous man, both for cheating and cosening, and has been whipped in Barnstable and should have whipped [as cheaters?] had she not come from thence when Sir George Smith was mayor there.

She says she knows one John Franckelon, a Somersetshire man who travels with a false pass made by the aforesaid Mr [Dea] a minister dwelling in Pilton. *She says he is a glimmer maunderer* and begs for that he had his house burnt and four children, having yet six with him, whereof four she thinks to be he own, but the other two he has stolen.

And further that she knows one Anne [?] and Anne Lowe who travel with a pass made by the aforesaid Oliver Oake, and also one Fraunces Maunder late wife of John Maunder, but now goes under the name of William Edwards. His wife who travels with a pass made by William Martin of Axbridge with the names and seals of Sir George Trenchard and Sir John Browne, knights, and begs for the burning of the town of Dorchester.[79] And further says that she is to be known by a blemish in one of her eyes. Her apparel is commonly a purple waistcoat with a small wing with three green laces on the shoulder and laced about the skirt. And being further examined where she knew any of the places where these people do usually resort, says that at [Yeovil?] at Weaver's house at the sign of the Cup is a place of receipt where John Martin and Pickes with others do mean to keep their Christmas this year, and also at one Davis his house in Axbridge who keeps an alehouse there and is the mayor's man in Axbridge, who also harbors them secretly, sometimes a week together and is acquainted with that William Martyn that is a *feaker* aforesaid. She says also that at Cheddar at a widow woman's house who professes surgery for them that are lame of these wanderers, there is entertainment for them but she keeps no alehouse and dwells almost in the middle of the town. Also in Glastonbury at one Owen's house, a Welshman, there is entertainment for them; there is also money for those things that they shall bring with them, as likewise at the other places before mentioned.

Upon further examination what houses she knows of such receipt in Dorsetshire says that she knows none but those that are honest and good.

Being examined what places of such receipt she knows in Wiltshire, says that in Fisherton at the sign of the Green [?] at one widow Jones's there [lie?] all the disordered people that travel in the country. Also at one Ann Grosse's house in Fisherton and in the town of Salisbury at one Dickson's house in Winchester Street and at the Flying Horse in Catterne Street at one Benberye's house, who is also a *feaker* and also at Shedwell's house without Winchester Gate, who is also a notorious thief, and at one Cooke's by the [Pound; Pond?], who is a widow man. She says further that at this Cooke's house John [?] and his wife did appoint to keep their Christmas there; also at the Rose in [?] and the house right against it are places both of receipt for such people and such things as shall be stolen by them in their thievish wandering.

Hampshire

She says that at Romsey at one Hollowaie's house there resort all such persons, and especially one William Braye and his woman. This Braye is a counterfeit madman and a false pass carrier. She says that this Hollowaie's house is one licensed alehouse. Also at Fareham at the sign of the Lamb, being further examined of her further knowledge of these wandering rogues, says there is one Arthur Barrett, a glassman, whose wife carries small wares, notable rogue and a thief. He is a tall, big fellow with a red beard; his apparel is like a sailor.

She says also that there is one Michael White, a wandering rogue and dangerous. There is also one Mary Browne, bred a wandering rogue and a thief and does travel much the country aforesaid, and says that at Charmouth [Dorset]; with [?] of Lyme [Regis, Dorset] in the country aforesaid at one Jones's house there is a place of receipt for all such kind of people. There is also one Honor that is a Bedlam man, a most vile creature. All these rogues aforesaid this examinant says will be had about Lyme this Christmas. And says that at Dunster in the county of Somerset there is one John More; also at [Earningeton?], the clerk of the parish is a *feaker*; likewise at [blank] there is a *feaker* but she knows not his name.[80]

Notes

For their valuable comments on earlier drafts of this paper, I wish to thank Professors John M. Beattie, Peter Linebaugh, James Siemon, Lawrence Stone and William C. Woodson. They are, of course, not responsible for any of its failings.

1 John L. McMullan, *The Canting Crew: London's Criminal Underworld, 1550–1700* (New Brunswick, NJ: Rutgers University Press, 1984), 99.

2 Peter Trudgill, *Sociolinguistics: An Introduction to Language and Society* (Harmondsworth: Penguin, 1974); R. A. Hudson, *Sociolinguistics* (Cambridge: Cambridge University Press, 1980). It is obvious from the latter's discussions of 'language change' (85, 149ff) that historical development is accorded little or no role in this paradigm. Rather 'change' seems to mean variations within a language.

3 P. J. Corfield, 'Introduction: Historians and Language', in P. J. Corfield (ed.), *Language, History and Class* (Oxford: Blackwell, 1991), 21–2.

4 McMullan, *The Canting Crew*, 99.

5 Mary McIntosh, *The Organisation of Crime* (London: Macmillan, 1975), 22.

6 M. A. K. Halliday, 'Antilanguages', repr. in his *Language as a Social Semiotic: the Social Interpretation of Language and Meaning* (London: Arnold, 1978), 164, 166–7, 179.

7 M. T. Clanchy, *From Memory to Written Record: England, 1066–1307* (London: Arnold, 1979). But the recording of beggars' and thieves' jargon began much earlier in the Muslim world, in the tenth century: Clifford E. Bosworth, *The Mediaeval Islamic Underworld*, 2 vols (Leiden: Brill, 1976), i: xi and ch. 1.

8 Bronislaw Geremek, *The Margins of Society in Late Medieval Paris* (Cambridge: Cambridge University Press, 1987), 33, 43.

9 Robert Jütte, *Abbild und soziale Wirklichkeit des Bettler- und Gaunertums zu Beginn der Neuzeit* (Cologne: Böhlau Verlag, 1988), 105–9; John Camden Hotten, *The Book of Vagabonds and Beggars: With a Vocabulary of Their Language* (London: Hotten, 1860), 3. See also Robert Jütte, *Poverty and*

Deviance in Early Modern Europe (Cambridge: Cambridge University Press, 1994), 179–85 (quotation at 182).

10 Geremek, *The Margins of Society*, 127–9.

11 Jose Luis Alonso Hernandez, *El lenguaje de los maleantes españoles de los siglos XVI y XVII: La germanía* (Salamanca: Ediciones Universidad de Salamanca, 1979), *passim*.

12 Piero Camporesi, *Il libro dei vagabondi*, 2nd edn (Turin: Einaudi, 1980), xcii (I wish to thank Peter Burke for this reference), 351–61; also cited by Jütte, *Abbild und soziale Wirklichkeit*, 106, 225.

13 Late medieval information from Professor Barbara A. Hanawalf; F. W. Chandler, *The Literature of Roguery* (Boston: Houghton, Mifflin and Co., 1907), I, 205.

14 John Awdeley, *Fraternity of Vagabonds* (1561), and Thomas Harman, *Caveat for Common Cursitors* (1566), repr. in A. V. Judges (ed.), *The Elizabethan Underworld: A Collection of Tudor and Early Stuart Tracts and Ballads* (London: Routledge and Kegan Paul, 1930; repr. 1965), 24, 35–6, 51–108, 113–18.

15 Judges, *The Elizabethan Underworld*, 312, 511; cf. De Witt T. Starnes and Gertrude E. Noyes, 'The Development of Cant Lexicography in England, 1566–1785', in Starnes and Noyes, *The English Dictionary from Cawdrey to Johnson, 1604–1755* (Chapel Hill: University of North Carolina Press, 1946), 215–17. Students of canting should consider themselves extremely fortunate to have the valuable scholarship of Starnes and Noyes.

16 Judges, *The Elizabethan Underworld*, 406–11. The total of 363 is a conflation of Harman, *Martin Markall* and those listed as cant ones in Judges' own glossary, 522–32, and not listed by the former two authors. There might be further cant words in other examples of the literature in the period and in the drama (see Starnes and Noyes, 'Development of Cant Lexicography', 217, 285 n. 17). There are also some poems and songs to be considered: John S. Farmer (ed.), *Musa pedestris: Three Centuries of Canting Songs and Slang Rhymes (1536–1896)* (1896; repr. New York: Cooper Square, 1964). But it is unlikely these sources will greatly expand the vocabulary.

17 Richard Head, *The English Rogue Described in the Life of Meriton Latroon, a Witty Extravagant* (London: Routledge and Sons, 1928), 28–34.

18 Richard Head, *The Canting Academy, or, the Devils Cabinet Opened* (London, 1673), 34–56 (quotation at 56).

19 B.E., *A New Dictionary of the Terms Ancient and Modern of the Canting Crew, in Its Several Tribes, of Gypsies, Beggers, Thieves, Cheats, etc.* (London, n.d.; facsimile edn, n.p., 1899). The dating of this publication is difficult. Starnes and Noyes, in 'Development of Cant Lexicography', rather loosely assign it to 1690–1700, then suggest that it could not have appeared before 1694 (213, 220). They also say that Yale University Library has a copy dated 1699 and cite another authority who puts the publication date at 1698. My own reading turned up a reference (sig. I.8.b.) to 'anno 1695' as being in the past, suggesting that it was not published before that date.

20 A 'c.' after a word in B.E., *A New Dictionary*, is assumed here to designate a cant word.
21 A. L. Beier, *Masterless Men: The Vagrancy Problem in England, 1560–1640* (London: Methuen, 1985), 125.
22 McMullan, *The Canting Crew*, 97ff. Contrary to Dr McMullan, there is no evidence that canting was illegal. The more recent study by Ermanno Barisone, *Il gergo dell'underworld elisabettiano* (Genoa: Il melangolo, 1989), ignores judicial records and recent historical writing on the subject.
23 See the frontispiece to B.E., *A New Dictionary*, which was refreshingly frank in stating that it was intended to be 'very diverting and entertaining'.
24 Jütte, *Abbild und soziale Wirklichkeit*, 71–4.
25 Beier, *Masterless Men*, xx–xxi.
26 Essex Record Office, Q/SR 76/56.
27 *The Book of John Fisher, Town Clerk and Deputy Recorder of Warwick, 1580–1588* (Warwick: Henry T. Cooke, n.d.), 28.
28 Essex Record Office, Q/SR 113/40a.
29 Kent County Archives Office, QM/SB 643–4.
30 William Fleetwood, letter to William Cecil, 7 July 1585, in R. H. Tawney and Eileen Power (eds), *Tudor Economic Documents* (London: Longman, 1924), ii: 338–9. For Fleetwood's credibility as a magistrate, see Ian Archer, *The Pursuit of Stability: Social Relations in Elizabethan London* (Cambridge: Cambridge University Press, 1991), 204ff. For the canting words cited here, see Judges, *The Elizabethan Underworld*, 115 (nip; mill a ken), 408 (foist), 528 (lift), 530 (shave).
31 Somerset Record Office Q/SR 18/82, 19/126 (my italic). It seems that the documents appear in the records of another county, because the Dorset justice was informing Somerset officials of criminals working in their county.
32 Judges, *The Elizabethan Underworld*, 55 (Awdeley), 93–4 (Harman), 408, 522.
33 Ibid., 114 (Harman), 523.
34 Ibid., 114.
35 Ibid.
36 Ibid. 117; Head, *Canting Academy*, 56–7.
37 Beier, *Masterless Men*, 125, citing *OED*, 'cant'.
38 Judges, *The Elizabethan Underworld*, 114–15, 407–9, 522–32.
39 Jütte, *Abbild und soziale Wirklichkeit*, 119–24; Hernandez, *El lenguaje de los maleantes españoles*, 20ff.
40 Halliday, 'Antilanguages', 170–1.
41 Specific references to every cant word cited in the following would be out of the question. Readers are referred to the glossaries and dictionary cited in nn. 15–19.
42 Beier, *Masterless Men*, 74.
43 For an informed and cautious view, see Joan Thirsk, *England's Agricultural Regions and Agrarian History, 1500–1750* (London: Macmillan, 1987), esp. ch. 5.

44 J. C. Drummond and A. Wilbraham, *The Englishman's Food: A History of Five Centuries of English Diet*, new edn (London: Cape, 1958), pt 2.

45 Judges, *The Elizabethan Underworld*, 53–5, 67ff.

46 Beier, *Masterless Men*, 128–30, 134–7.

47 'Buttered bun' was not actually listed as a cant word, but it is in sufficiently bad taste by the standards of the time to be so classified.

48 Thomas E. Murray, 'The Folk Argot of Midwestern Gangs', *Midwestern Folklore*, 19, 2 (autumn 1993), 141–2.

49 B.E., *A New Dictionary*, title page.

50 J. A. Sharpe, '"Last Dying Speeches": Religion, Ideology and Public Execution in Seventeenth-century England', *Past and Present*, 107 (May 1985), 147–8; Peter Linebaugh, 'The Ordinary of Newgate and His Account', in J. S. Cockburn (ed.), *Crime in England, 1550–1800* (London: Methuen, 1977), 247; also Peter Linebaugh, *The London Hanged: Crime and Civil Society in the Eighteenth Century* (Cambridge: Cambridge University Press, 1992), *passim*.

51 J. A. Sharpe, *Crime in Early Modern England, 1550–1750* (London: Longman, 1984), 63–5; J. M. Beattie, *Crime and the Courts in England, 1660–1800* (Oxford: Clarendon Press, 1986), 470–4.

52 There is a paucity of discussion of gaols in recent monographs on crime and punishment.

53 Joanna Innes, 'Prisons for the Poor: English Bridewells, 1555–1800' *Labour, Law, and Crime: An Historical Perspective* (London, 1987), 77, 79; J. A. Sharpe, *Crime in Seventeenth-century England: A County Study* (Cambridge: Cambridge University Press, 1983), 151; cf. Beattie, *Crime and the Courts*, 498.

54 Beattie, *Crime and the Courts*, 461–8, 485–7; Beier, *Masterless Men*, 164–9.

55 I am grateful to Dr Derek Keene for valuable information concerning shops and booths.

56 Sharpe, *Crime in Seventeenth-century England*, 115–16, 189–90; Beattie, *Crime and the Courts*, 402.

57 Beattie, *Crime and the Courts*, 75–6, 401–2.

58 This is the position of a number of papers delivered at a session on 'Did Crime Modernize over the Long Term? Evidence since the Middle Ages', 16th annual meeting of the Social Science History Association, New Orleans, 1 November 1991.

59 Beier, *Masterless Men*, 142; John Styles, '"Our Traitorous Money Makers": The Yorkshire Coiners and the Law, 1760–83', in *An Ungovernable People: The English and Their Law in the Seventeenth and Eighteenth Centuries* (London: Hutchinson, 1980), 172ff; Alan Macfarlane, *The Justice and the Mare's Ale* (Oxford: Blackwell, 1981), 162ff.

60 Steven Michael, 'Criminal Slang in *Oliver Twist*: Dickens' Survival Code', *Style*, 27, 1 (spring 1993), 49.

61 Murray, 'Folk Argot of Midwestern Gangs', 114–15.

62 Vivien de Klerk, 'Slang: A Male Domain?', *Sex Roles*, 22, 9–10 (May 1990), 593.

63 Halliday, 'Antilanguages', 171 (my italics).

64 Ibid. 179.

65 Judges, *The Elizabethan Underworld*, 24, 114, 367; Head, *English Rogue*, 29.

66 Judges, *The Elizabethan Underworld*, 113; Head, *English Rogue*, 29.

67 Starnes and Noyes, 'Development of Cant Lexicography', 213.

68 Francis Grose, *A Classical Dictionary of the Vulgar Tongue* (London: Hooper, 1785; repr. Menston: Scolar Press, 1968), sig. K.2.a.

69 Michael, 'Criminal Slang in *Oliver Twist*', 45–7, 53.

70 Pascale Gaitet, 'From the Criminal's to the People's: The Evolution of Argot and Popular Language in the Nineteenth Century', *Nineteenth-century French Studies*, 19, 2 (winter 1991), 232.

71 *A Manifest Detection of the Most Vile and Detestable Use of Dice-play* (1552), repr. in Judges, *The Elizabethan Underworld*, 35.

72 E. P. Thompson, *The Making of the English Working Class* (New York: Vintage, 1966), 10–11.

73 B.E., *A New Dictionary*, sigs I.3.b., K.6.a.

74 Elisha Coles, *An English Dictionary* (1676), quoted in Starnes and Noyes, 'Development of Cant Lexicography', 220.

75 Starnes and Noyes, 'Development of Cant Lexicography', 220.

76 *Cocker's English Dictionary* (1704), quoted in ibid.

77 Starnes and Noyes, 'Development of Cant Lexicography', 221.

78 Ibid.; Samuel Johnson, *A Dictionary of the English Language* (London: Knapton et al., 1755; repr. New York: AMS Press, 1967), sig. I.4.a.

79 For the Dorchester fire of 6 August 1613, see David Underdown, *Fire from Heaven: Life in an English Town in the Seventeenth Century* (London: HarperCollins, 1992).

80 Somerset Record Office Q/SR 18/82. Punctuation has been modernized, as have place and personal names. Italics have been added to indicate where cant words are employed. Personal and place names were identified from John Paul Rylands (ed.), *The Visitation of the County of Dorset, taken in the year 1623 . . .*, Harleian Society, 20 (London, 1885); G. D. Squibb (ed.), *The Visitation of Dorset, 1677*, Harleian Society, 117 (London, 1977); F. T. Colby (ed.), *The Visitation of the County of Somerset in the year 1623*, Harleian Society, 11 (London, 1876); R. B. Pugh (ed.), *Victoria County History: A History of the County of Dorset* (Oxford, 1968), III; J. Hutchins, *History and Antiquities of the County of Dorset*, 3rd edn, 4 vols (Westminster, 1861–70); *Gazetteer of the British Isles* (Edinburgh; John Bartholomew & Son Ltd, 1972).

Another text citing cant words is found in J. H. Bettey (ed.), *The Case book of Sir Francis Ashley, JP, Recorder of Dorchester, 1614–1635*, Dorset Record Society (1981), 81–2. I owe this reference to the kindness of Professor David E. Underdown.

4

Caló: The 'Secret' Language of the Gypsies of Spain

JOHN GEIPEL

Ar pan le yaman *manró*,
Ar tocino *balebale*,
A la iglesia la *cangrí*
Y el *estaribé* a la carcé.

(They call bread 'manró',
Bacon 'balebale',
The church is the 'cangrí'
And 'estaribé' [stir] is the jail.)

Copla from a traditional *cante flamenco*

Some 400,000 Spanish citizens are currently recognized, by themselves and others, as Gitanos – Romanis or Gypsies. They thus represent a significant minority element in the country's population.

While the Iberian Gypsies (including the estimated 25,000 Portuguese Ciganos) constitute a mere fraction of the total world Romani population of some 6,000,000, they comprise, after the former Yugoslavia, Romania and Hungary (with populations of 900,000, 800,000 and 500,000 Romanis respectively), the largest concentration of their people in Europe.

Origins and language

Despite the persistent tradition which links them with Egypt (whence such ethnonyms as 'Gypsy' and 'Gitano'), the origins of the Romani people have been traced – though not by the Gypsies themselves, who know nothing of their remote antecedents – to the India of some thousand years ago. At that time, various groups of still largely unidentified, nomadic people, who may have included the ancestors of the later Romanis, left the region of the Punjab to cross Persia in the direction of Asia Minor and south-east Europe.

The Indian origins of the Gypsies, while partially confirmed by anthropological (mainly serological) evidence,[1] have been identified almost wholly on the basis of their use of a distinctive, in-group language, known by its speakers as Romani. This term, itself of Indian derivation, is from the root *rom*, which, in the speech of the Iberian Gypsies, means a married man, from which are derived the feminine *romí* (wife) and such compound forms as *romandiñar* (to marry) and *romandiño* (marriage). In spite of its lack of a standard, let alone a written, form and its fragmentation into many regional dialects (at least sixty of which have been distinguished in Europe), this idiom has retained a remarkable degree of conformity, especially in terms of its lexicon, from Turkey to Scandinavia and from the Atlantic to the Urals. This 'core' vocabulary of basic terms, common to all or most of the Romani dialects, is largely (some 65 per cent) of Indian inspiration. In Iberia, where the language is known as Caló, the original structures and much of the traditional lexicon have been replaced by those of the peninsular Romance languages (Castilian, Catalan and Galician/Portuguese). Nevertheless, the Gypsies of Spain and Portugal have retained sufficient of the *purí chipí* (old language) to enable us to relate this to other, more archaic Romani dialects spoken elsewhere in Europe and to hypothesize that, a mere eight or nine generations ago, the Gitanos must have spoken a much 'purer' form of their ancestral tongue than do their living descendants.

However, despite the attempts of such scholars as the Euro-MP Juan de Dios Ramírez Heredia (himself a Gitano) and Luís Tudela to re-create an idealized form of Romani[2] – a kind of 'Gypsy Esperanto' – with most of the traditional Indic vocabulary and inflections intact, this artifice bears little relation to the language as it is used by the Gypsies today. As Carlos Clavería remarks, 'What the Gitanos speak today is nothing more than the local dialect of Castilian, sprinkled with the odd Caló word.'[3] Even so, as Miguel Ropero Núñez points out: 'From the philological point of view [Caló] is a relic ... in imminent danger of disappearing, which serves as a link in the study of many (colloquial Spanish) words of Sanskrit derivation', while Clavería stresses that 'the importance of the Gitano element in the Spanish language is indisputable, as is the necessity for the lexicographer to study and classify it scientifically'.[4]

Almost as remarkable as the very tenacity of the Romani language within the Gitano community – however debased it may have become – is that this important linguistic influence on idiomatic Spanish emanates from the speech of those at the very bottom of the social scale.

The days when the Iberian Gypsies spoke Romani as their first language (if, indeed, such a time ever existed) are long gone. Today, and for countless generations past, they have learned Caló solely as a language secondary to Castilian or one of the other peninsular Romance vernaculars, acquiring it – as a cryptolect for exclusive use within the Gypsy community – on the street, in the market and in the home, from their elders and peers, along with all the imperfections, distortions, embellishments and individual quirks of usage and pronunciation that typify any such unwritten jargon. For a jargon it is or, rather, has become, in spite of the protestations of those who strive to resurrect it in its ancestral form, if we accept the dictionary definition of a jargon as a debased language or mode of speech familiar only to a specific group or profession.[5]

So what of those who first introduced this oriental language, in its archaic and inflected form, into the Iberian peninsula, the furthest west that the language penetrated in the Old World?

It has so far proved impossible to identify the 'proto-Romanis', the progenitors of the later Gypsies of Asia Minor, the Levant and Europe prior to the diaspora from India, with any specific group of nomads within the subcontinent. Attempts have been made to equate them with the Ḍoms, a caste of *harijan* (untouchable) peoples whose name appears to be etymologically akin to Rom/Roma/Romani, and to the Lohars, a nomadic sect who migrate seasonally across the Deccan of central India to the Western Ghats. As both these peoples speak Dravidian languages, some scholars have identified the proto-Romanis as the dispersed survivors (*dasas*) of the pre-Aryan Harappa or Mohenjo-Daro civilization which was overrun by Indo-Aryan invaders in the sixteenth century BC. However, the Romani language contains nothing of Dravidian derivation; it is classified as a distinct branch of the Neo-Indic family, derived from the Prākrit vernaculars spoken between about 500 BC and about AD 1000 and, ultimately, from the Sanskrit of the ancient Brahmin texts. Genealogically, Romani stands closest to the central Indian group (which includes Hindi and Panjabi), though it shows evidence of contact with the Dardic languages (including Kashmiri), indicating that the pre-diaspora 'proto-Romanis' may have sojourned in north-west India before embarking on their westward migration (see table 4.1).[6]

It is, of course, entirely possible that by no means all the original, pre-dispersal proto-Romani population took part in the migrations from India and that distant kinfolk of those who departed may have remained in the subcontinent. It has been suggested that a small, isolated community of speakers of an Indic language, Dumaki, may represent a surviving fragment of the Romani people who did not take part in the migration. The first part of the name, Dum-, has been compared with Dom/Rom and the language, spoken by a rapidly dwindling caste in the mountainous Hunza and Nagar regions of north-western Kashmir, is said to share certain features with some of the Romani dialects of the diaspora. As with the Gypsies of the West, the traditional trades of the Dumaki included blacksmithing and music-making. It is likely that most of the Dumaki speakers, who were already, twenty years ago (when their number was down to less than three hundred), bilingual in their own tongue and the surrounding non-Indo-European Burushaski, will by now have abandoned their ancestral speech – possibly the last surviving close linguistic link with Romani in the Gypsy cradleland.

As for the reason for the departure of the proto-Romanis from India, this can only be guessed at, though some authorities have identified them as camp-followers – a pariah caste of smiths, tinkers, petty traders, jugglers, musicians and dancers – who accompanied the warrior Jats and Rajputs who invaded the Turkish (Ghaznavid) realms of Persia and Afghanistan during the twelfth century AD.

Others claim that the ancestral Romanis may have fled west from the Indus valley during the fourteenth century, displaced from their ancestral homelands in the Punjab by the conquest of Timur the Mongol. Yet this would appear to be much too late, for the first positive sightings of Gypsies in Europe (the south-east Balkans) date from the mid four-teenth century (1348), half a century before Timur's invasion of India.

The migration of the Romanis out of Asia Minor into Balkan Europe, however, is almost certainly connected with the advance of the Rum (Seljuk) Turks, who, by the mid twelfth century, had occupied much of central and eastern Anatolia (the Sultanate of Iconium). Two centuries later the Ottoman Turks had established a bridgehead in the south-east Balkans and moved their capital to Adrianople (now Edirne) on the European side of the Bosporus. By that date (1365) the presence of Gypsies in the area had been noted for almost two decades.

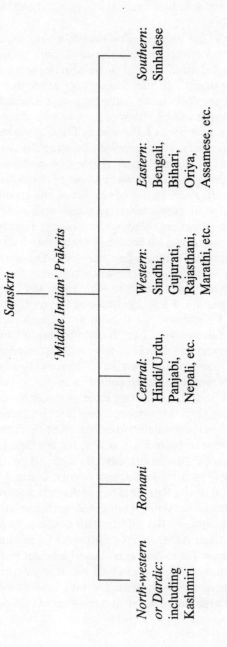

Table 4.1 The Indo-Aryan genealogy of Romani

Sanskrit

'Middle Indian' Prākrits

North-western or Dardic: including Kashmiri

Romani

Central: Hindi/Urdu, Panjabi, Nepali, etc.

Western: Sindhi, Gujurati, Rajasthani, Marathi, etc.

Eastern: Bengali, Bihari, Oriya, Assamese, etc.

Southern: Sinhalese

Arrival in Spain

The first wave of Egiptanos appears to have reached the Iberian peninsula in the second decade of the fifteenth century. Crossing the Pyrenees from France, they were recorded as having reached the kingdom of Aragón in 1425. By 1447 they were outside Barcelona and by mid-century had penetrated as far south as Andalusia, though they are not referred to in the Portuguese annals until the early sixteenth century.[7]

Their first incursions appear not to have aroused undue hostility. The roads of Europe were, at that time, full of landless, footloose souls uprooted from their farms and villages by famine, crop failure, fear of conscription, taxation, religious persecution and epidemic disease. By contrast, the Egiptanos, apart from their somewhat outlandish appearance, garb and speech, must initially have seemed much less threatening than many of the roving bands of dispossessed, for they travelled in well-organized troupes led by chieftains who proudly bore such regal titles as dukes or counts of Egipto Menor, a reference to Little Egypt, as western Asia Minor was then known, rather than to Egypt proper. In many districts they were received with much ceremony and greeted as welcome, though exotic, guests.

By the end of the fifteenth century, however, measures had begun to be taken to restrict their movements and the militia were frequently sent out to disperse the larger and more troublesome bands. From then on, the Gypsies found themselves living on the fringes of settled society, marginalized as much as a result of discrimination by the *gaché* (*payos*, or non-Gypsies)[8] as by their own distinctive lifestyle, customs, occupations, endogamous marriage practices and cryptic argot.

A race apart?

While the Gitano community has, in theory, long been assimilated into Spanish and Portuguese society at large, integration is still far from complete and an uneasy relationship between the two peoples has persisted to our own time, when many *payos* cannot tolerate the idea of living close to Gitanos or having Gitano children attend the local school. In Spain and Portugal, as in every country where they have settled, the Gypsies have always been regarded with a mixture of awe, suspicion, hostility and fascination. Miguel de Cervantes, in his exemplary novel *La Gitanilla* (1613), was by no means the first in a long line of writers who both vilified and romanticized the Gypsy, while Sancho de Moncada's *Discurso de la expulsión de los gitanos* (1618) was but one of many diatribes against them.

Nevertheless, it cannot be denied that the Gypsies have added a distinctive flavour to the popular culture of Spain, especially that of Andalusia, while their cryptolect, Caló, has contributed many colourful expressions to colloquial Spanish, mainly via the media of underworld slang and the special language of the *cante flamenco*.[9]

The first law restricting the movements of the newly arrived Egiptanos was passed by the Catholic monarchs Ferdinand and Isabella as early as 1494, while in 1525 the Cortés of Toledo petitioned that 'the Egyptians not wander through the realm, since they steal from the fields and destroy orchards and deceive people' – an allusion to the *jojanos* (deceptions) played on gullible *payos*. The most notorious of these was the trick of inducing the dupe to bury valuables in the ground on the promise that, when dug up after a stipulated time, the treasure would be found doubled or quadrupled. This *jojano baro* (great deceit) of the Gitanos is known under a variety of related names by all Europe's Gypsies: those of the British Isles, for example, call it *hukkapen*, *hokkaben* or *hukni*. The term, of Indian inspiration, was derived by the nineteenth-century gypsiologist Franz Miklosich from the Sanskrit verbal root *kakh* (to laugh at or deride).[10]

Ostracism, persecution and vilification have been the lot of the Gypsies ever since their arrival in Europe early in the fourteenth century, and it was not long before they began to experience the same reception from the Christian peoples of Iberia.

In 1558 Philip II took further steps to force them to abandon their peripatetic life and to settle in the towns and villages of the *payos*. Yet the Gypsies, then as now, were reluctant to integrate and in 1594 action was taken to separate male Gypsies from females 'para acabar con la raza' (to have done with the race), a precursor both of Hitler's attempted genocide of Europe's Gypsies and of the policy of sterilizing female Gypsies in the Romania of Ceauşescu and the Bulgaria of Zhivkov in the 1980s.

Despite such Draconian measures, the Gitano population continued to proliferate and by the seventeenth century large nomadic groups, consisting of several extended families and headed by a *brojeró* (*cabeza de familia*, or chieftain), were still wandering through the peninsula, living off the land, performing seasonal work and plying their traditional trades as *chalanes* (horse-dealers), vets, blacksmiths, fortune-tellers, scrap-metal dealers and pedlars.

Such was their reputation that, in the popular imagination, the Gypsy came to represent the embodiment of all that was sinister, blasphemous and satanic, and Gitanos were accused of every conceivable crime, from cannibalism to desecration of the host – accusations identical to those levelled at Judaizers and other heretics. Although they did not attract as much attention from the Inquisition as the Moriscos or the ex-Jewish Conversos, they continued to be the frequent target of the civil authorities. An edict of 1633, issued by Philip IV, ordered them to discard their distinctive dress, abandon their disreputable ways and forsake their impenetrable jargon. In 1692 Charles II ordered them to settle in towns with a *payo* population of not less than one thousand; he followed this with an edict forbidding them from continuing to practise their traditional trades and commanding them to devote their energies to settled, agricultural pursuits. Those who lapsed back into their old ways and refused to obey the edict faced, after a period of grace of six months, incarceration, exile (to the American colonies) or six years in the galleys.

1749 was the year of the great *redada*, or round-up, of all the Gypsies in Spain. Those classed as 'bad' were forced to perform public works, escapees were hanged and motherless girls were sent into service with 'honest' *payo* families.

Such was the lot of Spain's fast burgeoning and widely dispersed Gitano community until the reign of the more liberal and pragmatic Charles III, who, in 1783, granted them a modicum of freedom and restored to them the right to return to their traditional occupations; their wanderings were still prohibited. The very use of the name 'Gitano', which had been appropriated by many who (like the 'New Age Travellers' in Britain today) had adopted the nomadic life, but were not 'of the race', was forbidden – though it had never been applied by the Gypsies to themselves. It was, for a while, permissible to refer to them as 'New Castilians', but the currency of such sobriquets was much more limited than that of 'New Christians', as applied to Jewish Conversos.

By the start of the nineteenth century the great mass (some 88 per cent) of Spain's Gitano population (estimated at twelve thousand in a total population of ten million) had been forced to adopt a sedentary life, in contrast to most of the Gypsy communities of central and eastern Europe, which remained, until recently, at least semi-nomadic. Today an estimated 5 per cent of the Gypsies of Spain follow the migratory lifestyle of their 'wild' ancestors and most are settled in *barrios* close to, or on the fringes of, *payo* towns; only in a very few cases are the two communities – *payo* and Gitano – totally integrated, however, and a state of uneasy *convivencia* continues to exist.

Indeed, as Tomás Calvo Buezas's recent detailed study of *payo* attitudes towards the Gypsies, *¿España racista?*, demonstrates, the two communities still cherish the same stereotypes of each other as have persisted for centuries.[11] Most Gitanos hold themselves as aloof as possible from *payo* society, to the extent of disowning the offspring of Gitano – *payo* unions, whom they refer to as *payos rabudos* (long-tailed *payos*). They have maintained many cultural traits, such as styles of costume, decoration and dressing the hair, which, in addition to their physical appearance, tend to mark them off from the mass of the surrounding 'gentile' population.[12]

The many attempts on the part of the authorities, during the past five centuries, to disperse the Gypsies and sever their connections with their old occupations have largely proved futile; the Gypsies are still prone to concentrate in compact communities and to marry among their own kind. Ancient superstitions, including belief in such phenomena as vampires (*mulé*, or dead ones) and *nasula* (the evil eye), are extant among the largely illiterate masses; taboos against the eating of certain foods are still observed, as are traditional remedies and a number of rituals associated with such important life-events as birth, marriage and death.

Despite their legendary indifference to organized religion, the Gitanos are an intensely spiritual people. Their religiosity and the enthusiasm with which they have embraced the Pentecostal Church is acknowledged even by their most devout Catholic compatriots. They have also retained a body of traditional myths and legends which occur, in various permutations, in almost every European Gypsy society. While some of these have been attributed to Indian prototypes, the majority appear to be inspired by themes of European peasant provenance.

The cult of the Mother Goddess is particularly strong and accounts for the devotion to Ostalinda (the Virgin Mary) and to such saints as La Macarena, the Catholic counterpart of the Gitano Virgin Goddess Sara la Calí (who has been identified with Kali, also known as Satisara, consort of the Hindu god Shiva).[13] Many participate in the Catholic *romerías* (pilgrimages) and belong to exclusively Gitano *cofradías* (Christian fraternities), and while, during the past three decades, many have joined the evangelical sects, they have by no means abandoned such Catholic cults and frequently seek formalization of marriage by undergoing a second ceremony, conducted by a Catholic *araipo* (priest), as well as insisting on receiving the final sacraments.

In demographic terms, Gypsy communities may be found in almost every part of the peninsula: in the Basque country (where they are known as Ijitoak, or Egyptians), throughout Catalonia, in Galicia, León, Valencia, Murcia and Castile, where, as elsewhere in Spain, most cities in the nineteenth and early twentieth centuries still had their *gitanería*

(Gypsy quarter). Compact Gypsy communities are also to be found in parts of Portugal, including Lisbon and the Algarve and especially in the towns of the Alentejo, the province immediately adjacent to Extremadura.[14] This Spanish *autonomía* and its southern neighbour, Andalusia, are the two areas of Spain most closely associated with the Gypsies, and it is here that Gitano traditions – exemplified by the *cante jondo* (flamenco 'deep song'), of which the Gypsies are the acknowledged virtuoso exponents – are most in evidence.

In the face of discrimination and the animosity which frequently surfaces between them and their *payo* neighbours the Gitanos of Spain have maintained a strong sense of and pride in their own ethnic identity. The incidence of unemployment among them is high (over 90 per cent in Extremadura, where some 95 per cent live in *chabolas*, or shanty towns),[15] but many continue to ply the trades traditionally associated with Gypsies throughout the world; others are in seasonal employment, engaged in such temporary work as harvesting potatoes and sugar beet during the summer months. Although illiteracy rates are also high (an estimated two-thirds of Gypsies cannot read or write), a conspicuous few are entrepreneurs and self-made millionaires, often in retailing and the garment industry. A small minority have become professionals – doctors, lawyers, academics and even members of parliament.

Origin of the name Caló

The Iberian Gypsies do not refer to themselves as Gitanos, nor as Cíngaros or Ciganos, the alternative Spanish and Portuguese names respectively, which are related to such other European ethnonyms for the Gypsies as the German *Zigeuner* and the Russian *tsygán*.[16] Their own name for themselves is Calé, the plural form of Caló. This name is based on an identical adjective, of Indian derivation and meaning black (cf. Hindi: *kālā*), and is found among other Romani communities in Europe (where the form is *kaale*) and in the Middle East. It is evidently an allusion to the Gypsies' swarthy complexion compared with that of the *parnorré* (Sanskrit: *paṇḍarā*), 'whites' or non-Gypsies. In the United States Texan Chicanos, or Mexican Americans, whose jargon makes use of many Caló terms, such as *bato* (guy or dude) and *jalar* (to get drunk), claim that the name Caló (which they call their own argot) is an abbreviation of California – a classic case of folk etymology. The form *cañí*, often applied in Spain to both the Gypsies and their language, is believed to be nothing more than a deliberately distorted version of Caló, for the literal sense of *cañí*, in that language, is hen, which would be meaningless as an ethnic designation. Elsewhere in Europe the name *kalo* may be applied by Gypsies to persons outside their community: in parts of Serbia, for example, the word may refer to a policeman; in parts of central Europe a *kalo rashai* (black priest) is a monk; while in Britain the name gave rise to the now obsolescent term of address *cully* (mate).

George Borrow's contribution

Caló is also the name of the ancestral language of the Gypsies of Spain, a form of communication whose Indian antecedents were confirmed by a Jesuit, Lorenzo Hervás y Panduro, as early as 1802. The ultimate Indian source of Europe's Romani dialects had been known since the late eighteenth century and demonstrated by the seminal work of such pioneers as August Friedrich Pott, Franz Miklosich and Alexander Paspati (see table 4.2).[17] Three broad divisions of Romani are recognized: the European (of which Caló is the westernmost representative), the Armenian and the Syrian. These correspond to the three main regions of Romani settlement west of Iran. The European branch may be further subdivided into the Vlakh dialects (heavily influenced by Romanian) and the non-Vlakh dialects, in which Romanian is but one, relatively minor component. As a result of past migrations, many dialects have been introduced into areas where they did not evolve: thus, Vlakh dialects (such as Kalderash) are now used by groups as far from Romania as France, Spain, Great Britain and Scandinavia; Balkan dialects may be heard in Italy; and so on.

It was an Englishman, in the person of that prolific travel writer and Romani savant George Borrow, who provided posterity with its largest single source of information on the Indian roots of the 'secret' language of the Gitanos, in the form of the extensive glossary he appended to his seminal study *The Zincali: An Account of the Gypsies of Spain* (1841).[18]

George Borrow (1803–81), the son of an army officer, had spent much of his youth travelling around Britain with his father's regiment, and acquired his lifelong passion for philology at Norwich Grammar School. In his twenties, having disappointed his family by failing to take up the law, Borrow, who was at this time suffering from poor health, embarked on a long peregrination throughout rural England in the company of tinkers, Romanis and other itinerants. This experience provided him not only with his apprenticeship in the Anglo-Romani dialect, but also with the background for his first two books, *Lavengro* and *Romany Rye* (literally 'Wordsmith' and 'Gypsy Gentleman'). It also revitalized him,

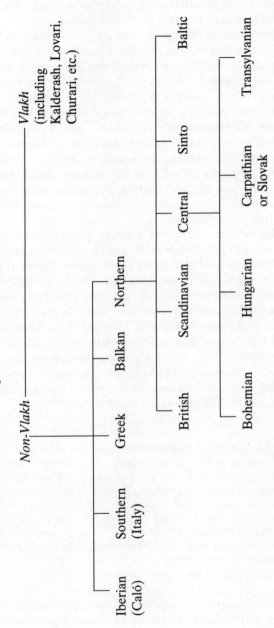

Table 4.2 Caló in the context of the European dialects of Romani

Source: T. V. Ventsel, *Tsyganskij Jazyk* (1964)

restored his health and whetted his appetite for a deeper knowledge of Romani life and language in other parts of Europe.

Borrow's basic mission, during his four and a half years in Spain, was to sell bibles for the British and Foreign Bible Society, but his already intimate knowledge of the customs, beliefs and language of the Romanis of his homeland enabled him to gain an entrée into the Gitano community, a privilege seldom accorded to an outsider. His very physical appearance – massive, ruddy skinned and so unlike the Spanish *payo* with whom the Gypsies were familiar – may have helped him to ingratiate himself into their society and gain their confidence. Whatever the reason for his acceptance, 'Jorgecito el Inglés', as his Gitano companions affectionately called him, was able to obtain from them a vocabulary of some four thousand terms, distinctive to their dialect and little known outside their community; the majority of them were of demonstrably Indian inspiration.

Borrow's glossary provided the starting point for all subsequent investigations of Caló and its speakers and showed that, far from being the rag-bag of underworld slang and substandard Castilian that many believed it to be, the language had an identity and a pedigree that were unique and well worthy of study. It remains the most compendious source of our knowledge of the 'primitive' Caló of the early nineteenth century and has, in the words of Carlos Clavería, 'been plundered, either first or second hand, by almost all those who have compiled Gitano–Spanish vocabularies'.[19] In Borrow's day, enough of the authentic, primeval Romani vocabulary of Caló survived to enable him to translate St Luke's Gospel into a remarkably 'pure' form of the language (*Embeó e Majaró Lucas*). 'The lost opportunities,' laments Clavería,

> for studying the Gypsies of Spain at close quarters, since the time when Borrow lived among them, are incalculable. Any attempt to reconstruct the old Gypsy way of life as it was during or before the time Borrow came into contact with it, or to study rigorously the folklore and speech of the surviving Gypsies, will inevitably lack the immediacy, life and colour which the English writer imparted to his description of his direct and intimate relationship with the Gypsies of Spain at a time when they unquestionably retained their customs and language with much greater purity than today.[20]

In Borrow's day, although the Gypsies still suffered much discrimination and abuse, they were, thanks to the more liberal legislation of Charles III, once again engaged in their old trades, though Borrow found fewer of them travelling the roads than he did among their brethren in Britain.

While never claiming that any one of his Gypsy informants was familiar with the entire content of his glossary, which was gleaned from a variety of speakers in many different parts of Spain, Borrow demonstrated that a far greater proportion of the Caló community was conversant with the old language than is the case today; indeed, José Carlos de la Luna's claim that the Gypsies of Estremadura regularly used, until as late as the 1950s, some three thousand words of Caló origin is almost certainly a gross exaggeration, and it is doubtful whether any individual of the present generation knows a fraction of that number.[21]

Húngaros, Bohemios, Quinquis and the Calé outside Spain

Borrow was well aware that, in addition to the Zincali – the Gitanos proper – other, more recent groups of Romanis had entered the peninsula at various times since the fifteenth century. Bands of so-called Húngaros or Bohémios (names indicative of their central European origin) are still recognized in Spain.[22] Some, such as those encountered by Borrow, had come with the armies of Napoleon early in the nineteenth century; others came after the emancipation of the Gypsy serfs in the Romanian provinces in the 1860s and continued to do so until a century later, when small groups of Balkan Gypsies were still seeking sanctuary in Spain. In the Basque country such comparative latecomers are often known as Motxailak (sheep shearers); they speak Basque, rather than Castilian or Caló, as their first language, and are distinguished from the Ijitoak, or Gitanos. The Húngaros arrived speaking a much more archaic and inflected form of Romani than Caló; communication in Romani between them and the longer-established Gitanos was limited, despite the survival of a common core vocabulary of several hundred words in the two dialects.

Communities of Romanis calling themselves Calourets (from the alternative plural, *calorré*) or Gitans are also found in the south of France and in Paris; they tend to speak French argot, heavily interlarded with Caló, as opposed to other forms of Romani, such as Kalderash and the central European Sinti dialects, although, more so than in Spain, they are in contact with those who do.[23]

In Spain itself such marginal groups as the Quincalleros (roughly tinkers), whose name is commonly abbreviated to Quinquis, also speak an argot which draws copiously on Caló, and yet the *Gitanos de raza* deny close relationship with this class of hawkers and petty criminals, whom they do not regard as *primos* (cousins) or *de la familia*. The Quinquis, who, surprisingly, were not mentioned by Borrow, are generally believed to be descended from Castilian *payos*, made homeless during the past three centuries as a result of famine and disease; ironically, they retained the migratory lifestyle for much longer than the Calé and many were fully nomadic until as late as the 1950s. It was around that time that a similar caste of itinerants, known as Mecheros, finally lost its identity, probably as a result of assimilation into the Quinqui community; the name alone lives on, in the sense of shoplifter.

One of the first scholars to draw attention to the important role of Caló in the argot of such fringe communities was Rafael Salillas, whose study *El delincuente español* (1896) revealed the pervasive influence of the Gitano and his language on every aspect of Spanish low life.[24]

The Indian roots of Caló

One of the features of this dialect which immediately stands out is the remarkable similarity of its core vocabulary to that of the other Romani dialects of Europe and the Middle East and, indeed, to those of such Neo-Indic languages as Hindi, Panjabi and Gujurati.

This is well illustrated by a comparison of the cardinal numbers, from one to ten (though not seven, eight or nine, which, in Romani, are of Greek derivation), in Caló, Common Romani, modern Hindi and Sanskrit (see table 4.3). Romani, it will be observed, is more conservative than modern Hindi in its retention of the Sanskrit initial *tr-* in

Table 4.3 Some cardinal numbers in Caló, Common Romani, Hindi and Sanskrit

	Caló	*Common Romani*	*Hindi*	*Sanskrit*
1	yequé (sometimes *yes*)	yek	ek	éka
2	dui	dui	do	dvá
3	trin	trin	tīn	trí
4	estar	štor	chār	chatúr
5	panche	panč	pãnch	pãncha
6	job	šov	chhai	sás
10	deque[a]	deš	das	dáça

[a]There is no š sound in Caló; see p. 120 below.

trin and of the medial *-t-* in *estar*. The archaic *tr-* (or *dr-*) also distinguishes Caló (and Romani in general) from the modern Indo-Aryan languages in such terms as *draca* (grape), which was *drâkshâ* in Sanskrit but is *dakh* in contemporary Panjabi.

Several other items of the Romani vocabulary are more archaic in form than their modern Indian counterparts: the words for dog and bird (*chuquel* and *chiricló* in Caló), for instance, are closer to their Sanskrit prototypes, *jakuta* and *ciritīka*, than are the Hindi equivalents, *kuṭṭa* and *chiriyā*.

Most Caló nouns, adjectives and verbs of Common Romani origin, and of demonstrably Indian inspiration, show a striking conformity with their cognates in other Romani dialects, as the examples in table 4.4 illustrate.

Some Caló verbs have acquired the additional syllable *-el-* (as in *manguelar*, *diquelar* for *mangar*, *dicar*). This was explained by the nineteenth-century gypsiologist F. Quindalé as a device for amplifying, extending or altering the semantic range of a verb.[25] Thus, *achinar* is simply 'to cut' in general, while *achinelar* is specifically 'to harvest'. It is possible, however, that the medial syllable *-el-* represents a survival of the old third person singular verb ending of inflected Romani, that is: *camel* (he loves), *camela* (she loves). The *-elar* suffix, unique to Caló among the Romani dialects, has been likened to the iterative (or frequentative) verbal ending *-erav*, found in many central European dialects of Romani. It is often used by Gypsies to 'gitanize' a Spanish or Portuguese verb, as in *tragelar* (from *tragar*, to swallow), *abaixelar* (from *abaixar*, to lower).

The verb ending *-av*, which, it will be noted, survives in central and eastern European dialects of Romani, is fossilized in such Caló infinitives as *puchabar* (to ask), *guillabar* (to sing) and *bichabar* (to send; cf. Anglo-Romani: *putch*, *gill*, *bitch*).

Very little of the highly complex syntax of Common Romani, as preserved in some of the archaic dialects still spoken in the Balkans and Carpathians, has survived in Caló. Like Anglo-Romani, the traditional inflectional structure of the language, inherited from Sanskrit, has largely been supplanted by that of the locally dominant *gachó* (non-Gypsy) language, in this case Castilian. Consequently, few of the 'structure words' (prepositions, personal pronouns, conjunctions) derived from Common Romani are still in use in Caló. Two exceptions, however, are *andoba* (literally, that one), which has passed into colloquial Spanish in the sense of bloke or individual, and *coba* (literally, this one), which, in street Spanish, means a fib or soft soap and is identical to the English 'cove' (a person) – both from the Romani *akova*.

Table 4.4 Some common terms in four representative dialects of European Romani

	Caló	German	English	Russian (Kalderash dialect)
Nouns				
iron	sas	saster	saster	sastrí
hunger	boquí	bok	bok	bok
knife	churi	churi	churi	churí
mouth	mui	mui	mui	mui
hair	bal	bal	bal	bal
mother	dai	dai	dai	dai
mud	chique	chik	chik	chik
kerchief	dicló	diklo	diklo	dikhló
gold	sonacái	sonnekai	sonakai	somnakái
fingernail	ñai	nai	nai	nai
water	pañi	pani	pani	paní
Adjectives				
drunk	mato	mato	mato	mató
red	lolo	lolo	lolo	loló
quick	sigó	sik	sig	sigó
rich	balbaló	barvelo	barvalo	barvaló
poor	chororo	choro	choro	chorró
Verbs				
buy	quinar	kinava	hin	khináv
make, do	querar	kerava	ker	keráv
beg	mangar	mangava	mang	mangáv
see	(en)dicar	dikava	dik	dikáv
sell	binar	bikinava	bikin	bikináv

Sources: F. N. Finck, *Lehrbuch des Dialekts der deutschen Zigeuner* (1903); S. A. Wolf, *Grosses Wörterbuch der Zigeunersprache* (1960); T. Acton and D. Kendrick, *Romani Rokkeripen To-divvus* (1984); B. C. Smart and H. T. Crofton, *Dialect of the English Gypsies* (1875); G. Borrow, *Romano Lavo-Lil: Word Book of the Romany or English Gypsy Language* (1874); R. S. Demeter, *Tsygansko-Russkij i Russko-Tsyganskij Slovar (Kalderarskij dialekt)* (1990)

The personal pronoun *menda* (I) has also been picked up by non-Gypsies, and one frequently hears *payo* children using the jocular form *mi menda* in the sense of 'I myself'.

Occasionally, other such retentions may be heard in the more archaic traditional *coplas* of the *cante jondo*; the line *Tú sin jucal* (You are beautiful) contains the original, inflected form of the verb *sinar* (to be), as also heard in the Anglo-Romani formula *Sar shan?* (How are you?).

Of the original Romani inflections, only the plural *-é* (as in *busné*: gentiles, literally goats; *gaché*: Gorgios, or non-Gypsies; *Calé*: Gypsies) and the feminine suffix *-í* continue to be productive. Examples of the latter are *chaborí* (daughter, from *chaboró*: son) and, in the extended form, *-ñí*, in *grasñí* (mare, from *graste*: horse) and *plañí* (sister, from *plal*: brother).

Among the other morphological elements surviving in Caló from Common Romani, only the nominal suffix, *-ipé(n)*, and the agentive suffix, *-engoro*, remain productive. The first, a reflex of the Prākrit termination *-ppaṇa*, occurs in such fossil forms as *chibibén* (life), *meripé* (death) and *chachipé* (truth, still current in colloquial Spanish in the reduced form *chipé*: true, authentic, 'great'). It may also explain the term *guripa* ('squaddy' or soldier, popular during the Civil War) and the short form *guri* (policeman or 'cop'). The term appears to be a Caló version of the Common Romani *kuripen* (*kuripa* in some Scandinavian dialects means fighting), from the verb *kur* (to fight), whose Caló reflex, *currar* (or *currelar*), has found its way into Spanish in the sense of to work.

However, this formant is unknown to many speakers; when one of McLane's Guadix informants wanted to say 'food', he coined a hybrid form, *jalancia*, of which the second part is Castilian, apparently unaware of such traditional Caló forms as *jalipén* and *jachapén*. It is likely that he also had in mind the existing Caló–Spanish hybrid *jamancia*, a jocular word for food, from the Caló verb *jamar* (to eat; cf. Hindi: *khānā*).[26]

The old agentive suffix, *-engoro*, still occurs in such compounds as *masengoro* (butcher, from *mas*: meat), identical to the Anglo-Romani *masengro*, though the alternative, *mascaruño*, in which the suffix has been deliberately distorted, is reportedly more frequent.

While Caló may at first seem somewhat eccentric in its pronunciation of certain Common Romani terms, it is soon clear that its apparent deviations from the 'norm' are regular and consistent; most of them reflect accommodation to the phonology of Castilian, which, as a result of centuries of intimate symbiosis between the two languages, has profoundly influenced the pronunciation of Caló.

The *sh* sound, for example, is absent from Caló, as from Castilian;

Table 4.5   Common Romani: š > j [x] in Caló

	Common Romani	Caló
cross	trušul	trejú
head	šero	jeró
year	berš	berji, breje
vinegar	šut	juti
flee, run	naš	naj(el)lar
deaf	kašuko	cajucó
listen	šun	junar
cold	šil	jil
rain	brišindo	brijindia

where this sound occurs in Common Romani, it is invariably treated in Caló as a *jota* (velar spirant), giving such correspondences as those in table 4.5. (Compare Castilian *jefe* from French *chef*.)

Many Common Romani words starting with a consonant have, in Caló, acquired an epenthetic *e-* or *a-*, a feature clearly modelled on Castilian practice. This process has led to such forms as *arachí* (night), *aruje* (wolf) and *araquerar* (speak), from Common Romani *rat*, *ruv* and *rakerav*.

Again in conformity with Castilian phonology, many common, especially monosyllabic words which end in a consonant in other Romani dialects are given a terminal *-e* or *-i* by Caló speakers: for example, *jebe* (hole), *caste* (stick), *chube* (louse), *lique* (nit), *rati* (blood) and *gate* (shirt), which are *hev*, *košt*, *juv*, *lik*, *rat* and *gad* in Common Romani.

Initial *d-* and *t-* often become *ch-* in Caló, whence such correspondences as *chibés* (day), *chutí* (milk) and *chubalo* (cigar) for Common Romani *dives, tud* and *tuv* (smoke, tobacco).

Common Romani final *-r* may, in some common words, become *-l* in Caló: *jel* (donkey) for Common Romani *kher* (Sanskrit: *khára*) and *cal* (penis) for *kar* (Hindi: *kārh*). This transposition of 'l' and 'r' is characteristic of many Andalusian and southern Extremeño dialects (for instance, *colol* for *color, borsiyo* for *bolsillo*: pocket) and it is doubtless from this source that Caló speakers acquired the tendency.

The termination *-av* (or *-ab*) of Common Romani terms is invariably pronounced *-ao* in Caló, giving such forms as *drao* (poison, medicine) and *gao* (town, place, also the Caló name for Madrid) for *drab* and *gav* (the 'drab' and 'gaff' of the English underworld).

It has long been popularly believed that the Gypsies lisp (that is, make use of the *zeta*, or voiceless dental fricative) when pronouncing 's', as in *Zí, zeñó'* for *Sí, señor*. However, this habit, though still used on stage by actors parodying Gypsy speech, is by no means characteristic of the pronunciation of today's Calé, whatever may have been the case in the past; it is certainly not a feature of the Caló spoken in the region of Córdoba, where *ceceo* (use of *zeta*) is also absent from the local *payo* dialect.

The specifically Indian associations of many Caló words are still transparently obvious. The Caló reflex of the Indian *rishi*, a Hindu sage, for example, is *arajay* (sometimes disguised as *araipo*), here applied to a Catholic priest, while the Indian *rajah*, variously represented in Caló as *rajo, eray, jere, elay, jari, jarai, gera* and so on, is used of a gentleman. As the old Caló verse has it:

> Yo no *camelo* ser *jarai*,
> Siendo *calé* estoy contento.
>
> (I don't want to be a gent,
> I'm happy to be a Gypsy.)[27]

The Indo-European identity of Romani is also evident from such Caló terms as *aquía* (eye), *dañí* (teeth, now used in the sense of saw), *nao* (name) and *nebo* (new). Caló *debel* (god) corresponds to Latin *deus*, *yaqué* (fire) to Latin *ignis* and *ruv* (wolf, from Sanskrit *vŕkas*) to Lithuanian *vilkas*, Russian *volk*, Greek *lukos*, Latin *lupus*, English '*wolf*' and so on.

Several Common Romani terms have acquired a specifically Spanish significance in Caló; the Common Romani name for a fiddle, *bašadi*, has become *bajañí* in Caló, in the sense of that quintessential Gitano instrument, the guitar, while the ancient Romany ethnonym *khorakhai*, applied in the Balkans to a Turk or Muslim Gypsy, is used, in the form *corajai*, by Caló speakers in the sense of Moor, the Arabic language being *corajano*. (In the archaic Welsh Gypsy dialect recorded by John Sampson in the 1920s *khorakhai* was used in the general sense of foreigner.)[28] The Common Romani term for a sausage, *goyi*, survives in Caló in the specifically Spanish sense of a *morcilla* (blood sausage), and the Common Romani word for an egg (*anro*) is, in contemporary Gitano idiom, mainly used in its plural form, *anré*, and then only in the secondary sense of testicles, in imitation of Spanish *huevos*.

Other terms have undergone radical changes of meaning over the course of the centuries. The word *quiribó*, for instance, no longer means godfather, as it did in Borrow's day, but is now used by most Gitanos to mean friend.

As Romani has never had a written (as opposed to an oral) literature, let alone a standard form, it is inevitable that differences in word usage and pronunciation have arisen over the five centuries and more during which its speakers have wandered the length and breadth of Europe. Within the Caló community of Spain, marked speech variations may be noted between different communities and even individuals of different generations within the same family.

While Caló has retained a number of archaic Romani terms which are apparently no longer used in other European Romani dialects, among them *barim* (bride), *rua* (virgin) and *fetén* (smashing),[29] it has lost many others which are still common currency elsewhere in Europe, such as *veš* (forest), *mokado* (ritually unclean) and *ruk* (tree), though the latter may survive as the second element in the hybrid *arberuque* (Spanish: árbol).

The meanings of many other Common Romani terms have undergone considerable semantic change. The adjective *tato*, meaning hot in most other Romani dialects, is used by Caló speakers only in such nominal senses as bread and fever, and the Common Romani adjective *gudlo* (sweet) survives only as the noun *gule* (syrup). The Common Romani adjective *korelo* (blind) survives in Caló as *corroró*, meaning one-eyed, and the noun *cacobí*, which Borrow recorded in the original Greek sense of kettle, is now more often applied to a ring, which Borrow recorded as *carobí*. *Mumeli*, which, in most other dialects, means a wax candle, has acquired the more general meaning of light in Caló.

The Romani identity of many other terms is greatly obscured by deliberate distortions and embellishments designed both to preserve the impenetrability of the language to outsiders and for reasons of taboo. Examples of this latter category include the disfigured names of God and the Devil. A wide range of variants of the basic name of the deity (*debel*, from Sanskrit *devá*) has been recorded, including *Undebel*, *Oncebel*, *Ostebé*, *Teblequé*, *Teblequeró* and *Terebideré*, while the Common Romani *beng* (the Devil) has become *mengue* (less often, *dengue*) in Caló, and is appropriated by non-Gypsies in the imprecation 'Malos *mengues* te lleven' (Go to the Devil). The word *beng* originally meant frog, as it still does in Hindi, from the Sanskrit *vyaṅga* (maimed or crippled one). The nineteenth-century gypsiologist Paspati suggested that the use of the word in the sense of 'Devil' was inspired by the ubiquitous paintings, which the Gypsies encountered in Greece, of St George slaying the Dragon. In Anglo-Romani the variants *bong* and *bonk* are heard alongside the base-form, *beng*, which is still known to some Gitanos.[30]

The wolf was also considered a dangerous being, and the taboo against uttering its base-name, *aruje*, gave rise to such distortions as *orú*, *orióz*, *ollarub* and, using the 'back-slang' technique, *yerú*.

A word may be disfigured by the application of a superfluous affix, such as *re-* or *ro-*, giving, for example, *retaja* for *chaja* (cabbage). Suffixes were similarly employed, producing such elaborations as *cachimaní* for *catuna* (tent), *lumiaca* and *lumiasca* for *lumí* (whore) and *abatico* for *bato* (father), while the base-form *naquí* (nose) spawned such variants as *nacrí*, *napia* and *ñacle.*[31] Anglo-Romani employs similar devices when, for example, it distorts *matcho* (fish) to *gratcho* and *dosta* (enough) to *goshta*.

Slang terms, children's play-talk, loan-translations from Spanish, underworld argot, 'pig Latin', a multiplicity of Ibero-Romance dialects and the speech of foreign soldiery all augmented the already multi-stranded vocabulary of Caló, enabling its speakers to refer to a single object or action by a variety of synonyms. A cat, for instance, may not only be a *machico* (its Romani base-form), but also a *marcurí*, *perpiché* or *chichojí*, of unknown provenance.

Superfluous syllables may be introduced to disguise a word, resulting in such extended Caló forms as *sarapé* (serpent) for Common Romani *sap*, *rapipocha* and *rabasunche* (fox) for Spanish *raposa* and *matagacno* for *mato*.

Many other Spanish terms are gitanized by the use of these devices. Back-slang accounts for such otherwise inexplicable terms as *esden* (ten), *chepo* (breast) and *brone* (man) for *diez*, *pecho* and *hombre*. *Caracol* (snail) may become *norical, peseta pacueca, Cuaresma* (Lent) *Cuarinda, gozo* (joy) *gozuncho* and *tarde* (evening) *tasarden*.

Popular quasi-Caló suffixes such as *-saro* and *-zuno* are used to create such forms as *unosaro* (one) and *calzonzuno* (pants). Conversely, a Spanish suffix may be added to a Caló stem: the colloquial Spanish *chorizo* (thief, literally a hard, pork sausage) contains the Common Romani term *choro* (thief), also familiar to Anglo-Gypsies (and the British underworld) as *chor*.

Much of the contemporary Caló vocabulary consists of words drawn from the non-Romani dialects of the Iberian peninsula, and many of these are considered, erroneously, to be of Gitano origin, much as *moyla* (donkey) and *mort* (woman), employed by Anglo-Romanis, are popularly believed to be 'Gypsy'. The non-Romani origins of *churumbel* (child), *clisos* (eyes) and *piños* (teeth), for example, have been conclusively demonstrated, though they are used by Gypsies and often attributed to Caló.

The Caló names of places and people deserve a special mention. Here again, the interaction between the Gypsy dialect and Castilian comes into full play: some names are translated from one language into the other, such as *Uchó* (dew) for Rocío, *Ujaranza* for Esperanza (from

Caló: *ujerar*, to hope), while others are puns, as in *Liyac* for Tomás, on the basis of Spanish *tomar* (to take), which is *liyar* in Caló.

Other names are specifically Caló. Spain is *Sesé* and Portugal *Laloró* (a Romani word meaning dumb), applied by Spanish Gitanos to a language which they found difficult to understand. The river Guadiana is *Lucalí*, believed to be derived from *L(a) (J)u(n)calí* (the beautiful), from the adjective *ju(n)cal* (Common Romani *šuker* < Sanskrit: *šukrá*, pure, white, clean) – yet another Caló term which has found its way into Spanish, in which a girl with a slim figure may be said to have *un talle juncal*. The French argot term *choucard* (beautiful) is from the same Romani root.

Even in Borrow's day, well over a century and a half ago, the original Romani syntactical structure of Caló had considerably disintegrated, to be replaced by that of Castilian. The process of hispanicization has continued to the stage where, in utterances containing Caló terms, the syntax and morphology are entirely Spanish.

Modern Caló has thus been reduced to the status of a mere 'sub-code' of lower-class Castilian, in which Romani and other non-standard lexical items are treated grammatically as if they were Spanish. An identical situation exists in Britain, where Anglo-Romani is now no more than a *poggerdi jib*, or broken tongue, in which English and Romani terms are used interchangeably in a grammatical context that is wholly English.

For example, the Anglo-Romani sentence 'Let's jal ta pee mull' (Let's go and drink wine) is echoed by its Caló counterpart, 'Chalemos ta piyar mol'; in both cases, the principal lexical items are Romani, but the grammatical structure and inflections are those of English and Spanish respectively, the Caló version following the Spanish example of casting the imperative of the verb *chalar* (go) in the subjunctive mode. (By contrast, in the much more archaic Bashaldo dialect of the Carpathians, the same sentence would be 'Muk amen te ǰau ta piyau mol', with the original Romani inflections intact.)

Similarly, the structure of the Caló sentence 'O chuque diqueló os jojoyes' (The dog saw the rabbits) is as grammatically, though not lexically, 'Spanish' as its Anglo-Romani equivalent, 'The jook dicked the shushis', is 'English'. (In traditional, inflected Romani the form would be 'O ǰukel dikhjá o šošojén'.)

Many Caló expressions are mirror images of Castilian prototypes. '¡Qué chutí abiyás!' (What a nerve – literally milk – you've got!) reproduces the Spanish 'Qué leche tienes!' while 'laches chibeses' (good day) echoes the Spanish plural form 'buenos días'. Conversely, the Andalusian formula to ward off the evil eye, 'Qué mis ojitos te vean'

(Let my little eyes see you), is a calque of the archaic Caló 'Sos minrés sacaitos tue diquelen'.

The non-Indic element in Caló

Despite the overwhelming preponderance of words of Indian provenance in Caló, the dialect is also indebted, as are all forms of Romani, to many other languages – those spoken in the lands through which the ancestral Gypsies passed on their migration routes from India to Europe. Of these, the most significant contributions were made by the Iranian languages (including Kurdish and Ossetian), Armenian, Greek, Slavonic (especially in its Balkan varieties) and Romanian. Caló has also inherited a small number of terms of Turkish, Hungarian and German origin.

According to a recent theory, the proto-Romanis were living in the Persian lands before the fourth century BC, possibly as a result of the invasions of Alexander the Great into north-west India. Their language might therefore have been exposed, at a very early stage in its post-Indian evolution, to the strong Iranian influence which still characterizes the language. In Caló, this element is represented by such terms as *cangrí* (church, also used in Spanish slang in the sense of 'nick' or jail), *chi* (nothing), *quin* (honey), *angustí* (finger, often disguised as *langustía*) and *quejesa* (silk).

Armenian has provided such terms as *cotor* (piece), *morchás* (skin, hide), *grasté* (horse) and *choré* (mule) and a word for witch, which occurs in Caló as *chuajañí* (cf. Anglo-Romani: *chovahauni*, *chuvni*, etc.).

The Greek component in Caló is particularly important; indeed, one sixteenth-century traveller in Spain claimed to have been able to converse with a tribe of Gypsies entirely in 'vernacular Greek', and emphasized that they knew not one word of 'Egyptian' (that is, Arabic), inspite of their popular association with Egypt.[32] The Egyptian connection has persisted to our own time: some Gypsy groups in the Balkans still claim to be 'descendants of the Pharaohs', while one school of gypsiologists, represented by Jean-Paul Clébert, José Carlos de la Luna and their protagonists, insists that the Gitanos entered Iberia from north Africa, even though Caló contains no identifiable words of direct Arabic derivation – apart, perhaps, from *lao* (word) and *quisobí* (a rare term for a purse, which may, in any case, have been acquired in Persia after its conquest by the Arabs).

The large Greek component in Romani indicates that Greece (and, perhaps, pre-Seljuk Asia Minor in general) represented an important staging-post on the migration route of the early Gypsies, and that they stayed there long enough to acquire a copious Greek vocabulary, including the names of the numerals seven, eight and nine (*efta, otor* and *enia* in Caló) and such essential terms as *foró* (town), *drom* (road), *cocal* (bone) and *zumí* (soup).

Many of the older Slavonic terms in Caló must be regarded as part of the legacy of the original language as spoken by the ancestral Gitanos when they first arrived in Spain. Representative of this older stratum of Slavonic terms are *cralis* (king), *clichí* (key), *bobis* (beans) and *dosta* (enough). Other Slavonic terms, by contrast, are demonstrably later arrivals from eastern Europe, perhaps introduced to Spain, and to Caló, by Húngaros or Bohemios. They include *machico* (cat), *jundo* (soldier or policeman), *ulicha* (street) and *pusca* (gun), which can be traced to the Balkans, while *guillar* (to walk) and *sejoña* (nowadays) have a more specifically Russian aspect (Russian: *gulyát*, walk; *segodnya*, today).

Of the other languages which have contributed to the core vocabulary of Caló, we may mention Afghan, from which a word for beard (*chon*) is derived; Ossetian, which has provided *berdo* (a Gypsy wagon, the 'vardo' of Anglo-Romanis; some Caló speakers use the term in the sense of boat, presumably because few of them now travel the roads in caravans); and Romanian, which has supplied *cornicha* (basket).

At some stage in their wanderings the ancestral Calé acquired terms from languages as far afield as English (such as *singa*: music), Hungarian (*jecó*: ice) and German (*gueltre*: *Geld*, or money), though some of these may have been picked up from foreign troops on Spanish soil or introduced by Romani conscripts in the armies of Napoleon.

However, despite the fact that many of these non-Indic terms have been used by generations of Gypsies throughout Europe, in chronological terms they are comparatively recent accretions, superimposed on the much deeper lexical 'bedrock' of the language, its common Indic heritage.

The Caló element in colloquial Spanish

The infiltration of 'gitanismos' (terms of Caló origin) into Spanish, which has been in progress for at least two hundred years, took place along three principal channels: the special language of the *cante jondo*; the jargon of the *hampa*, or underworld; and the popular novels and *sainetes* (sketches) of such Andalusian writers as José Sanz Pérez, F. Sánchez de Arco and Juan Ignacio González del Castillo, who spiced their dialogue with Caló expressions culled from the street-talk of Málaga, Seville, Córdoba and Cádiz. The great writer Don Ramón María Valle Inclán was another who was fascinated by Caló and did much to promote interest in the fast disappearing idiom; according to the Gitanos, 'Chamuyaba barsamía mistó o Caló' (He spoke Caló quite well). (The verb *chamuyar*, to chat, is a Caló reflex of the Common Romani *chamava*, to chew, from an Indian root meaning jaw; cf. Hindi: *jalhā*.)

The flamenco craze was at its height during the lifetime of Benito Pérez Galdós, whose novel *Fortunata y Jacinta* featured the heavily gitanized vocabulary of the young señoritos of mid-nineteenth-century Madrid, where such terms as *garlochín* (heart), *postín* (swanky, from the Caló *postí*: skin), *ful* (false) and *chungo* (bad)[33] were distinctly 'de moda'. Indeed, in Galdós's day the terms *Gitano* and *flamenco* had become virtually synonymous, but it must be pointed out that so great was the mania for all things Gitano, many of the popular *coplas* then in circulation were translated into Caló by *payo* aficionados familiar with the glossaries of Borrow and his epigones in order to make them appear more 'authentic'.

Caló is still confused by many with *germanía*, the argot of the underworld, to which it has contributed many expressions. The current edition of the *Larousse Dictionary of Modern Spanish* still defines *germanía* as the 'lenguaje de gitanos y rufianes', and many believe that the Spanish word for jargon (*jerigonza*) is an abbreviation of (*cin*)*gerigonza* (Cíngaro talk). In Portuguese *calão* is the general term for slang (in Brazil, the word means bad language), while *calô* is applied to the special jargon of thieves, fences, confidence tricksters and prostitutes.

Caló, however, is by no means identical to underworld slang, though, as Max Leopold Wagner pointed out in his seminal study *Notes linguistiques sur l'argot barcelonais* (Barcelona, 1896), the two have been exchanging items of vocabulary for centuries. Whereas Caló has inherited a core vocabulary of archaic, Indian words as part of its Romani legacy, *germanía*, like the German *Rotwelsch* and the Dutch *bargoens*, which also contain much Romani material, draws on many other sources and changes its word usage even more rapidly than the notoriously protean speech of the Gypsies. It is largely through the medium of prison and criminal slang that such Caló terms as *guillarse* (to go round the bend), *chala'o* (crazy), *ducas* (troubles, tribulations) and *gilipollas* (bloody fool, 'prat') have passed into general circulation. The last name is a compound of the Caló *jilí* (mad; cf. Panjabi: *jhāllā*) and the Spanish *pollas* ('prick'), while *achares* (jealousy), meaning, literally, something burning, is from the Romani verb root *ač* (to burn), familiar to Anglo-Romanis in such expressions as 'Atch the yog' (Light the fire).

It will be noted that the majority of the gitanismos in Spanish belong to what the lexicographer would class either as 'marginal' or 'substandard', and that they refer to commonplace actions, bodily functions and emotions, human types, basic adjectives and colloquial equivalents of words already present in the Spanish lexicon. All this is clear evidence of their origins in the street, the tavern, the *barrio chino* (red-light district), the thieves' den and the prison yard, and they have infiltrated idiomatic Spanish in much the same way as Yiddishisms infiltrated American English via the slang of the underworld in the early decades of this century.

Most of these Caló loans have become so intimately embedded in colloquial Spanish that their Romani origins generally go quite unrecognized; when Spaniards use such words as *chucho* (dog), *diñar* (give), *parné* (money), *lacha* (shame), *beata* (peseta), *bastes* (fingers) and *chinel* ('screw', or prison officer), they are using Romani words, though they may be no more aware of doing so than the English speakers who use such terms as 'dad', 'pal', 'lolly' (money), 'posh', 'cosh', 'moosh', 'cock' (mate) and 'minge' (vagina),[34] which are also of Romani origin. Interestingly, several of the Caló terms in colloquial Spanish have their exact counterparts in English slang: the English 'stir' (gaol), for example, is echoed by Spanish *estaribel* (from the Romani verb root *štar*, to capture, of Slavonic inspiration), 'nick' (steal) by *nicabar*, 'gaff' (place, hideaway) by *gao* (town, village) and 'shaver' (boy) by *chaval* (lad), both from Romani *chavo*.

Romani loans are, of course, by no means confined to Spanish and English. The Portuguese *pá* (mate) comes from the same Romani root as the English 'pal'; French argot makes use of such terms as *surin* (knife; Romani: *churi*), *chouraver* (steal; Romani: *chorava*) and *costaud* (heavy, strong; Romani: *kushto*, good – whence substandard English 'cooshti', recently popularized by David Jason in the television comedy series *Only Fools and Horses*, and its variant 'cushy', meaning easy, comfortable);[35] while the Romani *ker* (house; identical to the Caló *quer*) has entered German via *Rotwelsch* or underworld slang.

It is, however, Castilian, of all the European vernaculars, which has retained the largest number of terms of Romani inspiration; indeed, it may be predicted that colloquial Spanish – the language of the streets – will, within the next generation or so, come to represent the final repository of the largest number of Romani survivals in Europe.

As for Caló itself, it has long since passed the stage where it could be classed as one of the world's 'endangered' languages. Its total extinction is imminent; as Angus Fraser recently remarked, it has 'dwindled to a relatively small vocabulary which can be employed within the context of a national language or dialect', and thus typifies what Bernstein defined as a 'restricted code', a variety of a language (here, specifically Spanish or one of the other peninsular Romance vernaculars) interlarded with Caló expressions and used to stress the speaker's membership of the Gitano community and to exclude outsiders[36] – the speaker, of course, being able to 'switch codes' back to the local Romance dialect according to social context.

Yet, despite its dwindling use, what is remarkable about Caló is that it has managed to survive as long as it has, especially as its speakers have lived in almost total isolation, for the best part of five centuries, from the other, more archaic dialects of European Romani spoken north of the Pyrenees.

As Miguel Ropero Núñez concludes, 'If Sanskrit has been studied with such respect, I do not see why Caló should be so despised.'[37]

Notes

1 A. E. Mourant, *Blood Relations: Blood Groups and Anthropology* (Oxford, 1983).

2 J. D. R. Heredia, *Nosotros los gitanos* (Barcelona: Ediciones 29, 1978); J.-L. Tudela, *Tejiní a caló: Cours de caló* (Marseilles, 1985). See also I. V. Pathania, *International Romani Language* (Sarajevo: Institut za proučavanje nationalnih odnosa, 1989); V. G. Kochanowski, *Problems of the Common Romany* (Sarajevo: Institut za proučavanje nationalnih odnosa, 1989).

3 C. Clavería, Estudios sobre los gitanismos del español (Madrid: *La revista de filología española*, Anejo L111, 1951), 45.

4 Ibid., 71.

5 F. D. Mulcahy, *Studies in Gitano Social Ecology: Linguistic Performance and Ethnicity* (The Hague: Mouton, 1979); J. Ortega, *Los gitanos: guía bibliográfica y estudio preliminar* (Manchester: Manchester University Press, 1987).

6 R. L. Turner, 'The Position of Romany in Indo-Aryan', *Journal of the Gypsy Lore Society*, 3, 6 (1927), 129–38.

7 A. L. de Meneses, *La inmigración gitana en España durante el siglo XV* (Barcelona, 1968); B. Leblon, *Les Gitans d'Espagne* (Paris, 1985).

8 *Gadjo* (the *gachó* of the Spanish Gypsies and the *gaujo, gorjer, gorgio*, etc. of their British brethren) is the true Romani term for a 'gentile' or non-Gypsy, though the Galician word *payo* (a yokel or country bumpkin) is also widely used. The traditional Romani term is of Slavonic derivation (cf. the Serbo-Croat *gazda*: boss, farmer, master, landlord, possibly reinforced by the Sanskrit *gārhya*: domestic). The feminine form, *gachí*, has passed into

colloquial Spanish in the general and usually somewhat opprobrious sense of woman, while *payos* have adopted the masculine form, *gachó*, in the sense of chap or bloke.

9 R. Lafuente, *Los gitanos, el flamenco y los flamencos* (Barcelona: Bara, 1955); A. A. Caballero, *Gitanos, payos y flamencos en los orígenes del flamenco* (Madrid, 1988).

10 F. Miklosich, *Über die Mundarten und die Wanderungen der Zigeuner Europas* (Vienna, 1872–81).

11 T. Calvo Buezas, *¿España racista? Voces payas sobre los gitanos* (Barcelona: Antropos, 1990).

12 J. Yoors, *The Gypsies of Spain* (New York, 1974); B. Quintana and L. Floyd, *¡Qué Gitano!* (New York: Holt, Rinehart and Winston, 1972). See also F. de Sales Mayo, *Los gitanos, su historia, sus costumbres, su dialecto* (Madrid, 1869). The author also wrote under the Caló form of his name, Quindalé- = May; see n. 25.

13 C. Lal, *Gipsies: Forgotten Children of India* (Delhi: Ministry of Information and Broadcasting, 1962); J.-P. Clébert, *Les Tsiganes* (Paris, 1976).

14 F. A. Coelho, *Os ciganos de Portugal* (Lisbon: Imprensa nacional 1892); O. Nunes, *O povo cigano* (Oporto, 1981).

15 *Enciclopedia de Estremadura* (Mérida: Junta de Extremadura, 1992).

16 The name is a corruption of *athínganoi*, an heretical sect which flourished in the Byzantine Empire during the first millennium AD. The early Gypsies were often confused with this sect, because of a shared reputation for sorcery and fortune-telling, and by the eleventh century the term *atzínganoi* was applied solely and specifically to Gypsies. The Spanish *zíngaro* (or *cíngaro*) is based on the Italian form, and the Portuguese *cigano* on the French *tsigane*.

17 A. F. Pott, *Die Zigeuner in Europa und Asien* (Berlin, 1884); F. Miklosich, *Über die Zigeuner Europas*; A. Paspati, *Études sur les Tchingianés ou Bohémiens de l'Empire Ottoman* (Paris, 1870).

18 G. Borrow, *The Zincali: An Account of the Gypsies of Spain* (London: John Murray, 1841). The name 'Zincali', no longer in use, is probably a compound of the Romani *sinté*, applied to several groups of central European Gypsies, and the plural *Calé*. *Sinto* is a term of Indian origin, related to the Hindi *sānt* (group, band, union). In France the Sinté are commonly known as *manouche* (Romani: *manúš*, man), and several bands have settled in Spain.

19 Clavería, *Estudios sobre los gitanismos*, 63.

20 Ibid. 43–4.

21 J. C. de la Luna, *Gitanos de la Bética* (Madrid: ESPESA, 1951). See also B. Dávila and B. Pérez, *Apuntes del dialecto caló o gitano puro* (Madrid, 1943).

22 J. Hasler, *Los gitanos o 'húngaros'* (Madrid, 1970).

23 F. de Vaux de Foletier, *Les Bohémiens en France au 19e siècle* (Paris: Lattés, 1981); J.-P. Liégeois, *Tsiganes* (Paris: La Découverte, 1983); N. Martínez, *Les Tsiganes* (Paris, 1986).

24 R. Salillas, *El delincuente español*, 2 vols (Madrid: Suárez, 1896).

25 F. Quindalé, quoted in T. Rebolledo, *Diccionario Gitano-Español* (Cádiz: University of Cádiz, 1909).

26 M. F. McLane, *Proud Outcasts: The Gypsies of Spain* (Cabin John, Md, 1987).

27 M. R. Núñez, *El léxico caló en el lenguaje del cante flamenco* (Seville: University of Seville, 1978), 118.

28 J. Sampson, *The Dialect of the Gypsies of Wales* (Oxford, 1926), 183.

29 This may be a distortion of the Romani *feter, feder* (better; Sanskrit: *bhadratara*).

30 Paspati, *Études*.

31 The Romani word is the origin of the English (copper's) nark (literally nose).

32 L. Palmireno, *El estudioso cortesano* (Madrid, 1540).

33 The word appears in its diminutive form, Los Chunguitos (The Bad Little Boys), as the name of one of Spain's popular Gitano-rock groups.

34 The word, of Indian origin and present in all Romani dialects, occurs in Caló as *minchi*, and in such compound forms as *minchoró*, a *chulo de putas* (prostitute's pimp), and the verb *minchabar* (to give birth). The variant *mencha* may have inspired the ethnic name *mechero*.

35 The word also occurs in Spanish slang as *costo*, meaning drugs or 'dope'.

36 A. Fraser, *The Gypsies* (Oxford: Blackwell, 1992), 300; B. Bernstein, *Class, Codes and Control*, i and ii (London: Routledge and Kegan Paul, 1971 and 1973).

37 Núñez, *El léxico caló*, 22.

Suggested further reading

Baudrimont, A.: *Vocabulaire de la langue des Bohémiens habitant les Pays Basques français*. Bordeaux, 1862.

Besses, L.: *Diccionario de argot español o lenguaje jergal gitano, delincuente, profesional y popular*. Barcelona: Manuel Soler, 1906.

Botey, F.: *Lo gitano, una cultura folk desconocida*. Barcelona: Ed. Nova Terra, 1970.

Calvo Buezas, T.: *Los gitanos en la sociedad española*. Madrid: Cáritas, 1980.

Campuzano, R.: *Orijen, usos y costumbres de los jitanos y diccionario de su dialecto*. Madrid, 1848.

Cannizo, M.: *D'où viens-tu, Gitan?* Mémoire pour la CAEI d'instituteur, 1980.

Dávila, B. and Pérez, B.: *Apuntes del dialecto caló o gitano puro*. Madrid, 1943.

Diccionario del dialecto gitano. Barcelona, 1851.

Frere, J.-C.: *L'Énigme des gitans*. Collection Pensées et sociétés secrètes. Paris; Mani, 1973.

Hancock, I. F. (ed.): *Romani Sociolinguistics*. The Hague; Mouton, 1979.

Jiménez, A.: *Vocabulario del dialecto jitano*. Madrid: Imprenta de Don José María Gutiérrez de Alba, 1846.

Jung, C.: *Wortliste des Dialekts der spanischer Zigeuner*. Mainz: Flamenco Studio Verlag, 1972.

Quindalé, F.: *Diccionario gitano*. Madrid: Oficina Tipográfica del Hospicio, 1867.

Puxon, G.: *Rom: Europe's Gypsies*. Minority Rights Group Report, no. 14. London, 1973.

Starkie, W.: *Don Gitano*. Barcelona: Janés, 1944.

Vega, L. A.: *Nosotros los flamencos*. Madrid: Palacios, 1965.

5

Masonics, Metaphor and Misogyny: A Discourse of Marginality?

MARIE MULVEY ROBERTS

If it can be assumed that the primary function of language is communication, then the notion of a private or even secret language is surely paradoxical.[1] But in practice the public and the private may not be diametrically opposed. What will be considered here is the way in which a covert linguistic system can function as a discourse practised within, rather than outside, a mainstream language.

Secret languages or discourses are best facilitated or sustained, in such a context, by a secretive society or esoteric order.[2] Ironically, the *raison d'être* of many such clandestine organizations is the divulging of secrets. Exposure is implied by secrecy, and secrets, particularly as they relate to ritual, can be constructed for such purposes as rhetorical revelation.[3] Jargon can be empowering in a similar way for certain members of the professions, especially computer scientists, medical practitioners, lawyers and even, let it be said, literary critics and sociolinguists, as a means of marking out linguistic zones of inclusion and exclusion. It also functions as a form of shorthand. Yet the main difference between those belonging to a professional or certain inner social circle and initiates of a secret society is that for the latter form, mainly through the use of ritual and symbolism, tends to prevail over content.[4] In both cases, the linguistic forms tend to be the most prominent mainly because the lines of professional and social demarcation with regard to who is in the know and who is not can be drawn most effectively by language usage. The discourse of a secret society is a form of jargon which must appear to abide by the rules of secrecy. Beryl Bellman's treatment of secrecy as a communicative event in the anthropological study *The Language of Secrecy* (1984), by resolving the paradox posited in my opening paragraph, provides a focus for the approach to be taken here. This chapter will include an exposition and exposé of one particular secretive discourse or jargon and its place within the mainstream and margins of both language and society.[5]

The particular discourse chosen for this purpose is Masonic. Not only has Freemasonry survived the course of three centuries, but it currently has a worldwide membership of over five million and is also a metonym for secrecy and an all-male cabal. However tempting it might be for some to dismiss the Masons as a bunch of overgrown schoolboys rolling up their trouser-legs and engaging in verbal mumbo-jumbo, the potency of a secretive network which includes powerful members of the community cannot and should not be ignored. Furthermore, the role of language as a fraternal cement within the lodge-room itself and for linking members covertly with one another outside has received scarcely any serious historical attention, with the exception of Margaret Jacob's *Living the Enlightenment* (1991).[6]

Although nowadays Masons will insist that they belong not to a secret society, but to a society with secrets, it cannot be denied that secrecy has been an organizing principle within the lodges since the founding of the Grand Lodge in London in 1717, if not before.[7] In tracing the evolution of Masonic secrecy and its relationship to language, I shall confine most of the discussion of this enormous subject to England in the eighteenth century, a period when the foundations of present-day Masonry and of modern society were laid. Many of the examples which will be given of the Freemasons' use of language during their early history, however, are relevant to modern Masonic ritual in current use.

The central question to be raised here is whether Masonic rhetoric should be regarded as a discourse of marginality or as a mirror of the mainstream. The answer should not be ahistorical, since, throughout its history, Masonic language has spanned the political and social spectrum from the subversive to the subservient, and from the radical to the reactionary. Varying from lodge to lodge and from one country to another, the discourse of Freemasonry has responded to the political climate of the society outside in a number of different ways. For example, the Augustan rhetoric of English Freemasonry during the early eighteenth century reflected the values of a society intent upon harmony and stability. Later on the Continental lodges went a step further by becoming training grounds for the integration of the values of the Enlightenment with government.[8] According to Jacob, the lodges on the Continent adopted the language of constitutional government which they had imported from England. In British Freemasonry throughout the eighteenth century there operated a wide variety of discursive practices including Whig, republican, court, country and Jacobin. In France the language used by Freemasons from one eighteenth-century Masonic enclave to another ranged from reflecting the values of the *ancien régime* to an articulation of resistance to absolutism. Although, in general, the lodge has always given more than standing-room only to the aristocracy and the lower orders, it has at its core invariably represented a valorization of the values of the bourgeoisie expressed through language.

Some aspects of class, power and gender on the interface between the public and the private spheres will be highlighted here in terms of linguistic usage. I shall argue that, despite being a secretive subculture, the Masons (both with and without their aprons) are and for much of their history tend to have been part of the mainstream. There have been exceptions, but my concern is less with the subversiveness of the society throughout its history than with its orthodoxy. As a means of social control, Freemasonry works effectively in diffusing potentially radical elements by containing them within its own socially accepted secretive network, which no longer provides alternatives to the established values of society. In spite of a revolutionary and subversive pedigree, members of the Masonic brotherhood nowadays are conformist and even reactionary. Their membership is made up of predominantly white, middle-class males, even though Masonic membership is open to men of any religion, race, class or creed.[9] This very inclusiveness exacerbates the feelings of marginalization among those who are excluded: women, for example, are not admitted into the fraternity.[10]

Like most other linguistic systems, that of Freemasonry enshrines a discourse of difference.[11] The gendering of the language of ritual which invariably privileges the male is one example, while the rhetoric of misogyny which is textualized through bawdy songs, to be discussed later, has the effect of reinforcing not only the exclusion of women, but also male superiority. The point is that Masonic discourse is less an expression of marginalized secrecy than an open linguistic secret reinforcing the existing power relations outside in terms of both class and gender.

Before discussing power and gender, it is important to identify the areas where Masonic discourse operates in the public and the private spheres. Three broad areas are the language used within the lodge, that which is communicated outside for the purpose of identifying a fellow-

Mason and the points at which Masonic words and phrases have entered the mainstream. Examples of the Mason's infiltration into common language usage are such words and phrases as 'Masonics' and 'Masonry' (colloquialisms for secrecy), 'on the level' (a reference to the working tool of the Fellow-Craftsman or second degree Mason), 'square' (another term connected with the Fellow-Craftsman, meaning morally upright, though it degenerated into a synonym for bribery at a time when Masons were associated with corruption), 'Lewis' (a word meaning both the son of a Mason and a working tool) and 'to give the third degree' (an American term relating to the trials of endurance contained within the final initiation rite of the tripartite system of Craft Masonry). As Bernard E. Jones points out in his discussion of colloquial words derived from Freemasonry, the word 'square' must have predated the craft, because it and its synonyms in other languages had been used to mean just or proper since Ancient Egyptian times. But for most of the other words mentioned their primary association has been Masonic.[12]

The power of the spoken word has never been lost on the Masons, particularly since they have a ritual specifically concerned with finding the Lost Word. At any Masonic gathering language functions in a variety of specific ways, from oath-taking to the catechismic exchanges between questioner and respondent. Its ceremonial purpose, as in the opening or closing of the lodge, conveys the Masonic values of order, fraternity and moral rectitude. The solemnity of the occasion is constituted verbally as well as visually and sometimes music is used to achieve a similar effect. Singing actively demonstrated the fraternal spirit at work.[13] Traditions of rhetoric have been kept alive in the lodge-room and the physical movement of participants is choreographed to a Masonic script. Orators are sensitive to the rules of manner, tone and spirit most appropriate to whatever speech act is being carried out.

The recitation of narratives documenting the origins and history of the society usually involves an adaptation of a biblical passage. Much Masonic ritual is overlaid with scriptural allusions.[14] These theological borrowings amount to a pseudo-religious discourse which serves to validate the gravity of the occasion by transmitting a sense of authority and antiquity even to the point of travesty. Lodge lectures which trace the origin of the Freemasons as far back as the Solomonic period or even further, to Noah, Adam or Eve, are blatantly anachronistic. Although members identify themselves with the operative craft and there is evidence of Masons being organized along the lines of secrecy in the Middle Ages, the English society of speculative or non-operative Freemasons was a product of the early modern period. The invention of pseudo-histories during the eighteenth century was by no means exclusive to Freemasonry: at that time clubs and societies were reclaiming, inventing or borrowing a lineage from other traditions for their own edification. John Anderson was largely responsible for this creative accounting, being the author of the first *Constitutions* and official history of 1723, which had become increasingly elaborate by the time its second edition appeared in 1738. Masonic written language from the eighteenth century to the present day reflects this eclecticism. The rituals, histories and exegetical writings generated by Freemasonry have contributed to build a heteroglossic new Tower of Babel with the bricks of religious rhetoric, the Bible, liturgical and sacred drama and esoteric and occultist jargon. All these appropriations are orchestrated within the layers and levels of Freemasonry in the best spirit of syncretic plagiarism.

Building metaphors, or rather archaeological digs, provide the best analogy for the construction of Masonic myths, symbolism, rituals and degrees. The historian, when having to excavate through the layers which have been built on to the fraternity, will find that some have fallen into decay and been discarded while others have flourished and become permanently established.

The Ancient and Accepted Rite, for example, consists of thirty-three degrees, most of which are not worked at the present time. Candidates who have passed through the tripartite system of Craft Masonry can proceed through the Rite in name only, leap-frogging from the fourth to the seventeenth degree in order to reach the next degree to be worked in full: the exotically named Knight of the Pelican and Eagle, Sovereign Prince Rose Croix of Heredom, or eighteenth degree. The next worked degree is the thirtieth, the Grand Elected Knight Kadosh, Knight of the Black and White Eagle; the remainder become more and more elevated and exclusive, culminating in the thirty-third degree of Grand Inspector General, which is the highest rung on the Masonic ladder. As these degrees reveal, there are layers within layers of secrecy even within the lodge itself.

The secrets which are presumably of most interest from the point of view of language are concerned with the revelation of specific words.[15] These are usually Hebraic, being often of biblical or cabalistic origin. Although they function as passwords for the purposes of identification and unlocking the details of the ritual concerned, the existence of secret words relates to certain occult traditions, like the Renaissance Neo-platonists, whose revival of the *Corpus hermeticum* and the Cabala had an effect on some influential Masonic thinkers.[16] Power words have connotations not only of operative magic, but also of gnostic and cabalistic creation myths whereby in the beginning was the word, *Logos*.[17] Within the higher degrees, which were developed during the eighteenth century in France, is a hunt for the Lost Word (the eighteenth degree). What could be regarded as an allegory of the hermetic quest for lost knowledge required physical exertion, since initiates were expected to climb up and down a ladder collecting a letter at a time in order to piece together the missing word.[18]

Being given, taking, losing and finding words is characteristic of the ceremonies for the first four degrees of Freemasonry. The first (Entered Apprentice) and second degrees (Fellow-Craftsman) of Freemasonry are given the passwords respectively of 'Boaz' and 'Jachin', the names of the pillars of King Solomon's Temple. In order to impress upon the candidate the importance of concealment, the Worshipful Master insists that 'Too much caution, therefore, cannot be observed in communicating it: it should never be given at length, but always by letters or syllables.'[19] When asked by the junior Warden, a lodge official, for the password during the initiation rites, the candidate reminds him that the words must be halved or split into their lettered components. For the third degree of Master Mason a ritual re-enactment of the murder of the legendary founder of Freemasonry, the architect of King Solomon's Temple, Hiram Abif, takes place, resulting in the loss of a secret word. This is recovered in the fourth degree of the Royal Arch, where it is revealed that the word is the composite sacred word 'Jah-Bul-On'. This syncretism is derived from four languages: Chaldee, Hebrew, Syriac and Egyptian.[20] The divinities referred to include Iahova, the pagan female deity Baal and the Egyptian god Osiris. Anti-Masons have regarded Jah-Bul-On as denoting an unholy trinity and the existence of this word within the rites of Freemasonry has led to the accusation of heathenism or even devil worship. Its roots are more likely to be in the hermetic or cabalistic tradition, where the Tetragrammaton is revered as the Ineffable Name of God. More prosaically, it represents a houyhnhnm parodox in being the word which cannot be spoken. Elaborate lore also surrounds the mysterious Mason Word, particularly in seventeenth-century Scotland,[21] where it was believed by non-Masons that the Word was linked to the supernatural and so fed into local superstitions connected with the Devil.

The 'Mason Word' was used as a general term for the initiation rituals and included the passwords for the first two degrees, 'Jachin' and 'Boaz'. These function to protect the secrecy of the specific degree in which they are given from outsiders and Masons who may not yet have advanced to that stage of initiation. Within the Masonic hierarchy, one may proceed laterally as well as vertically, since Master Masons can be admitted into other branches of the craft, such as Mark Masonry and the Knights Templar. Templarism cultivates its own phraseology and lexicon. The

Grand Password for this chivalric order, 'Maher-shalal-hash-baz',[22] scarcely trips off the tongue, while Mark Masons have less trouble getting their tongues around the more easily pronounceable password 'Joppa'. This is a place-name associated with Hiram Abif during the building of King Solomon's Temple, which is the setting for the central legend of their degree involving the discovery of the keystone to an arch. Words are also indicated by letters in many Masonic handbooks in order to preserve their secrecy in case they should fall into the wrong hands. In the Mark Masons' degree, for example, the letters 'H.T.W.S.S.T.K.S.' stand for 'Hiram Tyrian's Widow's Son, Sent to King Solomon', which forms the semi-secret motto that is inlaid on the keystone jewel of the degree. For all Freemasons the most prominent example of the use of an initial is the letter 'G' displayed on the aprons of Scottish Master Masons since the 1850s and also situated in the centre of the lodge ceiling. It is believed to denote the initials of both God and Geometry.[23] In addition to being known as the Great Architect of the Universe and prototype for all builders, in Masonic circles God is also called the Grand Geometrician.

The candidate for initiation makes his Solemn Obligation in the presence of the assembled brethren and God, using the more familiar title of Great Architect of the Universe. Before reaching this stage, however, he must give the correct ritualized reply at the door of the lodge in order to gain both symbolic and physical entry. Language unlocks the door to initiation. The testing out of the candidate includes a viva voce. If the answers are satisfactory, the oath of allegiance is taken by the neophyte, who, in promising to maintain the secrecy of the society, agrees to a ritual penalty in the event of perjury. The severity of the sanctions for disclosure, ranging from disembowelment to throat-cutting, are intended for rhetorical effect only.[24] Apart from deliberate transgressive revelations, which do incur penalties, secrets can also be revealed accidentally to the wrong person. Precautions against this are taken by teaching Freemasons to identify one another through a set of secret visual, physical and verbal signals.

How seriously Masons have taken these secret communications outside the lodge cannot be fully determined. That there have been countries and periods in history which have seen the persecution of Freemasons is undeniable. In such hostile environments the main-tenance and strict practice of secrecy would be imperative. Apart from instances when Masons' secrecy was regarded as subversive or self-serving, their secret signals were probably little more than etiquette, conforming to conventions which had arisen from the traditions of the stonemason who wanted to protect the building secrets of the craft from outside competition.[25] Such secretive messages abide by certain rules which prompt furtive disclosures as to name, rank and number. The grip, sign and word of a degree are used both inside and outside the lodge to test out strangers, though nowadays in Britain there is greater openness about Masonic membership. A covert approach in public is to refer to phrases taken from ritual or even to make an indirect enquiry as to the identity of a stranger's mother lodge by asking him, 'Who is your mother?' Since it is more normative to enquire of another man, 'Who is your father?', the question about maternity is designed to arouse suspicion. By deconstructing and decoding, it becomes apparent that the real question is not about a woman, but about a male collective. This encoded question furnishes an example of metacommunication, which is the knowledge shared by the questioner and respondent that information is being restricted. What links the epistemological concerns of Masonic signs to the power dynamics implicated in concealment and revelation is the way secret semantic signals are used in such a manner as to alert outsiders to the existence of a secretive network from which they are excluded.

In contrast to overt signalling are phrases which are intended to warn that a spy, known Masonically as a cowan, is close at hand. During the eighteenth century the expression 'it rains' was used in the case of a man (and 'it snows' for a woman) to indicate the presence of an intruder.[26] This innocuous-sounding phrase was in fact an adumbrative for a ritual punishment which insisted that anyone eavesdropping on a Masons' meeting was to stand below the eaves of a house while it was raining, until water ran out of their shoes. The name 'eavesdropper' alludes to someone lurking within the 'eves-drop', the space between the wall of the house and the line where the rain water drops from the eaves. In William Hogarth's engraving *Night* (1738) a Freemason is depicted below the eaves from where a chamber-pot is being emptied into the street below thus raining down its contents on his head and shoulders. In this print Hogarth, a prominent and active Freemason, depicted Sir Thomas De Veil, his former Grand Master.[27] De Veil, who was also a magistrate, had been appointed to enforce the Gin Act, which he did through a network of spies, hence the connection with a cowan. He engaged not only in espionage, but also in hypocrisy, since instead of helping to curtail the abuse of alcohol, he was one of the greatest violators of his own law enforcement. The image of him tottering along a London street propped up by Sir Andrew Montgomery after indulging himself in the convivialities of a lodge meeting illustrates the lines in Henry Fielding's play *The Coffee-house Politician (Rape upon Rape): or the Justice Caught in His Own Trap* (1730), where Sotmore declares in

Act 4 Scene 9, 'I must give the justice one wish. May Heaven rain small-beer upon thee, and may it corrupt thy body till it is as putrefied as thy mind.'[28] Because De Veil was a corrupt justice, the variation on the traditional punishment for an eavesdropper adopted for him was a scatological outpouring.

Wordplay is represented visually elsewhere in the engraving, for example by the words *Ecce signum* (Behold the sign), which refer to the secret signs Masons use to identify one another. That the directive is in Latin implies further mystification, but, if translated, the injunction to behold the sign is rather redundant, since it is written on the sign itself anyway. Rather it is a signal to another meaning. This is the point at which the brethren in the lodge simultaneously 'cut the penal sign', that is, make a gesture of cutting the throat from left to right to symbolize the ritual penalty for perjury. Contained within the oath is the threat of the tongue being torn out. In Hogarth's engraving the finger in the picture on the barber-surgeon's sign is pointing not, as one might expect, to a tooth, but to a tongue. Samuel Prichard, in his pamphlet *Masonry Dissected* (1730), explains how the secrets of Freemasonry are kept in a bone box that neither opens nor shuts except with ivory keys. He reveals this to be a metaphor for the tongue and mouth. As demonstrated by his exposé, Prichard the renegade Freemason had failed to keep his own mouth shut. A false rumour circulated that he paid the full ritual price for his perjury by having his heart and tongue torn out in open lodge.

Four years after the Abbé Larudan wrote about this Masonic revenge in 1747, Hogarth engraved *The Reward of Cruelty* (1751).[29] Here Tom Nero, the convicted murderer, after being taken down from the gallows, is being dissected by the Royal College of Physicians in the aptly named Cutlerian theatre. This print is susceptible to a number of different readings, including a Masonic interpretation which draws on metaphor and textuality. In a reply to Prichard's exposé ascribed to Daniel Defoe and entitled *The Perjur'd Free Mason Detected* (1730) the suggestion is put forward that the original exposé should not be named the '*Free Mason* Dissected but *Mr Samuel Prichard* Dissected'.[30] As the new title indicates, in the context of Hogarth's engraving and the rumour mentioned by Larudan, just as Prichard had dissected the Masons, they have taken apart not only the offending text, but also, quite literally, the author – a far more drastic measure than the most hostile of reviewers could ever achieve. Instead of writing the body, as in *écriture féminine*, here, in Hogarth's allegorical engraving, we are invited to read the corpse. What this reveals is that the figurative oath has been made literal.

In terms of Masonic iconography the hangman's noose denotes the

Masonic cable-tow. This is the rope placed round the neophyte's neck
with which he is led round the lodge-room. The cable-tow is also a
signifier for the penal sign, which, as mentioned earlier, relates to the
part of the oath which says, 'All this under no less Penalty than to have
my Throat cut.' The text accompanying the print, written by the Revd
James Townley, is a commentary on Nero's just desserts, 'Torn from the
root that wicked tongue'. This is a punishment more appropriate for a
perjurer than for a murderer. The third stage of the Masonic penalty
depicted here as recited in the oath is that the heart is being 'pluck'd
from under [the] left breast',[31] where the secrets of a Mason are said to
be kept. Hiram Abif's assassins were punished in this way by having
their breasts torn open and hearts and vitals ripped out. In later exposés
it is revealed that if a Master Mason dared to divulge the secrets of
initiation, his ritual penalty would be specified as dissection.[32]

What Hogarth is doing in *The Reward of Cruelty* is to parody the
tropological language of Masonic ritual by making literal the figurative
blood-curdling oath and thereby recuperating the power of metaphor.
In his two engravings Hogarth has revitalized metaphor within a ritual
context. In doing so, he has also exposed Masonic secrets for those who
are able to decipher the visual signs which refer to the language of
initiation.

Bellman distinguishes between two forms of secrecy which manifest
themselves in her study of the Poro tribe – that which is known but
cannot be spoken and that which can be spoken, which she defines as
'the metaphorical expression of the secret'.[33] She goes on to point out
how the Poro tribe, while performing certain ritual acts, use metaphors
creatively in order to produce specific rhetorical effects.[34] The ability to
use metaphors creatively is shared by the Freemasons through the
dramatization of their history, like the re-enactment of the murder of
Hiram Abif, and in their rituals of initiation, as in the experiential rites
of illumination.

The main metaphor of Freemasonry is a rite of passage from darkness
into light. It is significant that Masons embody the values of the *Siècle
des lumières* and *Aufklärung* and, as Margaret Jacob points out in her
book on eighteenth-century Freemasonry, they have been speaking in
the language of the Enlightenment.[35] ('Liberty', 'Equality' and 'Fraternity' are watchwords of Freemasonry as well as of the French Revolution.) The trope of enlightening is experienced literally by the neophyte,
who is described as 'a poor candidate in a state of darkness',[36] having
been confined to a dark room for a few hours. From there he is taken to
the lodge-room blindfolded and led by the cable-tow. When asked what
his dearest wish is, he replies, 'Light', at which point the blindfold is

removed. In early workings of this ceremony the lodge-room was blazing with candles and the brethren displayed uplifted shining swords.

The request for 'light' is part of the tropological language of rebirth, as when the candidate is torn from comforting darkness into the searing light of illumination by Masonic midwives. In terms of psychoanalysis the cable-tow becomes a 'symbolical umbilical cord'.[37] The dissemination of the language of motherhood in order to enunciate that the candidate has been reborn into Freemasonry is an appropriation of the female reproductive role. As such, it is a symbolic form of empowerment in an area from which men are biologically excluded. Their figurative reclaiming of this territory reinforces the existing power structures predicated upon gender.

Where lodges were mixed, the use of mystical language transcended gender. In La Loge du juste, in France, the implications of such language were so radical with regard to egalitarian social behaviour that it was too subversive to be implemented beyond the lodge. As Margaret Jacob explains, a different criterion for judging individual worth had been adopted from the hermetic traditions of the Renaissance, based not on gender, but on intellect.[38]

The boundaries of Freemasonry in Britain have remained different from the Continent; it is inscribed by a more tribal notion of masculinity in that it has remained exclusively male. The lodge is traditionally an environment that is alien to women. As its name implies, the lodge is a place of repose and, as it turned out, a sanctuary from women. It has always granted men a legitimate space within which to exercise their masculinity. During the eighteenth century this manifested itself in the manly pursuits of transgressive swearing and gaming. In a comic dialogue between a Master Mason called Level and Sir Timothy Tattle, described as a fop, the latter opposes the inclusion of women in the lodge since he believes that it would inhibit the brethren from blaspheming or gambling:

> No cards! No scandal! now you've spoiled the Whole
> A pretty meeting under such control
> A modest set who neither game nor swear,
> Egad, I fancy you'll not catch me there.
> In search of Joys I vanish to Soho,
> But stay – I'll leave one secret e'er I go
> I find your Order suits not Lads of Spirit.[39]

The lodge-room itself is arrayed with phallic symbols, ranging from pillars to columns, candlesticks and masculine tools such as the level and the gavel (hammer shape), while the Masonic configuration of the point within the circle has been interpreted as a sacred hieroglyphic signifying the worship of the phallus.[40] Within its system of signification, Masonry and its rites of initiation may be seen as a celebration and recapitulation of the entry into the realm of the Lacanian symbolic (language), thereby embodying a structure which generates the discourses and practices of the phallocentric.

Developing from this sense of difference is the discourse of misogyny which assumes a power and authority through the genre of pornographic verse.[41] Bawdy lodge drinking songs are the discursive practices which most reinforce sexual differentiation. Whether they were actually sung in the lodge while 'at rest' or were a product of anti-Masonry is difficult to determine. But it is likely that they were the equivalent of modern-day rugby songs. Appended to rituals and exposés and included in collections of Masonic songs, they represent a form of virulent misogyny which was strongly associated with Freemasonry. At the very least, the crude and exuberant puns used have been provided by a Masonic discourse or jargon. The authors, who were usually anonymous, enlisted the corrective stance of the satirist as a means of diffusing that which they feared most through comedy. In this case, the objects of fear were women. Felicity Nussbaum, in her book on English satires of women from 1660 to 1750, *The Brink of All We Hate* (1984), puts forward the suggestion that a writer of such satire is able to express such misogyny through the creation of a rhetorical stance which 'releases him and like-minded readers from the charms of a woman' and 'simultaneously absolves him and his readers from all that he finds reprehensible'.[42] The narrator is forced to confront his own desires through his assaults on female autonomy in his rebarbative verse.

In some of the wordplay of the bawdier drinking songs the language of initiation, as used in the expression to be 'made' a Mason, is employed to describe both the loss of virginity ('make a maid a Mason') and the acquisition of occult or mystical knowledge involved in the rites of Masonic initiation. Discernible in this poem are the erotic wordplay and *double entendres* associated with the Freemasons' working tools. Even degrees of the craft, like Entered Apprentice, were subject to eroticized allegory exploiting the metaphors of penetration. Some Caledonian verses attributed to Robert Burns include sexual puns on 'tools' referring to the working tools, 'illumination' on initiation, 'grip' for secret hand shake and 'slip' denoting the skin that comes away from the finger of Hiram Abif's corpse, since his body has been found by his disciples in a state of decomposition. This macabre episode is play-acted in the raising of the master by using the prescribed grip in the third degree:

> So pleased was I to see him ply
> The tools of his vocation
> I beg'd for once he would dispense
> And make a maid a mason.
>
> The more and more the light did pour
> With bright Illumination
> But when the grip he did me slip
> I gloried in my mason.[43]

The word 'mason' in this context is being used as a metonym for male sexuality. Conveyed in the lyrics were tales of courtship, Masonic erotica and the idea that Masonry enhances male sexual potency. These were strategies of appeasement that could be offered to female partners abandoned night after night because of lodge convivialities; they could be reassured that their neglect was in a good cause, and one from which they would eventually benefit. Bawdy drinking songs may have functioned as an aphrodisiac aperitif for homebound brethren. That Masonic membership enhanced masculine potency and virility was mysterious indeed when one considers the amount of alcohol Masons were reputed to consume during lodge meetings.

In a series of eighteenth-century Masonic epilogues wives of Masons appear to break their traditional silence by speaking publicly. These theatrical pieces spoken by female players began as protests against the exclusion of women, but ended up as anthems to the joys of marriage to a Mason. The language of homespun wisdom is used to great effect in Mrs Thurmond's eulogy:

> Ye marry'd Ladies, 'tis a happy Life,
> Believe me, that of a FREE MASON's Wife,
> Tho' they conceal the Secrets of their Friends
> In Love and Truth they make us full Amends.[44]

Confiding to the audience her fears that her husband's initiation into the fraternity would result in his castration, she then discloses her pleasure in discovering not a loss of manhood, but a veritable improvement in her spouse:

> When he came back, I found a Change, 'tis true,
> But such a change as did his Youth renew.
> If magick Charms they practis'd, it must be
> In Æson's chauldron, that they made him free;
> With rosy Cheeks, and smiling Grace, he came,
> And sparkling Eyes, that spoke a Bridegroom's Flame.[45]

The anxieties about castration expressed by this complacent Masonic wife would indicate that this epilogue, along with all the others composed by the grateful wives of Freemasons, had been written by men, since voicing their spouses' approval for their nightly jaunts served their purpose well. In another epilogue Mrs Gifford's fears that her initiated husband would return as an emasculated version of his former self is allayed later that evening with the result that she desires 'That to increase our mutual delight, / Would he were made a Mason every night'.[46] Likewise, in the pornographic song 'Kate and Ned', included in the Masonic pamphlet *Jachin and Boas* (1762; New York edition of 1797), an example of transference from the desiring subject to the object desired, the eagerness for initiated Masons reaches fever-pitch when Kate announces her willingness to 'pawn my gown, my robes and coat / My cardinal with lace on'[47] if Ned can be a Mason every night.

The identification between the Freemason as procreator and the operative skills of the Mason as creator is made in the lines spoken in a theatrical monologue by Mrs Younger, whose loyalty as a Mason's wife is exemplary:

> They're able Workmen, and completely skill'd in
> The deepest – Arts and Mysteries of Building;
> They'll build up Families, and, as most is,
> Not only will erect, – but people, Cities:
> They'll fill, as well as fabricate, your Houses,
> And found a lasting Race of strong built Spouses.[48]

The workman has advanced to being the creator not merely of buildings, but also of urban communities and, more particularly, of individuals. The images of potency and virility are evoked by the word 'erect'. And what does the Mason do for his mate? The answer can be found in the 'Kate and Ned' song, where the woman is seen metaphorically as a broken building with a breach which is in need of attention. The female is represented as an imperfect male in need of the craftsman's skills to repair her. Through the imagery of stonemasonry she is at best a desirable property and at worst a ruin. The metaphors of Masonry may be deconstructed to reveal a buried recognition that power and gender are socially constructed in such a way that privileges the male.

When men get together, they can be made to feel under pressure to live up to an image of exaggerated heterosexuality to conceal any suggestion of homo-eroticism. This may be one reason for the Free-masons' boast of their increased virility, which is ridiculed as self-parody in the songs. Such sexual bragging also functioned to deflect any suspicion that their secrecy veiled illicit practices like homosexuality or paedophilia. Even in the bawdy Hudibrastic poem *The Free Masons* (1722–3), with its buttock-branding and 'bumbarding', we are told 'none but females have the power / Their breeches and their purse to lower'.[49] The punning on purse refers to the female genitalia as well as to the greater earning power of men, while the combination of both is a recipe for prostitution.

Apart from such denigrations, another strategy for excluding women from the lodge was to insist that they were incapable of keeping secrets. This is expressed in the lodge drinking songs, where a favourite motif was to draw a parallel between Masonic concealment and the enclosure and exposure of sexual secrets in their revelation through pregnancy. In an epilogue by a Freemason's wife, Mrs Horton, we are told of 'A charming secret, but I must conceal it, / If time, at nine months end, does not reveal it'.[50] This alludes to the tell-tale signs of pregnancy which show that sexual intercourse has taken place. The divulgence through the sight of a swollen belly and eventual presence of a newly born infant confirms the inability of women to keep secrets. The foetus is the secret planted by the man, who loses control of its secrecy once it becomes public knowledge.

Similarly, the author of Masonic satires has the power to mine the text with secret meanings to which the reader has private and privileged access, rather like a husband who has exclusive rights over his wife's body, a recurring theme in some of the bawdier lyrics. Meaningless to the uninitiated, the sharing of codes and mastery of secrets reinforce the solidarity of those in the know. Readers of erotic verses equipped to decipher the double meanings are already party to the kind of encodings taking place within Masonic symbolism itself.

Secrecy functions as a form of empowerment for the reader of Masonic exposés in all their forms. But invariably there are secrets which are dependent not upon their continuing concealment, but upon their impending exposure. These are the time bombs waiting to be detonated at the appropriate time, since the *raison d'être* of a secret is its eventual revelation. An early example of this may be found in the brethrens' claims for their virility, which was rarely the best kept of secrets. Instead it was closer to an open boast. Masons were attributed with having the secret of defloration as revealed in a collection of songs of 1734:

> None shall untye my virgin zone
> But one to whom the *Secret's* known,
> Of famed *Free-Masonry*.[51]

When attached to exposés of the craft, these songs give outsiders access to Masonic secrets and also supposedly to the mysteries of female sexuality, which, by remaining secret, threatened to undermine male sexual authority. Men were able to respond to any such threat by consolidating their power in maintaining the secrets of their all-male club.

Traditional female curiosity in the activities of the lodge is likely to have been a collective male fantasy fuelled by the self-importance of its members. The idea that women were aching to discover the secrets of Freemasonry because they were an excluded group smacks of a constructed and scripted female response, the sacred text of many bawdy songs being that female charms will be deployed in a bartering of sex for knowledge. But no Mason is so easily duped by these womanly wiles. Fickleness and female charm would never tempt the cautious stalwart of male integrity, loyalty and solidarity.

Mrs Horton, in her epilogue, fears initially that Masons are a species of monster comparable in brutishness only to Italian tenors. Later she renounces her misapprehensions on realizing that the seeming misogynists are, in fact, lovers of the fair sex – a misunderstanding to which women are prone. In a prologue written by F. Blythe in 1753 (published in the *Gentleman's Magazine*), which had been intended for a Masonic bespeak at a theatre, the scientific method of experience and observation is advocated as a means of discrediting such misleading assumptions: 'For tho' some dames suspect: we hate their sex; / Those dames who've tried us, own: – they're gross mistakes.'[52]

The discourse of misogyny has not been the exclusive purview of the Masons, but is a reflection of anti-women attitudes in a male-dominated society at large. As a microcosm of outside society mirroring the binary oppositions which underpin gender roles, Masonry is an exaggerated statement of the unequal power relationships existing between the sexes. As is self-evident, this is by no means a construction of gender peculiar to Freemasonry. Rather it is a reinforcement of existing stereotypes. The rhetoric of male power and privilege which exists in the mainstream language services Freemasonry in the articulation of its ritual and symbolism. One example of the way in which the fraternity has enhanced its own status is by identifying with the concept of the Brotherhood of Man through its songs. Such an equation could have the effect of making outsiders, especially women, feel relegated to the margins of society. Many of the non-bawdy songs associated with Freemasonry are a celebration of masculinity, while the initiation ceremonies can be seen as rites testing out manhood. The man as an active achiever and as a bearer of the values traditionally associated with the male, rather than with the female, is valorized. In view of this, it would appear that Masonic discourse is less a rhetoric of marginality than a mirror of the mainstream. Such a claim is not intended to be ahistorical, since admittedly there have been periods in history, such as the time of the French Revolution, when Freemasons stood apart from the status quo as a radical body. But this radicalism was, itself, an embodiment of the *Zeitgeist*.

Language is not only the indicator of political affiliations of a lodge at a given time and place, but also a facilitator for change. The protean quality of Masonry, in absorbing and reproducing the values around itself, has ensured its continuing survival. Obviously there have been exceptions, as when Freemasons were banned by totalitarian regimes like Hitler's Germany and Stalin's Russia. But for the most part Freemasonry has been tolerated because of its interactive nature with society outside and its ability to maintain an ongoing dialogue. The ritualized speech, rhetoric and metaphors of Freemasonry since the Enlightenment tend to articulate the values of the dominant culture. Included in these are a deference to authority, a maintenance of hierarchy (albeit a different one from that operating outside), middle-class ideologies and a rigid adherence to the demarcation of gender roles. Harmless joking by outsiders about rolled-up trouser-legs and the phrases and expressions which have found their way into the mainstream language are, in themselves, peripheral. What is more significant has been the process of linguistic symbiosis that has passed through the membrane of the lodge. This has inculcated a culture of masculinity and cultivated a discourse of empowerment which has had repercussions both in and outside Freemasonry.

This analysis of the relationship between a secret discourse and the public language has attempted to shed light upon the nature of metaphor and reality, particularly within the context of ritual. George Lakoff and Mark Johnson argue that the metaphors we live by are present in ritual, which reinforces and propagates those values so that 'Ritual forms an indispensable part of the experiential basis for our cultural metaphorical systems.' They go on to state, 'There can be no culture without ritual.'[53] The way in which the rites of Freemasonry have helped shape the cultural spaces, both within and outside itself, has been, in part, through the adoption of the linguistic transmissions from the mainstream language. What this has opened up for the Freemasons is a means of reinforcing their own assumptions of power and privilege. That Masons are not being marginalized by society and are not presently engaged in its subversion, but have in many respects continued to help ratify establishment values, has been one of their less well kept secrets.

Notes

I would like to thank Hugh Ormsby-Lennon, J. C. Smith, Maurice Hindle, Margaret Jacob, David Lamb, David Stevenson and Charlie Butler for invaluable comments on this chapter and John Hamill, the librarian of Freemason's Hall, for supplying me with some very useful material.

1 For some interesting details about secret languages, see R. M. W. Dixon, *The Languages of Australia* (Cambridge: Cambridge University Press, 1980), 65–8.

2 A seminal sociological approach to secrecy has been made by G. Simmel, 'The Sociology of Secrecy and Secret Societies', *American Journal of Sociology*, xi, 4 (1904), 441–98. See also H. Ormsby-Lennon, 'Nature's Mystick Book: Renaissance *Arcanum* into Restoration Cant', in M. Mulvey Roberts and H. Ormsby-Lennon (eds), *Secret Texts: The Literature of Secret Societies* (New York: AMS, forthcoming), and Thomas Willard, 'Rosicrucian Sign Lore and Origin of Language', *Theorien vom Ursprung der Sprache*, i (1989), 131–57, and Frank Kermode, *The Genesis of Secrecy on the Interpretation of Narrative* (Cambridge, Mass.: Harvard University Press, 1979). Peter Burke looks at hidden meaning in art and literature and asks why there is so much secrecy in *Culture and Society in Renaissance Italy 1420–1520* (London: Batsford, 1972), 159.

3 A useful study is Sissela Bok, *Secrets: Concealment and Revelation* (London: Oxford University Press, 1984). Harvey Sacks writes about the parodox of a secret whereby its divulgence is inevitably an exposure of it. The way in which this contradiction is negotiated linguistically and psychologically is explored in his essay 'Everyone Has to Lie', in M. Sanchez and B. Blount (eds), *Sociocultural Dimensions of Language Use* (New York: Academic, 1975), 57–80.

4 See C. S. Lewis's memorial oration at King's College, University of London (1944), on 'The Inner Ring', in *Transposition and Other Addresses* (London: Geoffrey Bles, 1949), 55–64. Here he claims that 'the genuine Inner Ring exists for exclusion', 63.

5 See B. L. Bellman, *The Language of Secrecy: Symbols and Metaphors in Poro Ritual* (New Brunswick, NJ: Rutgers University Press, 1984), and Peter Burke, *The Historical Anthropology of Early Modern Italy: Essays on Perception and Communication* (Cambridge: Cambridge University Press, 1987), 223–38.

6 M. C. Jacob, 'Speaking the Language of the Enlightenment', ch. 6 in *Living the Enlightenment: Freemasonry and Politics in Eighteenth-century Europe* (Oxford: Oxford University Press, 1991), 143–61. See also Revd M. Rosenbaum, 'Masonic Words and Proper Names', *Transactions of Leeds Installed Master's Association*, vi (1909–10), and Bro. Oldroyd, 'Masonic Words and Proper Names', *Transactions of Humber Installed Masters Lodge*, pt 1, v (1908–12), 504–16. A linguistic model for discourse analysis is provided by W. Labov in 'Rules for Ritual Insult', in *Studies in Social Interaction* (London: Collier-Macmillan, 1972), 120–69.

7 J. Hamill, in *The Craft: A History of English Freemasonry* (London: Crucible, 1986), has contested this description of Freemasonry in the following comment: 'Freemasonry is neither a secret society nor, as it has sometimes been characterized recently, a 'society with secrets'. The only 'secrets' in Freemasonry are the traditional words and signs of recognition and, as a careful reading of the obligations taken in each degree shows, these are the only secrets that a Freemason binds himself to keep' (146). This seems to me to be rather contradictory. That the secrecy is 'only' a matter of form rather than content and concerned with codes of recognition and allegiance should not detract from the fact that these pieces of information are still technically secrets. In the light of this, it seems unduly defensive to try to deny their essential nature and argue, on these grounds, against the description of Freemasonry as a society with secrets.

8 See Jacob, *Living the Enlightenment*, 20.

9 In his *Constitutions* (1723) John Anderson specifies that bondsmen are excluded and that members must be freeborn. This refers to slavery and also to the specifications made in the Old Charges or rules for operative Masons formulated during the Middle Ages, when feudal serfdom existed. Nowadays black lodges do exist in the United States.

10 As M. Jacob has shown, this was not the case on the Continent. See her article 'Freemasonry, Women and the Paradox of Enlightenment', *Women and History*, 9 (1984), 69–93. See also E. L. Scott, *Women and Freemasonry* (Enfield: privately printed, 1988); D. Wright in *Women and Freemasonry* (London: William Rider, 1922); and F. W. G. Gilby in *Women and Freemasonry in the Past and in the Present* (Birmingham: privately printed, 1925). Co-Masonry was founded in Britain around the turn of the century. On 26 September 1902 the Lodge of Human Duty was consecrated in London; it attracted members of the Theosophical Society, such as its president, Annie Besant. In 1908 a breakaway group formed the Honourable Fraternity of Antient Masonry, which developed into an all-female society and was later renamed the Order of Women Freemasons. These female orders are not under the jurisdiction of the United Grand Lodge and as such are not officially recognized or integrated into the fraternity of Freemasons.

11 See B. Thorne and N. Henley, *Language and Sex: Difference and Domination* (New York: Heimele and Heimele, 1975); R. Lakoff, *Language and Women's Place* (New York: Harper, 1975); D. Spender, *Man Made*

Language (London: Routledge, 1980); and the classic collection of essays on this subject in B. Thorne, C. Kramarae and N. Henley (eds), *Language, Gender and Society* (Cambridge, Mass.: Newburn House Publishers, 1969).

12 See B. E. Jones, *Freemasons' Guide and Compendium*, rev. edn (London: Harrap, 1977), 301–2. Jones lists the slang words derived from Freemasonry and registers his regret that not all are complimentary to it. He assigns the term 'third degree' to a Masonic derivation and not to the torture inflicted by the Spanish Inquisition as has been claimed.

13 See H. Poole, 'Masonic Song and Verse of the Eighteenth Century', *Ars quatuor coronatorum*, xi (1927), 7–29. Here he deduces from the exposure *Hiram, or the Grand Master Key* (1764) that there were two classes of Masonic songs; those sung after the lectures and those sung during lodge hours.

14 See Bro. R. Baxter, 'Masonic Words and Their Meanings: Biblical, Hebrew and Other Words Used in the Literature and Terminology of Freemasonry', *Transactions of the Manchester Association for Masonic Research*, xxiii (1933), 203–16. See also Bro. Sir L. Brett, 'The Vocabulary of the Ceremonies', *Ars quatuor coronatorum*, 101 (1989), 2–3. In the dedication to *Long Livers: A Curious History of Such Persons of both Sexes who have liv'd several Ages, and grown Young again:* ... by Eugenius Philalethes, FRS, author of the *Treatise of the Plague* (London, 1722), repr. in D. Knoop, G. P. Jones and D. Hamer (eds), *Early Masonic Pamphlets* (Manchester: Manchester University Press, 1945), there is an account of what the goals of the fraternity should be. The opening is of interest in regard to language: 'I address my self to you after this Manner, because it is the true Language of the Brotherhood, and which the primitive Christian Brethren, as well as those who were from the Beginning, made use of, as we learn from the holy Scriptures, and an uninterrupted Tradition ... The Style I shall make use of is most Catholick, primitve and Christian; it is what is extracted from the sacred Scriptures' (43–4).

15 See Rosenbaum, 'Masonic Words and Proper Names', 30–53.

16 Hamill, in *The Craft*, classifies some interpreters of Freemasonry into the non-authentic school, which includes four approaches: the esoteric, the mystical, the symbolist and the romantic. The most colourful example he cites is that of John Yarker, who attempted to introduce into Freemasonry the Antient and Primite Rite, which Hamill describes as 'a pot-pourri of Egyptology, Gnosticism, Rosicrucianism, Cabala, Alchemy, Eastern Mysticism, and Christianity' (23).

17 In the cabalistic tradition, it is claimed that the universe was created out of the twenty-two letters of the Hebrew alphabet.

18 See W. Hannah, *Darkness Visible: A Revelation and Interpretation of Freemasonry* (London: Augustine Press, 1952).

19 Ibid., 101.

20 Ibid., 181.

21 See D. Stevenson, *The Origins of Freemasonry: Scotland's Century*

1590–1710 (Cambridge: Cambridge University Press, 1988), 125–34, and D. Knoop and G. P. Jones, *The Scottish Mason and the Mason Word* (Manchester: Manchester University Press, 1939).

22 This is taken from Isaiah, viii, 1. See Hannah, *Darkness Visible*, 199.

23 See J. T. Thorp, 'The Origin and Meaning of the Letter "G" in Free-masonry', *Transactions of the Merseyside Association for Masonic Research*, iii (1924–5), 51–7.

24 The oath has been modified and toned down so as not to offend modern sensibilities; it is still retained, though not recited by the neophyte.

25 On the origins of the craft, see D. Knoop and G. P. Jones, *The Genesis of Freemasonry* (Manchester: Manchester University Press, 1947), and the more recent history by Hamill, *The Craft*, which focuses on English Freemasonry and argues that it has its origin in speculative Masonry.

26 See Jones, *Freemasons' Guide and Compendium*, 424, where he refers to the gendered encodings of 'it rains' and 'it snows' and to a description of the ritual punishment for an eavesdropper in an old catechism dated 1730.

27 See E. Ward, 'William Hogarth and His Fraternity', *Ars quatuor coro-natorum*, lxxvii (1964), 1–18, and G. W. Speth, 'Notes and Queries: Hogarth's *Night*', *Ars quatuor coronatorum*, ii (1889), 116–17.

28 H. Fielding, *The Coffee-house Politician (Rape upon Rape)* (1730), in his *Complete Works*, ed. W. Ernest Henley, 16 vols (London: F. Cass, 1902; repr. 1967), ix: 140.

29 See Abbé de Larudan, *Les Francs-Maçons écrasés: suite du livre intitulé; l'Ordre des Francs-Maçons trahi, traduit du Latin* (Amsterdam, 1747), 57–60, 103–6.

30 D. Defoe, *The Perjur'd Free Mason Detected: and yet the Honour and Antiquity of the Society of Free Masons Preserv'd and Defended* (London: T. Warner, 1730), 18. See also J. Moore, *A Checklist of the Writings of Daniel Defoe* (Bloomington: Indiana University Press, 1960), 227.

31 Defoe, *The Perjur'd Free Mason Detected*, 16.

32 This ritual penalty has carried through into modern workings. See Hannah, *Darkness Visible*, 136.

33 Bellman, *The Language of Secrecy*, 83.

34 Ibid., 138. Paul Ricoeur argues that true metaphor is 'the rhetorical process by which discourse unleashes power that certain fictions have to re-describe reality'. What he means by living metaphors is that they generate a perception that had not existed before. A distinction is made between creative living metaphors and dead ones as polysemic in regard to the role of metaphor in ritual. See P. Ricoeur, *The Rule of Metaphor: Multi-disciplinary Studies of the Creation of Meaning in Language*, trans. R. Czerny with K. Mclaughlin and J. Costello (London: Routledge and Kegan Paul, 1986), 7.

35 See Jacob, *Living the Enlightenment*, 143–61.

36 Hannah, *Darkness Visible*, 95.

37 Quoted in M. Short, *Inside the Brotherhood: Further Secrets of the Free-*

masons (London: Grafton Books, 1989), 76, 102.

38 See Jacob, *Living the Enlightenment*, 128–9.

39 *Freemasonry for the Ladies dedicated by permission to her Royal Highness the Duchess of York* (London: Thomas Wilkinson, 1791), 61.

40 See Short, *Inside the Brotherhood*, 101–2.

41 Mark Madoff delivered a fascinating paper drawing on this material called 'Erection and Detection: Masonic Secrecy and Sexuality' at the annual conference of the American Society of Eighteenth-century Studies at Minneapolis in 1990.

42 F. Nussbaum, *The Brink of All We Hate* (Lexington: University of Kentucky, 1984), 4–6.

43 G. Legman, *The Horn Book: Studies in Erotic Folklore and Bibliography* (London: Jonathan Cape, 1970), 140–1.

44 Knoop, Jones and Hamer, *Early Masonic Pamphlets*, 210.

45 Ibid., 209.

46 Ibid., 291.

47 *Oriental Masonic Muse* (Calcutta: Joseph Cooper, 1791), 3.

48 Knoop, Jones and Hamer, *Early Masonic Pamphlets*, 285.

49 *The Free Masons: An Hudibrastic Poem* (London: A. Moore, 1722–3), 11. This is an anti-Masonic obscene poem which makes charges of indecency against the Freemasons.

50 *Oriental Masonic Muse*, 145.

51 Knoop, Jones and Hamer, *Early Masonic Pamphlets*, 320.

52 Ibid., 326.

53 G. Lakoff and M. Johnson, *Metaphors We Live By* (Chicago: University of Chicago Press, 1980), 234.

6

Jargon of Class: Rhetoric and Leadership in British Labour Politics, 1830–1880

TIMOTHY R. BURNS

Men of the Working Classes, your delivery is in your own hands – the freedom or slavery of millions yet unborn hangs upon your breath. By every principle of virtue, by all your hatred of slavery, by all your hopes of freedom, by all your love of country and children, I invoke you to be firm, unflinching – in short, to Do Your Duty! For myself, I nail the flag of 'No Surrender' to the mast, and though the good ship democracy should sink beneath the fire of open enemies and treacherous friends, my last cry, ringing from the waves of popular delusion should still be 'Vive, Vive la Charte'.

George Julian Harney

The trenchant and uncompromising rhetoric of the Chartist-socialist Harney, in this letter to 'Brother Democrats and Chartists of Sheffield' of March 1842, illustrates the rich strain of figurative language within nineteenth-century British labour politics. Working-class radical speeches and articles were enlivened by images of manhood and parenthood, punctuated with historical allusions and sustained through entangled metaphors of suffering borne with heroic fortitude. Themes of martyrdom and deliverance, corruption and regeneration, true and false community interacted to produce a common jargon of political struggle.[1]

In comparison with modern party politics, of course, the political language of nineteenth-century Britain appears devoid of jargon, at least in the contemptuous sense of excessive and meaningless terminology. Political jargon, however, is more than the mere production of terminology for and by specific groups. Indeed, Pierre Bourdieu argues that jargon aids the definition of group membership, establishing roles and hierarchies, and acting as a powerful device for the communication and persuasion of values and policies within the wider community. As such, the use of jargon is a key means to being political, in the sense of both speaking politically (using the recognized language of politics) and acting politically (seeking to draw and redraw the meanings of central political concepts).[2] In this way, the rhetorical construction of forms of political allegiance and leadership that were central to working-class radical language could also act as intrusions into the wider currents of political debate over modes of strategy, organization and legitimation. The jargon of political struggle could demarcate as well as integrate plebeian radicalism within the broader language of nineteenth-century politics.

Political languages are attempts at understanding, defining and creating the scope of debate, albeit within the context of prevailing economic and political conditions, and the guiding values by which society is structured.[3] It is from this perspective of the strategic nature of political discourse that this chapter sets out to explore aspects of the rhetoric of nineteenth-century working-class radicalism. The first section considers the role of terminology, modes of address and radical names in the rhetoric of leadership. The second section examines more directly the generation of political allegiances and the articulation of what could be termed the metaphors of political engagement that ran through labour politics. The rhetorical means of speaking and acting politically are explored. Finally, the relation of this jargon of class to broader developments in British political discourse and the shifts in labour politics are considered.

Leaders have been axiomatic in developments of forms of political organization and expression. Popular political assessments are to a significant degree based on perceptions of the personality traits of local and national leaders. These perceptions, for a generally politically disinterested populace, are rarely founded upon personal insight, but instead are developed from the public imagery of leadership. Nineteenth-century leadership, lacking the sanitized party political broadcast and orchestrated media soundbite, was sustained through the less tangible interplay of verbal and non-verbal forms of expression. Historians have sought to decipher the coded messages within the clothes, rituals and gestures of plebeian politics.[4] What concerns us here, however, are the means by which the rhetoric of leaders articulated and structured political allegiances and outlined modes of political engagement.

Political discourse is the arena in which relations between leaders and followers are most clearly displayed. Political language seeks to animate ideas, reducing the infinitely varied nature of human experience to a manageable level of types and processes, locating the role of the political speaker in relation to his or her audience and placing words relevantly within the wider context of social and political discourse.[5] In the nineteenth century uneven and diverse communal and work experience, the related absence of clear linear political and social cleavages of class and party, and the limited scope of national communication hampered the growth of organizations and political ideologies tied to discernible mass constituencies. National political rhetoric was thus crucially involved in the production of collective political identities. The nascent development of formal party structures before the 1860s and the pervasive distrust of sectional, party and class politics, in contrast to the principle-politics of statesmanship, served to underline the unifying power of the charismatic and highly figurative language of the popular champion. To achieve national political and economic changes popular leaders had to tether a diverse and regionalized base of support to transitory and fledgling political organizations. A simultaneous appeal, both as a representative of a movement and as someone transcending the narrow confines of any specific organization, was necessary.[6]

This dual appeal was reflected in the open-ended and adaptive quality of popular radical terminology and identities. Intermixing with more populist idioms of rich and poor, and people versus privilege, by the 1830s the rhetoric of class had been emergent in political debate for over a century. Chartists and later radicals repeatedly employed the terminology of 'the working class' and 'the working classes'.[7] By the 1850s the discourse of Harney's *Red Republican* newspaper was saturated with references to proletarian and bourgeoisie, revolution and class war. Such terms, however, were far from rigidly defined. The chaos of terminology in the nineteenth century provided no simple social classifications around which to structure political movements. The use of class or classes, proletariat or people, in political discourse therefore probably held limited ideological significance to plebeian radicals themselves. Where employed, the terminology of class pivoted on contingent political considerations, notably the divisions of the 1832 Reform Act, and thereby attested more to the adaptability of popular radicalism than to any precise shift in political identities. Indeed, given the complex nature of Victorian social relations, the eclectic and imprecise use of terminology by popular radicals was a more effective representation than the rigid categorizations of class.[8]

Moreover, as Crossick notes, the choice of terminology primarily 'reflected the politics for which it was used'.[9] Less concerned with exact definitions than with forging political alliances, plebeian leaders used language strategically, rather than purely descriptively. Without the means to mass communication, the dissemination of political ideas inevitably centred on the universal and familiar terms of political debate. The production of terminology was thus an evolutionary process, adapting established vocabularies to new purposes. 'Shopocrat' and 'millocrat' could be used to bridge gaps between evolving economic relations and a relatively static language of social description.[10] Political terms were turned to popular radical advantage, challenging the libertarian and enlightened claims of the new manufacturing classes. The 'steam aristocracy' of the Anti-Corn Law League was thereby damned as a 'new race of feudal lords', distinguished solely by the extent of their power and corruption. Even radicals immersed, however superficially, in the language of class saw clear political gains in the employment of ideas of a 'new aristocracy'. Harney, in the *Democratic Review* in February 1850, placed capitalists and middle-class radicals on a continuum of political and economic tyranny, decrying their claims to be progressive. 'The proletarians,' he wrote, 'need another sort of reform. The feudal aristocracy being doomed to expire, care should be taken that no new aristocracy be allowed to take their place.' What was seen to distinguish working-class radicalism was not the appropriation of a new language of class, but the rejection of an aristocratic mode of politics. This rejection was centrally concerned with the political delineation of plebeian radicalism as the true centre of progressive politics in opposition to the sectarianism of middle-class parliamentary and extra-parliamentary radicalism.[11]

Beneath the imprecision and contradiction of radical terminology, a pervasive language of political identity evolved. The force of political language, Bourdieu argues, resides not in the essential truth or accuracy of words, but in the 'power of mobilization' words contain. This mobilization may of necessity be in part built on the resonance of radical discourse with the perceived experiences of plebeian life, but the essential nature of this discourse is to persuade. The engaged nature of popular politics, and yet the diverse character of plebeian organization and identity, reiterated the tactical purpose of rhetoric, and, almost to the exclusion of more formal political ideas, popular radical discourse sought to construct boundaries of allegiance.[12]

A central medium of political mobilization is the identification of individual leaders with specific programmatic demands and strategies. One channel for such identification is the leader's form of address. The manner of address can emphasize or de-emphasize personal function and responsibility, ironically challenge or reinforce the relations of power.[13] The employment of 'Fellow Citizens' and 'Fellow Countrymen' could conjure up different but connected allusions to the threat of republican revolution and the evolutionary, redemptive potential of English manhood. Moreover, the predominant use of the first person 'I' or 'we' tethered the leader to the collective audience or readership. This served to reinforce the legitimacy of a style of leadership, creating the sense of collective values and endeavour held in the personage of the leader. Such modes of address, of course, are dialectical, given meaning in the unstable relationship between speaker and audience. As a result, they are resistant to simple categorization. Taken in the generality, however, they point to the ways in which specific political movements identify their relation to the prevailing political system. There was, for example, clearly an important distinction of political ideals contained in O'Connor's self-description as an 'unyielding and incorruptible shepherd' and the London Democratic Association's addresses to 'Brother Proletarians'. Moreover, O'Connor's association as the 'Lion of Freedom' held a less prosaic and potentially divisive set of allusions than Harney's 'L'Ami de peuple', with its connotations of Marat and the French Revolution, or indeed O'Brien's assumption of the name Bronterre. Despite this, whether in the Owenite 'Social Father', O'Brien's 'Schoolmaster of Chartism', O'Connor's 'Lion of Freedom' or Harney's 'Friend of the People', the universal location of the leader as enabler of the people's cause essentially reasserted the guiding paternalistic imagery of prevailing social and political ideas of leadership.[14]

Political namings and allusions were effective means of communication beyond the potentially divisive and alienating discussion of formal political ideas. 'Political Corrector', 'Regenerator', 'Reformator', 'Scourge' and 'Common Sense' (with its link to Painite republicanism), for instance, carried messages as to the temperament and scope of popular politics, in ways similar, say, to the use of the unwavering authoritarianism of 'Iron Lady' in the 1980s. Plebeian politics was thereby constantly portrayed as a responsive, regenerative force, correcting a state of political corruption; a powerful and radical imposition, but essentially redemptive and integral.[15] Irony, as a form of internal political challenge, was also widely employed, from the naming of the *Poor Man's Guardian* at the height of the anti-Poor Law campaign to the ironic signing as 'One of the Know Nothings', or 'One of the

Unshorn Chins and Battered Hands'. Following Bourdieu, such ironic
assertion of the characteristics of subordination, like 'queer' and 'radical' in the modern context, can be seen to shift between positive and
negative connotations, depending on individual standpoint and collective use. Just as 'queer' has become a label of distinction and pride for
part of the gay community and 'radical' has been co-opted by the new
right, so lack of formal education and the roughness of plebeian life
could be employed by radicals to contrast the honest, simple 'useful
knowledge' and liberating, though brutalizing, toil of labour with the
corrupt pretension and sterile indolence of the ruling orders. As in all
use of irony, however, the mocking of official language and hierarchies
through their reworking contains the implicit acceptance of an official
language and set of hierarchies against which opposition is measured.
Irony, therefore, as a mode of political naming, tends to be ultimately
integrative.[16]

Yet these distinctions masked a more straightforward tactical purpose. Radical leaders experimented with modes of address in order to
stress differing aspects of the leader-led relationship. Hence the liberal
mix of forms of address by O'Connor and the *Northern Star*'s editorials
during the politically charged second half of 1842, with O'Connor's
famous speeches 'To the Fustian Jackets, the Battered Hands and
Unshorn Chins' being underscored by his generally less paternalistic
addresses to 'My Devoted Friends' from their 'Devotedly attached
Servant' and 'ever faithful friend'. The fragmentation of O'Connor's
leadership, simultaneous to the decline in Chartism's sense of political
direction in the mid-1840s, saw an increasing use of a more chastising
and despairing tone tied to addresses to 'My Children', from their
tireless 'Father'.[17] Furthermore, with the splintering of Chartism after
1848, rival groups sought to supplement ideological debates with more
direct rhetoric. The O'Connorites portrayed themselves as 'Plain Chartists', the 'Old Guard', whose service to the cause, financial ruin and
periods of imprisonment symbolized the continuity of the basic political
message of popular radicalism. They endeavoured to protect their
crumbling power base through an essentially emotive appeal to the basic
values of Chartism, as jointly defined in the Six Points of the Charter and
the personage of O'Connor. However, the Six Points and O'Connor had
always functioned as rallying points for a far more diverse and pervasive
set of plebeian radical issues. The appeal to orthodoxy constituted a
reduction of Chartism to limits by which it had never previously been
defined.[18] On the other hand, Chartist-socialists, like Harney, Campbell
and Murray, sought to equate the cause to the ideas and plight of key
European exiles, including Marx, representing themselves as 'true

democrats', 'men of the future', of a coming dawn; their present 'gentle murmurings' presaged the 'humane roar' of the evolving vision of 'Chartism and something more'.[19] And yet the appropriation of ideas from European socialist émigrés, as Marx noted, tended to be so indiscriminate and superficial as to betoken more the desire to be deemed progressive than the assimilation of any specific new socialist vision. Indeed, even amongst the ideological left of working-class radicalism the tactical potential of names and addresses outweighed their formal content. Thus, when in the late 1840s members of the Fraternal Democrats assumed control of the National Charter Association Executive, an immediate measure was to change the Chartist flag from green to red. And yet, by the early 1850s Harney had become convinced of the necessity of realigning Chartism with trade union and co-operative groups, to politicize the latter while reactivating the former. Consequently, he changed the name of his newspaper from *Red Republican* to *Friend of the People*, due to the alienating effect of the former in the process of infiltrating non-socialist and trade union organizations.[20]

Given these tactical purposes and the overall decline of direct political confrontation from the 1850s, the growing predominance of addresses such as 'Brother Workers' and 'Brother Proletarians' doubtlessly continued to mask a subtler diversity of identities.[21] Certainly, the greater prevalence of class terms could be swiftly suspended, as by the *People's Paper* during the Crimean War, and replaced with more patriotic addresses to 'Fellow Countrymen' and 'Workingmen of England'. Here too, however, tactical considerations took precedence over ideological purity. Hence the 'slaughter' of British troops in the Crimea could be depicted as a governmental crime against a patriotic people equatable to the brutality of the 'Shopkeeper Patriots' against the working people of England. 'Will they talk', chastised Ernest Jones, 'about subsidizing for the widow and orphan of the soldier of hireling murder, but pocket the first pence in daily pay to themselves, will they think of the widow and orphan of the soldier of toil's illustrious army? Will they gaze on the bloodless slaughter at their sides, and will not a "patriotic" thrill arise in their hearts?' The meaning of patriotism was thereby manipulated, redefining true patriotism as the 'just rewarding' of the 'soldiers of toil'. The power of the terms of political debate resided in their tactical potential, in their capacity to galvanize popular support through the appropriation and reworking of the broader jargon of British politics.[22]

The central importance of modes of political address and namings lay in their capacity to mobilize popular support, and thereby maintain both a sense of the movement's momentum and its collective identity. Historians have noted the importance of the radical mass platform and gentleman leadership of Hunt and O'Connor in delineating a distinct plebeian radicalism.[23] Underscoring and supplementing these organizational factors were rhetorical reorderings of predominant images of community and legitimate hierarchies of power and responsibility. Paternal and familial images challenged the self-legitimation of existing political authority, promoting a plebeian sense of community. The government, millowners and monarchy were attacked as 'false parents' abusing the trust of their 'timid and childish' subjects, whose obedience was dependent on the provision of the means to physical and spiritual well-being.[24]

Existing political and social relations were characterized as 'a state of cannibalism' in contrast to the brotherhood of plebeian politics. A sense of familial and religious disquiet, of false relations born from the imposition of unnatural political and economic change, underpinned plebeian radical ideas of society. 'The child is made the machine,' wrote John Oxford in 1854, 'wholly subservient to the basest of all purposes, selfishness. Society is burthened with a fearful amount of juvenile crime, intemperance, theft and prostitution, and the unfailing footprints left on society's face by the god, Capital ... And the time must come when capital, the offspring of Labour, must succumb to Labour, the legitimate parent.' Similarly, Ernest Jones portrayed the 'Mammon-Capital', beneath whose hoofs the working classes languished 'like human offal amid the living heaps of the Bastille'.[25] Cutting through more orthodox political and economic analysis, such rhetoric sought to create images of legitimacy and normality, in which the natural state of social harmony in England was equated to the paternal image of labour. Consequently, all societal ills could be traced to the perceived shifts towards a more competitive and selfish society, as symbolized by the metaphor of the disintegrating family. This discourse did not rely on precise arguments of exploitation, but rather worked at a more intuitive and pervasive level. As the authors of the political and economic state of society, the middle and upper classes were deemed incapable of restoring harmonious social relations: 'Children of corruption,' as Ernest Jones put it, 'they become fathers of corruption.' Redemption, it followed, could only come through the efforts of the subordinated and dispossessed, who, being denied the just rewards of their labour, were not tarnished by the corruption of power and wealth.[26]

Indeed, direct political appeals to the working classes emphasized their national and parental duty to act on behalf of their children. John Campbell, for example, called upon the working men of Nottingham in

June 1842 to act 'as men, as fathers, as husbands, as patriots, and as good, true and sterling Chartists'. Notions of manhood and parenthood were used to reinforce the moral duty and redemptive power of labour politics. Such appeals to manliness and parental sacrifice on behalf of future generations were especially prevalent within the republican and socialist left of plebeian radicalism, as in this address by the Fraternal Democrats 'To the Working Classes of Great Britain and Ireland' during the 1848 revolutions:

> Will you rear children to enjoy no better heritage than that you received from your fathers – unrequited toil and undeserved misery? . . . We know that there are thousands of your order ready with an answer worthy of men . . . it is from the hut and the hovel, the garret and the cellar must come the regeneration of this order, and the social saviours of the human race.[27]

Moreover, manhood increasingly served as a symbol of strength and fortitude against which to judge political movements. The supposed want of manhood and the timidity of 'hugging one's chains' were liberally referred to in Chartist tirades against popular apathy. Similarly, 'An Old Chartist' felt unmanned by his association with the failure of the National Charter Association Executive to either endorse or direct the 'General Strike' of 1842.[28] The imagery of unmanning was pervasive. 'The philistines of capital are upon the shorn and blinded Samson of Labour,' wrote the leading mid-Victorian popular radical and newspaper owner G. W. M. Reynolds, following the vain attempt to secure working men representatives after the 1868 Reform Act. This biblical metaphor, of course, left the cause of working-class electoral failure distinctly ambiguous, though it reaffirmed the sense of a dignified plebeian strength enervated by the avarice of capital. In general, moral and biblical images of manhood were employed to distinguish between the 'true working man' and the apathetic, brutalized and immoral underclass so prevalent in mid-Victorian social debates. 'Ignorance, immorality, drinking and drudgery prevail,' lamented the *Beehive* in 1876. 'Such people may be called the savages of civilization and are bred in certain districts as plagues and pestilencies; but, however their existence or the cause of their creation may be explained, they are not the working people of England.'[29]

By the 1870s, however, the positive image of 'arising sons' and awakened manhood predominated in descriptions of working-class action. 'But the class from whence the pauper was taken', wrote the *People's Advocate* in July 1875, 'has begun to feel the promptings of a

noble manhood . . . Manhood has arisen and, with honest outspoken-
ness, declares its wants . . . The warm blood of freedom is coursing
through our veins, and our resolve is to conquer, and conquer we shall.'
Plebeian manhood was deemed both the true representation of English
qualities and the source for the regeneration of Englishness *per se*.[30] The
imagery of manhood and parental responsibility acted as a generalized
metaphor for the emergence of the redemptive politics of the disenfranchised and dispossessed. Moreover, the developing ideas of the
dignity of labour in the 1870s were predicated on established themes of
noble manhood, the purity of nature and the reliberation of England
through the toil of the masses. As the *People's Advocate* asserted in
1875:

> The muscles are strengthened, the blood is purified, and the boisterous
> play of the child will help to make it healthy and vigorous as it ripens into
> maturity. We could have no consciousness of any powers, no endurance,
> no force, no energy, no will, were we not called into exercise by the
> resistance of all the forces of nature. The barren waste becomes the
> fruitful garden through labour . . . If labour is necessary it must be
> honourable, it must be dignified, and he who tries to skulk through the
> world without labouring is unworthy of the name of man: he is the true
> pariah of society.[31]

The restorative quality of labour was more than a social and moral
necessity for all classes and individuals. It symbolized the regenerative
force of plebeian radicalism itself. The toil of labour was thus equated
with the imagery of suffering of political leadership and movements,
combining metaphors of adversity and fortitude. Traditions of popular
leadership were drawn from eighteenth-century ideas of true patriotism.
The leader was deemed independent (often due to financial security) of
sectional interests, yet tied to the people's cause through personal
sacrifice of wealth, status or health. The symbolic or real martyrdom of
the gentleman leaders, O'Connor and Hunt, their financial or physical
ruin, reinforced in the popular imagination their right to lead, reflecting
the disinterestedness of the cause they championed.[32]

All political movements are sustained by their heroes and betrayers,
and the accompanying language of martyrdom and treachery. O'Connor, for example, deliberately constructed his own leadership around
the image of former martyrs, seeing direct parallels between the 'faithful
and ill-used Hunt' of 1819 and the undermining of his own leadership in
1839.[33] Images of betrayal were used to condemn both internal squab-
bles and the attacks of political opponents. Hence the use by O'Brien, in

a speech to the Chartist Convention of 1842, of the images of Socrates forced to eat hemlock and Christ upon the cross to define his increasing marginalization in plebeian politics. A similar reference to crucifixion was made upon the arrest of M'Douall in 1848. 'Stick up a man in the dock,' opined the *Northern Star*, 'and call him "Christ", that is enough; the brutal bourgeoisie will howl unanimously, "Away with him, away with him! Crucify him! Crucify him!"' Leaders thereby symbolized the suffering of the people, uniting disparate hardships in their own misfortune, and, in their often autobiographically attested resilience, representing the strength of purpose the people as a whole desired but lacked. The guiding imagery was of reluctant heroes, proven service, men of the people whose ruin or success, imprisonment or triumphal release, death or defiance attested to the sufferance, resilience and ultimate deliverance of an unheard and disenfranchised people.[34]

The suffering of leaders represented in radical political rhetoric the broader endurance of working-class radicalism. This sense of endurance was pivotal to the rhetorical construction of a language of political engagement. Thus, whereas the sacrifice of leaders had the power of martyrdom, the rhetorical depiction of political movements concentrated more on the strength of purpose of the people's cause. Working-class radicalism was portrayed as a force born and sustained through hardship. 'In the ranks of the Chartists, Trades, etc.,' asserted Harney in 1849, 'very many talented men are to be found – men not college-bred, but taught in the school of suffering.' Truth and manhood were associated with images of distress, born from the subordinated life of labour.[35] The metaphor of a ship on rough seas was employed to describe the heroic fortitude of the plebeian radical's struggle against all odds. The progress of the 'labour movement' was thus depicted by Ernest Jones as the convergence of his own efforts with those of the people, in which his role had been 'the rudder in the vessel of Democracy – the hand of truth has been upon its keel, the waves of a faction have divided before it and gallantly have we made way, despite both storm and calm'. Written in 1854, with the collapse of Chartism heralding an age of relative political quiescence, such imagery betokened more than its author's naïve optimism. Plebeian radicals sought to cover the absence of effective national political organization through metaphorical constructions of political struggle, in which the ultimate attainment of objectives was integrally linked to the experience of setback and defeat.[36] Hence, for the *Western Vindicator* the abortive uprising at Newport in late 1839 was in no sense indicative of the fragmentation of Chartist organization. Rather, it betokened the hidden strength of working-class action, which 'like a smothered flame would burst forth with renewed vehemence'. Biblical similes were foremost here, with plebeian politics likened to the preacher in the wilderness, heralding in each conflict the roots of political salvation. Similarly, the future regrouping of labour politics in the wake of the Chartist defeat could be prophesied as 'the Ararat of Labour's Ark, the promised land of Labour's hope'.[37]

The connection of a future salvation with the imagery of long, often arduous struggle was a central rhetorical device in the cultivation of a collective identity within labour politics. It underpinned the predominant constitutional idiom of plebeian politics, which posited a return to a prior state of social and economic harmony as the central legitimation of political struggle. Encapsulated in the myth of the Saxon Parliament of freeborn Englishmen and its nemesis, the Norman Yoke, this highly symbolic and historically confused appeal to a lost golden age of English liberty acted as a metaphor for existing society. It articulated an historical justification for armed resistance of prevailing illegitimate political power. This justification was supported by literary and historical allusions, providing moral examples as to the legitimacy of force. Aristotle, Elizabeth I, Cromwell, Sir William Blackstone, Hume and Locke, for example, could be employed to legitimate mass arming in 1839. Indeed, constitutional rhetoric was essentially a mode of tactical reasoning. It enabled the threat of force to be deployed and armed drilling carried out without the necessity of an open declaration of revolutionary intent upon which the State could act. Moreover, as John Belchem notes, popular constitutionalism, in subverting the anti-monarchical language of eighteenth-century Whig radicalism, 'contested the very language of the ruling classes, confronting the establishment within the popular interpretation of the dominant value system'.[38] Organizational and tactical effectiveness, therefore, were secured through the subsuming of opposition in a language structured within wider political currents. One crucial consequence of the predominance of the constitutional idiom in popular radical rhetoric was thereby the re-emphasis of the essentially integrative nature of plebeian politics. In its vision of a lost golden age redeemable through the reasserting of the popular will popular constitutionalism reiterated the common sense of the moral superiority of Englishness, with its freeborn rights and malleable, responsive politics. The predominance of the constitutional idiom combined a tactical purpose with an overall reaffirmation of the integrative nature of British society.[39]

On the other hand, the sense of the collective independence of working-class politics was reasserted in a rhetoric of natural development. Throughout the nineteenth century radical movements were placed into a causal relation, in order to create a sense of a discrete and permanent plebeian political presence. This could take the form of the rewriting of political and trade union defeats as valuable and necessary lessons in the development of political strategy.[40] Underscoring this were metaphors of nature, representing the progressiveness of plebeian struggle. In the 1850s Chartism, as the heir of the platform radicalism of the late eighteenth century, could be seen as the latest wave crashing against the barriers of economic and political monopoly, its 'fertilizing tide filling the lowlands of society'. Similarly, trade unionism and popular radicalism were deemed discrete parts of the common advance of the working classes. Hence, in 1854 Ernest Jones outlined the people's cause as 'wave rolling over wave':

In the onward march of public opinion, one fresh thought sweeps over each old one, obliterating for a time the traces of the precursor, but all rising from that ocean of progress, all coming from that great tide of human intelligence, that sets in steadily and eternally, bearing in its agitated surfaces the destinies of man. At times chaffing amid the rocks – at times foaming over the shallows – at times swelling on in a calm majestic inundation over worn-out notions and things obsolete – at times returning to the bosom of that mighty deep, a People's heart – but never receding without leaving behind it the fertilizing traces of its presence – and preparing the soil for the glorious and easy harvest of the coming generation.[41]

Such imagery of progress, like popular radical tactical assessments themselves, placed greater emphasis on the continuity of political development than on the point at which tangible objectives would result. It construed political struggle in an evolutionary and progressive light, comparable to the wider ethos of mid-Victorian Liberalism.[42]

Political identities, of course, are relational, worked out in opposition. Overtures from middle-class radicals and Liberals, when not openly striven for, were denounced, as in 1831 by the National Union of the Working Classes, as 'that kind of friendship which a humane and considerate slave-owner entertains for those who are by their toil acquiring him a fortune'. Despite considerable overlap of personnel and values, middle-class radicalism and later Liberalism were perennially described in the deliberately authoritarian and immoral terms of the 'slave-owner' and the 'mammon worshipper', with the supposedly effete 'spouting saloons' of middle-class politics contrasted to the earnest integrity of the working classes.[43] The purity of plebeian radicalism was compared, as by 'X' in 1856, to the common politics of Whigs, Tories and Liberals, which had sprung from 'a diseased and putrescent state of the body politic'. Middle-class radicals were portrayed as 'the assiduous political pimps of the Whig Party'.

Moreover, the moral purity of plebeian radicalism was contra-distinguished from the 'Cesspool House' of parliamentary politics. Labour politics was described by Ernest Jones as cleansing the corrup-tion of government, as Hercules had cleansed the Stable of Augeas.[44] Such moral rhetoric could be turned on plebeian radicals themselves, as when O'Connor's supposedly demagogic leadership was portrayed by opponents within Chartism as a pestilence, a corrupting offshoot from the virus at the heart of British politics which, in the words of the anti-O'Connorite Nathaniel Morling, 'gnawed at the very vitals of the Movement'. Similarly, Chartist prisoners were condemned for their return in the 1840s as weak-willed sycophants of middle-class measures: 'These are the prodigal son Chartists; and these are pedlaring, or prostitute Chartists, and pussycat Chartists.'[45] Common to condemna-tions of both middle- and working-class radicals, however, were the same central images of moral and physical depravity and unmanning which were cast in opposition to the fortitude and selflessness of plebeian radicalism. They served to reinforce the sense of false relations, treachery and suffering that were the necessary counter-images of the redemptive force of working-class radicalism.

Motifs of corruption and redemption, subordination and deliverance through hardship animated the imagery of true and false community that demarcated the progress of plebeian radicalism from wider devel-opments in British politics. An open and adaptive definition of political allegiance galvanized an ideologically diffuse and organizationally amorphous working-class radicalism around powerful images of social relations and metaphors of engagement that stressed the fertilizing effect of both manual work and the toil of labour politics upon society. Rhetorically driven, these emphasized distinctions between a future true, incorruptible and unsullied plebeian politics able to restore the integrity of British life, and a corrupt present, reinforced by middle- and upper-class reformers.

Nineteenth-century labour politics were concerned more with the generation of persuasive and activating political appeals than with the production of precise representations of political identities. As I. A. Richards noted, language is always as much persuasion as exposition, and persuasion in political discourse relies heavily upon the use of figurative techniques (notably simile and metaphor) in order to bridge the gap between an idea and its expression. Norman Fairclough argues that although discrete political 'metaphors have different ideological attachments', they tend to be predicated upon a predominant master narrative.[46] At a crucial level, political struggle constitutes the competing attempts to rework, reinforce and negate the ruling narratives and images around which national political debate is structured.[47] Just as political opposition had been expressed through competing interpretations of religion in the 1670s, so political struggle in the nineteenth century pivoted on rival constructions of the boundaries of constitutionalism, community and liberty. Working-class radicalism had to confront the political system and modes of legitimation in which it functioned, and, like most Victorian ideologies, was expressed in the jargon of the freeborn Englishman. Certainly, in relatively stable polities oppositional political movements face conflicting impulses to ideological purity and the engaged politics of mass status, which in turn encompass the rhetorics of sectarianism and compromise. Though not mutually exclusive, these impulses tend to alternate according to assessments of the potential of working within or without the prevailing political system.[48]

British labour politics evolved integratively within wider political currents, and from the Huntite platform of 1815–21 were primarily concerned with the pragmatic search for political power. This pragmatism was reflected and articulated in the highly adaptive rhetoric of political allegiance and engagement.[49] The engaged character of labour politics accorded with broader trends in British political rhetoric and reasoning. The 'vulgar style' of Paine's *Rights of Man*, for example, combined lucid directness with emphatic allegories drawn from nature in order to produce political slogans and to create a robust plebeian mode of speech, which highlighted the writer's links to his audience. Criticized at the time for its specious jargon, Paine's language was itself an argument against the exclusivity, pomp and ceremony of established politics, using common phrases and simplified metaphors to expose the learned sophistry of the elitist defenders of the status quo. References to the Norman Yoke were thus employed to satirize the fallacious constitutionalism at the heart of Burke's case. Moreover, the use of common language and accessible imagery underscored the democratic appeal, implying all political discourse should be judged on its intelligibility to the mass population.[50]

Olivia Smith argues that ideas on refined and vulgar language, and on cant and meaningful words, were further politicized by late eighteenth- and early nineteenth-century radicals. Spence, Tooke and Cobbett attempted, through experiments with phonetic alphabets, to attain a 'linguistic levellering', by which the association of language use and social status would be undermined. Yet although by the 1820s a

discernible plebeian political vernacular was in place, most popular
radical discourse remained centred on the radicalization of the established language of the political literati.[51] It was primarily concerned with
the appropriation and reworking of established political jargon. In
political struggle, writes Lecercle, 'one gives battle to appropriate the
words of one's opponent, to deprive him of his words'. Hence, while
Burke used the image of 'drunken women' demanding the 'blood of our
children' to denounce the destruction of national customs and values in
the social anarchy of revolutionary zeal, so Paine and plebeian radicalism also described the American and French revolutions in familial
terms. For radicals, though, the demand for natural rights of political
reason were portrayed through the image of children of enlightenment
breaking free from their infanticidal parents. Ideas were confronted in a
shared rhetoric of political description, in which the family, however
subverted, was the guiding metaphor of political legitimacy.[52]

Similarly, the narrative of corruption and regeneration that underpinned plebeian political rhetoric for much of the nineteenth century
functioned through the appropriation of the jargon and metaphors of
wider political debate. This served several purposes. Firstly, the ideals of
the ruling classes were satirized and lampooned through the ironic use
of political names, through the reworking of economic and political
arguments in radicalism's alternative political economy and through the
mocking of the very images of community that animated ruling ideas of
national and political identity. Thus the language of patriotism could be
reworked, as by the *People's Paper* in 1854, to expose the selfishness and
corruption that sustained social divisions: 'John Bull is not one individual. Neither is he twenty millions united as one animal. But he is
congeries of most dissimilar and multifarious beings.' Social distinctions
were framed as variations upon the central national representation of
John Bull; 'LAND-BULL', 'MONEY-BULL', 'PULPIT-BULL' and
'LAW-BULL' were parasitic caricatures of Englishness growing fat on
the starvation of the working classes. Being labourers and operatives,
the working people were united, in their common subjection, as the true
representation of English manhood, as symbolized by the 'LABOUR-
BULL' – 'the most inoffensive of them all, who has his horns pretty well
blunted by class laws, and the log of poverty tied to his legs. Indeed, the
others have sought to mutilate him to a kind of OX, whom they muzzle
when he treadeth the corn.' Government was deemed the subservient
'British Lion', whose power was bought by the wealth of the ruling
classes. Political power was harnessed to the task of maintaining the
enslavement of labour's mind and body, and thereby of the degrading of
true Englishness.[53]

The second purpose of the rhetoric of labour politics, therefore, was the creation of a sense of social division in which the working classes were demarcated from the rest of society and tied to the oppositional politics of plebeian radicalism. Social cleavages and the unity of labour politics were sustained through a language of false community and economic and political toil and slavery, rather than by a strict terminology of class. Central was the appropriation of the imagery of enlightenment and progress that animated middle-class radical and Liberal debate.[54] The simplified biblical and natural metaphors of suffering and progress both created a popular political identity through the plainness of radical speech and, by the sense of ideas coming naturally out of their 'commonsensical' language, positioned plebeian radicalism as the true representation of moral and political progress.[55] The reworking of the language of true patriotism and the self-description through modes of address and familial imagery of plebeian leaders as paternal guardians of the people sought to play upon the sense of social decay in order to relocate radicalism as the upholder of ideals of a lost age of harmonious national unity. As a result, popular radicals felt able to denounce Conservatives as the 'true revolutionaries' undermining the traditional values of British society and to condemn middle-class radicals as 'half-hearted' and 'sham-Liberals'.[56] Plebeian radicalism was defined not only as the true manifestation of the politics of conventional values and social relations, but also as the natural home for the politics of liberation and progress.

Thirdly, the regenerative appeal of labour politics held a specifically tactical purpose. Images of cumulative, evolutionary change and the constitutionalist and historical modes of legitimation placed popular radical tactics precariously on the edge of legality. The success of the post-war mass platform of 1815–21 was thus effectively to distance labour politics from the images of sectarianism and destructive excess that had been drawn from the French and English Jacobins of the 1790s and the Cromwellian Long Parliament, and which had stigmatized more overtly revolutionary tactics and discourse from the early nineteenth century onwards.[57] This is not to imply that popular politics never indulged in the rhetoric of armed confrontation free from 'constitutional' limitations. Constitutional arguments were often mocked, with the moral right to revolution based jointly upon the legitimation of the popular will and the likelihood of success. However, here again the essentially tactical nature of radical language is manifest. For if popular radicals were not naïve constitutionalists, nor were they in the main at ease with historical associations to revolutionary precedents. Despite seeking profound political and economic changes, and notwithstanding the zealous defence of francophiles like O'Brien and Harney, popular radical rhetoric was remarkably free of positive images of the French Revolution. Similarly, the constitutional return of plebeian radicalism was seldom linked to levellerism or seventeenth-century parliamentarianism. In conjunction with the Jacobin reign of terror and the Napoleonic wars, the precedents of English revolutionary history continued to be used most often as symbols of the immoderate, essentially un-English nature of sectarian politics.[58]

The assertion of plebeian radicalism as a constitutional political opposition reflected the context in which labour politics evolved. Whereas political and economic chaos in 1780s France created a power vacuum, facilitating a shift to revolutionary politics, the overall cohesion of British society favoured more integrative tactics. Lynn Hunt has argued that the collapse of political power in France resulted in a fragmentation of the hierarchies and modes of legitimation around which society was structured. As ruling values and their rhetorical representations 'lost their givenness', oppositional politics were both compelled and enabled to explore political metaphors beyond the established imagery of the family. The rhetoric of revolution experimented with images of political community, often, in what Hunt terms its 'mythic present', negating both the hierarchies of the family and the legitimacy of historical precedent. The British State, on the other hand, was never threatened with economic collapse during the eighteenth and nineteenth centuries and was unvanquished by either revolutionary or nationalist war. The impulse to political reform had broad roots facilitating a relatively responsive parliamentary system which, especially in the wake of the psychological shock of Peterloo, was less prone to displays of repression and more adaptable towards political and economic unrest. Hence, oppositional rhetoric remained within the grain of British politics, seeking to appropriate the metaphors and idioms of political engagement that ran through the language of public debate.[59]

Appropriation was not limited to working-class radicalism. Disraeli, for example, used the mass circulation and more effective national reportage of the mid-Victorian press to create rhetorically a popular perception of Toryism as speaking to the 'One Nation' of palace and cottage alike, and as distinctly linked to national pride and the Britishness of the hearty life of joviality, beer and roast beef.[60] Popular Toryism was reasserted as the guardian of the essential customs and basic values of English life. Following the splintering of Chartism in the early 1850s and the subsequent process of political realignment which culminated in the 1867 Reform Act, however, it was Gladstonian Liberalism that emerged as the predominant political representation of popular political identities in the 1860s and 1870s. The logic of Lib–Labism was reinforced by overlaps in political traditions, with the Liberal Party combining the common plebeian and middle-class radical ideas of anti-statism, nonconformism and free trade with a re-emphasis, in the wake of the upheavals of the 1830s and 1840s, on the social responsibility of the individual. Such ideological realignments were underpinned by a growing disillusionment with popular radical leadership. The emergence from the 1860s of modern forms of national party organization exposed the essentially localized and dispersed base of popular radicalism. Indeed, following the calamitous Chartist meeting at Kennington Common in April 1848, the inadequacies of the main outlet to national political action, the constitutional mass platform, were finally and irrevocably laid open. From the mid-1860s Liberalism was thus able to represent the aspirations of a majority of plebeian radical and trade union opinion to a greater and more practical degree than any other political force.[61]

Yet although popular radicals had limited alternative national outlets to the Conservative and Liberal parties during the mid-Victorian period, their support remained conditional on the perceived accommodation of issues of popular concern. Tangible political and social reforms had to be underscored by a rhetorical redrawing of political identities. Significantly, at the heart of popular Liberal rhetoric were the familiar biblical and regenerative themes, the same ideas of heroic English manhood encapsulated in the charismatic leader and the established metaphors of evolutionary progress that had underpinned the rhetoric of plebeian politics throughout the first half of the century. Moreover, Gladstone, with his appeals to people above parliament and party and his play of imagery from corruption-felling axeman to the prophet-like paternalism of the Grand Old Man, assumed the mantle, vacated by O'Connor, of the gentleman-leader whose victories symbolized a deeper triumph of the people against privilege and vested interest. Liberalism, freed from the extremes of its early nineteenth-century utilitarian and libertarian associations, was thus rhetorically re-created in the mid-Victorian period as the embodiment of true community and the central force of political enlightenment.[62]

The organizational collapse of plebeian radicalism after 1848 was accompanied and reiterated by the marginalizing of its versions of the common jargon of political identity and tactical engagement. Radicalized metaphors of true and false community, which held powerful strategic appeal during the economic and political tumult of the Chartist period, were reappropriated by the Conservative and Liberal parties.

The vibrant ambiguity of popular radicalism's guiding images of corruption and redemption were narrowed to the 'dead metaphors' of the increasingly defined appeals of the two dominant national parties.[63] Popular radicals were often acutely aware of the need to reassess and demarcate the language in which their political ideas were framed. In fact, from the 1850s the increasing sectarianism of the O'Brienites and the metropolitan socialist clubs reflected as much a search for new modes of expression as any profound ideological realignment. Despite the appropriation by the O'Brienites and the Social Democratic Federation of the jargon of Continental socialism, however, mainstream labour politics continued to be articulated in the integrative language of radicalized Liberalism.[64] As David Howell has argued, the shift away from Liberalism and the formation of the Independent Labour Parties in the changed circumstances of the 1890s and 1900s drew together trade unionists, O'Brienite socialists, Fabians and radical Liberals through the politics of the 'broad church'. Working within the grain of British politics, such a realignment was facilitated by Labourism's adaptive rhetoric as encapsulated in 'its Labour title which camouflaged its formal commitment to socialism'.[65]

The jargon of labour politics therefore continued to be predicated on the appropriation and radicalization of the wider language of political allegiance and public debate into the closing decades of the nineteenth century. Rhetoric, of course, does not in itself create political identities. But deeper economic, political and cultural shifts are perceived and articulated, and their impact mediated, reinforced or abridged, through more or less persuasive political representations. In this respect, what remains remarkable about the rhetoric of British labour politics is its continuing attempts to radicalize the jargon of its political opponents. Indeed, there are distinct echoes of the more imaginative imagery of nineteenth-century labour politics in the rhetoric of community that has underwritten much of the Labour Party's response to the Thatcherite rejection of society and the subsequent retreat of Conservatism into the murky waters of Englishness and 'basic values'.

Notes

1 G. J. Harney, 'Brother Democrats and Chartists of Sheffield', *Northern Star* (hereafter cited as *NS*), 5 March 1842, 4. My approach to the rhetoric of labour politics owes an intellectual debt to the work of J. Epstein and J. Belchem, notably J. Belchem, 'Henry Hunt and the Evolution of the Mass Platform', *Economic History Review*, 93 (1978), 751–67; J. Epstein, 'The Constitutional Idiom: Radical Reasoning, Rhetoric and Action in Early

Nineteenth-century England', *Journal of Social History*, 23 (1990), 77–83.

2 See P. Bourdieu, *Language and Symbolic Power*, ed. J. B. Thompson (Cambridge: Polity Press, 1992), 37–65, 106–13.

3 A suggestive discussion of the nature of political language and its relation to historical enquiry is contained in P. J. Corfield (ed.), *Language, History and Class* (Oxford: Blackwell, 1991), 1–27.

4 See J. Gaffney, *The Language of Political Leadership in Contemporary Britain* (London: Macmillan, 1991), 1–20, 186–95; M. A. K. Halliday, *Language as a Social Semiotic: The Social Interpretation of Language and Meaning* (London: Arnold, 1978), 21–35; W. P. Robinson, *Language and Social Behaviour* (London: Penguin, 1972), 34–7; on the symbolism of verbal and non-verbal 'languages', see J. Epstein, 'Understanding the Cap of Liberty: Symbolic Practice and Social Conflict in Early Nineteenth-century England', *Past and Present*, 122 (1989), and P. A. Pickering, 'Class Without Words: Symbolic Communication in the Chartist Movement', *Past and Present*, 112 (1986), 144–62.

5 Gaffney, *The Language of Political Leadership*, 11; Robinson, *Language and Social Behaviour*, 34–7.

6 See P. Joyce, *Visions of the People: Industrial England and the Question of Class, 1840–1914* (Cambridge: Cambridge University Press, 1991), 27–55; see also E. F. Biagini, *Liberty, Retrenchment and Reform: Popular Liberalism in the Age of Gladstone, 1860–1880* (Cambridge: Cambridge University Press, 1992), 369–85, and Gaffney, *The Language of Political Leadership*, 19–20.

7 See G. Crossick, 'From Gentlemen to the Residuum: Languages of Social Description in Victorian Britain', in Corfield, *Language, History and Class*, 151–61; for examples of the use of class terminology in the *Red Republican* (hereafter cited as *RR*), see 'L'Ami de peuple', *RR*, 30 November 1850, 188–9.

8 See P. Calvert, *The Concept of Class: An Historical Introduction* (London: Hutchinson, 1982), 12–14, 95–114; P. Joyce, 'In Pursuit of Class: Recent Studies in the History of Work and Class', *History Workshop Journal*, 25 (1988), 174–7; B. Waites, *A Class Society at War: England, 1914–1918* (Leamington Spa: Berg, 1987), 71–5, 113–78, 271–80; on the relation of terminology to the assertion of political authority, see Bourdieu, *Language and Symbolic Power*, 37–44, and R. Harris, *The Language Myth* (London: Duckworth, 1981), 131–9, 150–5, 165–8; still the most effective discussion of the political contingencies of class identities and language is G. Stedman Jones, *Languages of Class* (Cambridge: Cambridge University Press, 1983), 1–24, 90–178.

9 Crossick, 'From Gentlemen to the Residuum', 158.

10 Ibid., 161–77; Harris, *The Language Myth*, 131–9, 150–5.

11 See *NS*, 16 March 1839, 3; G. J. Harney, *Democratic Review*, February 1850, 349–50; on the class nature of plebeian political language, see Epstein, 'Understanding the Cap of Liberty', 117–18; Pickering, 'Class Without Words', 160–2; J. Belchem, 'Radical Language and Ideology in Early

Nineteenth-century England: The Challenge of the Platform', *Albion*, 20, 2 (1988), 247–59.

12 See Bourdieu, *Language and Symbolic Power*, 182–8, 229–51; for valuable and suggestive comments on the political nature of language, see D. Mayfield and S. Thorne, 'Social History and Its Discontents: Gareth Stedman Jones and the Politics of Language', *Social History*, 17, 2 (May 1992), 181–6.

13 See J. Wilson, *Politically Speaking: The Pragmatic Analysis of Political Language* (Oxford: Blackwell, 1990), 77–103.

14 See, for example, 'L'Ami de peuple', *NS*, 28 October 1848, 5; *NS*, 16 July 1842, 1; *People's Paper* (hereafter cited as *PP*), 4 November 1854, 1; G. J. Harney, *Democratic Review*, February 1850, 349–50; 'L'Ami de peuple', *Friend of the People*, 19 April 1851, 165; for discussion of paternalism in early nineteenth-century socialism, see G. Claeys, *Citizens and Saints: Politics and Anti-politics in Early British Socialism* (Cambridge: Cambridge University Press, 1989), 63–105; on the importance of paternalism in the mid-Victorian period, see P. Joyce, *Work, Society and Politics: The Culture of the Factory in Later Victorian England* (London: Methuen, 1980), 134–54.

15 See J. J. Lecercle, *The Violence of Language* (London: Routledge, 1990), 211–13.

16 Bourdieu, *Language and Symbolic Power*, 37–44.

17 See O'Connor's addresses in *NS* between 1842 and 1847.

18 See, for example, O'Connor in *NS*, 10 December 1842, 4, 24 March 1849, 1, 3 March 1849, 1; on O'Connor's paternalistic leadership style and its part in constructing plebeian political organizational unity around the tactical shorthand of the Six Points, see J. Epstein, *The Lion of Freedom: Feargus O'Connor and the Chartist Movement, 1832–1842* (London: Croom Helm, 1982), 220–57.

19 See G. J. Harney, *RR*, 12 October 1850, 131; 'L'Ami de peuple', *NS* 17 February 1849, 5.

20 For Marx's criticism of Harney, see P. Cadogan, 'Harney and Engels', *International Review of Social History*, x (1965), 72–99; on Harney's tactical shift from *RR* to *Friend of the People*, see G. J. Harney, *RR*, 30 November 1850, 1.

21 See Crossick, 'From Gentlemen to the Residuum', 161–77.

22 Ernest Jones, *PP*, 18 November 1854, 4; see also use of patriotic modes of address in *PP*, 28 October 1854, 4; *PP*, 4 November 1854, 1; *PP*, 2 December 1854, 1; *PP*, 30 December 1854, 1; for discussion of the development of plebeian ideas of Englishness, see H. Cunningham, 'The Conservative Party and Patriotism', and E. Yeo, 'Socialism, the State and Some Oppositional Englishness', in R. Colls and P. Dodd (eds), *Englishness: Politics and Culture, 1880–1920* (London: Croom Helm, 1986), 299–302, 355–62; M. Taylor, 'Radicalism and Patriotism, 1848–1859', Ph.D. diss., University of Cambridge (1989), 272–8.

23 Epstein, 'The Constitutional Idiom', 77–83; Belchem, 'Henry Hunt', 751–67.

24 See Henry Vincent, *British Statesman* (hereafter cited as *BS*), 8 May 1842, 10; also *BS*, 29 May 1842, 6.
25 John Oxford, *PP*, 28 January 1854, 1; *The Democrat and Labour Advocate*, 17 November 1855, 1; Ernest Jones, *PP*, 4 February 1854, 1.
26 Ernest Jones, *PP*, 19 August 1854, 1.
27 John Campbell, *NS*, 11 June 1842, 7; Fraternal Democrats, 'Address to the Working Classes of Great Britain and Ireland', *NS*, 8 January 1848, 1.
28 See 'L'Ami de peuple', *NS*, 28 October 1848, 5; 'An Old Chartist', letter to editor, *BS*, 27 August 1842, 9.
29 G. W. M. Reynolds, *Reynolds Weekly News*, 14 June 1868, 1; *Beehive*, 23 September 1876, 9.
30 *People's Advocate and National Vindicator of Right versus Wrong*, 10 July 1875, 4; Ernest Jones, letter to G. J. Holyoake, 28 April 1855, Holyoake Papers, H761; see Taylor, 'Radicalism and Patriotism', 278–425, for a suggestive discussion of the ways by which this plebeian patriotism merged with Palmerstonian and Gladstonian Liberalism.
31 *People's Advocate*, 28 August 1875, 4; see also letter to editor, *People's Advocate*, 18 September 1875, 5; 'L'Ami de peuple', *RR*, 17 February 1849, 5.
32 See Harney, 'Brother Democrats and Chartists of Sheffield', 4; see also Belchem, 'Henry Hunt', 751–67; for discussion of the role of charisma in political leadership, see C. Geertz, 'Centres, Kings and Charisma: Reflections on the Symbolics of Power', in J. Ben-David and T. Nichols Clark (eds), *Culture and Its Creators* (Chicago: University of Chicago Press, 1977), 152–69; R. Michels, *Political Parties: A Sociological Study of the Oligarchical Tendencies of Modern Democracy* (New York: Free Press, 1968), 98–104; J. Vernon, 'Politics and the People: A Study in English Political Culture and Communication, 1808–1868', Ph.D. diss., University of Manchester (1991), 516–18; for representations of popular suffering and the potential of working-class 'self-help', see W. Lovett, *Life and Struggles of William Lovett in his Pursuit of Bread, Knowledge and Freedom* (London: McKibbon and Key, 1967), and T. Cooper, *The Life of Thomas Cooper* (London: 4th Edition, 1883).
33 O'Connor, *NS*, 14 December 1839; on O'Connor's use of martyrdom and charismatic language in the construction of his leadership over Chartism, see Epstein, *The Lion of Freedom*, 90–9, 216–19; for an account of the leadership of Henry 'Orator' Hunt, see Belchem, 'Henry Hunt', 81–92; for a wider discussion of the role of heroes and villains in the sustaining of a popular political movement's momentum and direction, see Michels, *Political Parties*, 92–7.
34 O'Brien, Convention Speech of 3 March 1842, *NS*, 14 May 1842, 7; *NS*, 14 May 1842, 7; *NS*, 22 July 1848, 4.
35 G. J. Harney, *Democratic Review*, June 1849, 4.
36 Ernest Jones, *PP*, 7 January 1854, 1; *NS*, 15 November 1845, 1; John Campbell, letter to editor, *NS*, 21 May 1842, 9.

37 *Western Vindicator*, 30 November 1854, 1; *Home Office Papers*, HO40, 46; *PP*, 14 January 1854, 1; Ernest Jones, *PP*, 21 January 1854, 4.
38 Belchem, 'Radical Language and Ideology', 256; on the constitutional idiom, see Epstein, 'The Constitutional Idiom', 358–69; A. Briggs, 'Saxons, Normans and Victorians', in *Collected Essays*, ii: *Images, Problems, Standpoints, Forecasts* (Brighton: Harvester, 1985), 215–32; J. Belchem, 'Republicanism, Popular Constitutionalism and the Radical Platform in Early Nineteenth-century England', *Social History*, 6 (1981), 3–11, 22–5, 30–1.
39 Epstein, 'The Constitutional Idiom', 358–69.
40 See, for example, P. M. M'Douall, *NS*, 23 August 1842, 5; R. J. Richardson, *NS*, 9 February 1839, 5; O'Brien, *NS*, 13 October 1838, 4; Ernest Jones, *PP*, 17 June 1854, 1.
41 Ernest Jones, *PP*, 20 May 1854, 1, and 14 January 1854, 1; *Labourer*, January–June 1847, 34–9.
42 See Biagini, *Liberty, Retrenchment and Reform*, 31–83; Joyce, *Visions of the People*, 27–47; for discussion of the broader nature of mid-Victorian parliamentary politics, see M. Bentley, *Politics Without Democracy, 1815–1914* (London: Fontana, 1984), 161–230.
43 National Union of the Working Classes, Report of Meeting of 14 September, *Poor Man's Guardian*, 17 September 1831; see Ernest Jones, *PP*, 4 February 1854, 1; on the overlap of ideas and values between popular radicalism and popular Liberalism, see A. J. Reid and E. J. Biagini, 'Currents of Radicalism, 1850–1914', in A. J. Reid and E. J. Biagini (eds), *Currents of Radicalism: Popular Radicalism, Organised Labour and Party Politics in Britain, 1850–1914* (Cambridge: Cambridge University Press, 1991), 1–17.
44 'X', *Reynolds Weekly News*, 14 December 1856, 1; Ernest Jones, *PP*, 10 June 1854, 4; see also 'Address of the Bristol Radicals to O'Connor, Stephens and Oastler', *NS*, 19 January 1839, 8.
45 N. Morling, National Charter Association Sub-secretary, *BS*, 29 October 1842, 9; *NS*, 11 February 1843, 7; hence also the use of rhetoric in the condemnation of individual leaders in order to explain political defeat, as against M'Douall, Leach and Campbell in 1842, *NS*, 10 December 1842, 4; and the use of images of corruption and illness to denounce popular apathy, as in *Notes to the People*, 3; William Hill, *NS*, 27 August 1842, 4.
46 I. A. Richards, *The Philosophy of Rhetoric* (Oxford: Oxford University Press, 1936), 23–5; N. Fairclough, *Language and Power* (London: Longman, 1989), 119.
47 See Gaffney, *The Language of Political Leadership*, 186–95; on the normative assumptions underpinning the apparent contestability of the meanings of political metaphors, see I. Meszaros, *Philosophy, Ideology and Social Science: Essays in Negation and Affirmation* (Brighton: Wheatsheaf, 1986), 232–52; there is a danger, however, in linguistic-based analysis of approaching historical explanation through a functional-evolutionalism; on the importance of the historical context of economic, social and political power in the generation of ruling political narratives, see G. Williams, *Sociolinguistics: A*

Sociological Critique (London: Routledge, 1992), 235–41; Fairclough, *Language and Power*, 31–41.

48 Bourdieu, *Language and Symbolic Power*, 188–92; Epstein, 'Understanding the Cap of Liberty', 84–6; Claeys, *Citizens and Saints*, 17–19; F. Jameson, *The Political Unconscious: Narrative as a Socially Symbolic Act* (London: University Paperbacks, 1983), 84–102; Lecercle, *The Violence of Language*, 196–213.

49 On the integrative development of the 'focused radicalism' of plebeian politics, see J. Brewer, *Party, Ideology and Popular Politics at the Accession of George III* (Cambridge: Cambridge University Press, 1981), 18–24, 163–200, 268–9; J. Belchem, *'Orator' Hunt: Henry Hunt and English Working Class Radicalism* (Oxford: Clarendon Press, 1985) 1–13.

50 J. T. Boulton, *The Language of Politics in the Age of Wilkes* (London: Routledge and Kegan Paul, 1963), 134–50; O. Smith, *The Politics of Language, 1791–1819* (Oxford: Clarendon Press, 1986), 44–52.

51 Smith, *The Politics of Language*, 1–34, 110–53, 248–51.

52 Lecercle, *The Violence of Language*, 208; S. Blakemore, *Burke and the Fall of Language: The French Revolution as a Linguistic Event* (Hanover: University Press of New England, 1988), 33–40.

53 *PP*, 17 June 1854, 4; on popular radicalism's alternative political economy, see N. Thompson, *The People's Science* (Cambridge: Cambridge University Press, 1984).

54 On the dominance of languages of illusion and revelation in modern ideologies, see Blakemore, *Burke and the Fall of Language*, 3, 67–73; hence the use of the language of light and reason against the 'blinding custom' and 'rotting corpse' of Disraelian Conservatism employed in *Liberty*, 28 April 1883, 1.

55 Smith, *The Politics of Language*, 44–6.

56 See, for example, the critiques of Conservatism in *PP*, 3 January 1857, 1; *Reynolds Weekly News*, 11 July 1858, 7; for condemnations of 'sham' and 'colourless' Liberalism, see, for example, G. J. Harney, *NS*, 17 February 1838, 6; *Reynolds Weekly News*, 31 January 1869, 7; *People's Advocate*, 6 May 1875, 4; *Radical*, 5 March 1881, 4.

57 Epstein, 'The Constitutional Idiom', 366–8; F. K. Donnelly, 'Levellerism in Eighteenth and Early Nineteenth-century Britain', *Albion*, 20, 2 (1988), 142–57; J. P. D. Dunbabin, 'Oliver Cromwell's Popular Image in Nineteenth-century England', in J. S. Bromley and E. H. Kossman (eds), *Britain and the Netherlands*, i: *Some Political Mythologies* (The Hague: Martinus Nijhoff, 1975), 261–6; C. Hill, 'The Norman Yoke', in J. Saville (ed.), *Democracy and the Labour Movement: Essays in Honour of Dona Torr* (London: Lawrence and Wishart, 1954), 66.

58 For example, H. Vincent, Great Suffrage Meeting Speech in Birmingham, *BS*, 16 April 1842, 5; *Reynolds Weekly News*, 11 February 1866, 1; and yet even the most fervent advocates of armed confrontation for natural rights became convinced as to the necessity of a more tactical use of 'violent talk',

with a programme of civil disobedience supported by a constitutional rhetoric; see, for example, P. M. M'Douall on the 1842 'General Strike', *NS*, 23 August 1842, 5.

59 L. Hunt, *Politics, Culture and Class in the French Revolution* (Berkeley: University of California Press, 1984), 1–16, 24–32, 48–51; L. Hunt, *The Family Romance of the French Revolution* (London: Routledge, 1992), 196–9; on the political, economic and ideological restrictions to revolutionary and Marxist politics in Great Britain, see R. McKibbin, 'Why Was There No Marxism in Great Britain?', *English Historical Review*, 391 (1984), 306–26.

60 H. C. G. Matthew, 'Rhetoric and Politics in Britain, 1860–1950', in P. J. Waller (ed.), *Politics and Social Change in Modern Britain: Essays Presented to A. F. Thompson* (Brighton: Harvester, 1987), 34–56; Joyce, *Work, Society and Politics*, 187–91, 201–21; Cunningham, 'The Conservative Party and Patriotism', 355–62.

61 Biagini, *Liberty, Retrenchment and Reform*, 84–253; see also J. Vincent, *The Formation of the Liberal Party, 1857–1868* (London: Constable, 1966), 257–8; for discussion of shifts in forms of party organization, see M. Weber, *Selections in Translation*, ed. W. G. Runciman (Cambridge: Cambridge University Press, 1978), 43–56; Michels, *Political Parties*, 205–11; J. Zvesper, *Political Philosophy and Rhetoric* (Cambridge: Cambridge University Press, 1977), 5; on shifts from a 'focused' extra-parliamentary to a parliamentary radicalism, see Brewer, *Party, Ideology and Popular Politics*, 17–25; Taylor, 'Radicalism and Patriotism', 102–61; on the continuities within nineteenth-century radical politics, see M. Taylor, 'The Old Radicalism and the New: David Urquhart and the Politics of Opposition, 1832–1867', and R. McWilliam, 'Radicalism and Popular Culture: The Tichbourne Case and the Politics of "Fair Play", 1867–1886', in Reid and Biagini, *Currents of Radicalism*, 41–3, 52–64; for a discussion of the constitutional mass platform and its irrevocable decline by 1848, see T. M. Parssinen, 'Association, Convention and Anti-parliament in British Radical Politics, 1771–1848', 504–33.

62 Biagini, *Liberty, Retrenchment and Reform*, 31–83, 379–85, 395–405; on the disassociation of Liberalism from its libertarian and utilitarian extremes in the mid-Victorian period, see Joyce, *Work, Society and Politics*, 152–4; Bentley, *Politics Without Democracy*, 203–19.

63 The term 'dead metaphor', meaning the limitation of a metaphor to a single commonly accepted association, comes from P. Ricoeur, *Hermeneutics and the Social Sciences: Essays on Language, Action and Interpretation*, ed. and trans. J. B. Thompson (Cambridge: Cambridge University Press, 1981), 169.

64 On popular radical assessments of the power of rhetoric, see O'Brien, *BS*, 9 July 1842, 6; G. J. Holyoake, *Sixty Years an Agitator's Life*, (London: Unwin, 1893), 119; on the O'Brienites and later nineteenth-century working-class socialism, see J. Davis, 'Radical Clubs and London Politics, 1870–1900', in G. Stedman Jones and D. Feldman (eds), *Metropolis-London: Histories and Representations Since 1800* (London: Routledge, 1989), 110–23; M. Bevir, 'The British Social Democratic Federation, 1880–1885', *International Review*

of Social History, xxxvii (1992), 212–25.
65 D. Howell, *British Workers and the Independent Labour Party, 1888–1906* (Manchester: Manchester University Press, 1983), vii, 389–97.

7

'The Jargon of Indostan': An Exploration of Jargon in Urdu and East India Company English

JAVED MAJEED

The outlines of the history of Urdu's development, its contentious relationship with Hindi and the impact of British policy on its status as a language have been studied by a number of scholars.[1] It is not the aim of this chapter to cover this ground once more, but instead to explore certain areas which might throw light on the nature of Urdu at different times in its history. In particular, it uses the notion of 'diglossia' to attempt to understand Urdu at these points in its history, as well as to consider the question of jargon from the perspectives which can be developed from this notion. The notion of 'diglossia' which this chapter works with is that termed 'broad diglossia' by Fasold, who defines it as:

> the reservation of highly valued segments of a community's linguistic repertoire (which are not the first to be learned, but are learned later and more consciously, usually through formal education), for situations perceived as more formal and guarded; and the reservation of less highly valued segments (which are learned first with little or no conscious effort), of any degree of linguistic relatedness to the higher valued segments, from stylistic differences to separate languages, for situations perceived as more informal and intimate.[2]

While the question of jargon in Urdu might in part be connected to its problematic relationship with its Perso-Arabic heritage, let us seek to remind ourselves of how the jargon in the administrative English of the East India Company in the late eighteenth and early nineteenth centuries reflected the continuing powerful influence of Persian as the Mughal language of administration.[3] This administrative language had begun to change in important respects by the 1830s, especially after the supplanting of Persian as the language of the courts in 1837. The premises on which this decision was based are examined briefly. Broadly speaking, whereas before 1837 the use of different languages for administration (and indeed writing generally) and for oral purposes could be considered a South Asian norm,[4] after 1837 this norm came under increasing pressure as British policy sought to make the language of the administration of a region continuous with what were defined as 'the vernaculars' of that region. This roughly fits in with Ernest Gellner's thesis regarding agro-literate polities, in which the languages of administration are discontinuous with the great majority of the languages of the speech communities in that polity, as opposed to post agro-literate polities, in which the need for a homogeneous idiom cannot tolerate such a discontinuity.[5]

The varying and often problematic relationship between Persian and Urdu is explored here in relation to Urdu legal petitions of the 1860s. Since the prestige of Urdu was intimately bound up with its definition by the British as the official language of Bihar, the United Provinces and Punjab, these petitions afford us interesting examples of what the character of this Urdu was. The abolition of Persian as the language of the law courts in 1837 seems to have had a significant effect on the form of this legal language. More importantly, the legal petitions also afford us striking instances of what has been called 'leaky diglossia'; 'leaky diglossia' refers to cases in which one linguistic variety (an idiom, dialect or language) 'leaks' into the functions formerly reserved for another variety.[6] This 'leaky diglossia' reflects the processes underlying the internal switch from Persian to Urdu within an influential part of the Muslim community, as well as among the specialist Hindu castes who had served as scribes.[7] The concept of diglossia as first defined by Ferguson,[8] and then modified by Fasold, is shown to have suggestive resonances in the context of Urdu's development. In particular, the concept of diglossia is fruitful in considering the whole question of jargon in Urdu, especially as it relates to the works of indigenous literati on Urdu language and literature. One important case considered here is the genre of the *tazkirā*, or biographical and stylistic mentions of poets. Two examples are considered: the *tazkirā* by the famous poet Mīr Taqī

Mīr written in Persian in the 1750s and entitled *Nikāt ul Shuʿarā* (The subtleties of the poets) and another Persian *tazkirā* by Kiyām, entitled *Makhzan-e Nrkāt* (A treasury of conceits), which was also composed in the 1750s. Apart from telling us much about the nature and place of Urdu poetry in eighteenth-century India, both these works are evocative of a complicated and often contradictory context which can be partially understood in terms of some types of diglossia.

A similar context is also implicit in one of the first grammars of Urdu, the *Daryā-e Latāfat* (The sea of elegance), written in Persian in 1808 by Inshā Allāh Khān. Its circular and sometimes convoluted arguments are suggestive both of one of the stages of diglossia and of Urdu's struggle to establish itself as a language in its own right. Mirzā Baig's later *Tashīl ul Balāghat* (The facilitation of rhetoric), like Inshā's work, pays much attention to dialectal variety, though with sometimes differing results. These works support the general conclusion that it is difficult to say what exactly constitutes jargon in Urdu during the nineteenth century, since there was no standard Urdu to invoke in this period. Furthermore, the grammatical and rhetorical works examined suggest that dialectal variety, while noted, was considered not so much a problem as an indispensable part of the flexibility which made 'Hindustani' (as the British first termed it) a lingua franca in polyglot northern India.

However, *Tashīl ul Balāghat* also bears the marks of the increasing role of language issues in the communal politics of the subcontinent, and the struggle for authority within parts of the Muslim community. The last part of the chapter touches upon the relationship between the All-India Muslim League and Urdu as a growing marker of Muslim identity. In this context, the notion of 'Dummy High' may be a useful one to use. 'Dummy High' refers to 'speech varieties of which some of the members have a certain knowledge, and which are given prestige ratings by the speakers ... but which are not in fact utilized extensively in any domain'.[9] It is suggested that Urdu sometimes mimics a 'Dummy High', while simultaneously remaining 'Low' in relation to classical Arabic and Persian. It is Urdu's ambivalent status in relation to its heritage which makes the 'Persianization' of Urdu a patchy and uneven process, as well as one which results in a variety of stylistic registers in which the notion of jargon remains a shadowy one.

Administrative idioms

Scholars have stressed how the East India Company sought to legitimize itself through indigenous idioms in the late eighteenth and early

nineteenth centuries, and how, as an Indian power, it built itself upon
the administrative and revenue systems of its Mughal predecessors;[10] in
doing so, it also drew upon their linguistic systems.[11] Documents such as
a Select Committee 'Fifth Report' of 1812 on the East India Company's
affairs reflect the experimental and cautious nature of British rule at the
time, and also an awareness of the complexities of local polities and the
company's relation to them.[12] It was partly as a result of the legacies of
its Indian predecessors that the administrative language of the East
India Company was replete with indigenous judicial and revenue terms,
or, as the Sanskritist H. H. Wilson put it, 'thickly studded with terms
adopted from the vernacular languages of the country'. It was because
many of these terms were 'commonly inserted without any explanation
of their purport' that Wilson felt it necessary to compile his *Glossary of
Judicial and Revenue Terms*.[13]

Wilson's introduction to his *Glossary* points to some of the preoccupations behind the British administrative language's engagement
with the previous administrative idioms of the subcontinent. There is a
predictable concern with authority. Wilson stresses the importance of
ensuring that documents 'emanating from authority' which intend to
'communicate information on which implicit reliance may be placed'
should be free from 'grave blemishes'.[14] More interestingly (and less
predictably), by 'blemishes' Wilson intends in the main 'blunders of
transcription of typography'. There is a long description of how these
blunders might arise in the life of each document as it is relayed to and
from Britain and India. At every stage of each document's development
errors in the transcription of indigenous words might occur. These
errors might arise from the English official's rendering of the term on
the basis of 'native enunciation', or from the transcription by native
copyists of terms written by native amanuenses, or from the recopying
by English clerks in Britain, or from the typesetting of the document for
the printing press. As Wilson concludes, each time the indigenous term
is rewritten there is a 'renewed possibility of error'.[15] Wilson accepts that
there is often no precise English equivalent to an indigenous term, such
as 'ryot' or 'ryotwar'. He argues that 'the only trustworthy representation of an Indian word is its native costume: it can never be thoroughly
naturalised in any other'. None the less, to reduce the number of
blemishes in each document there is an urgent need to standardize
transliteration.[16]

There are a number of points to note about Wilson's introduction to
his work, not least in terms of some of the premises underlying it. First,
there is a strong predilection for the printed word. The strength of
British rule is identified with the nature of its documents and the

reliance which can be placed on them. This points both to the central role of information gathering and analysis in the maintenance of British rule and to the different character of this archive of information from that of its predecessors in the subcontinent.[17] Indeed, the long list of glossaries, dictionaries, reports, records and documents in English which Wilson refers to as his source material suggests a strong sense of the almost autonomous life of an archive, with its network of references and cross-references.[18] Secondly, Wilson's identification of British rule with the unblemished records of its archives raises a concern for the way in which these archives might be undermined. The main issue here, however, is not the relationship between those archives and the various types of societal realities they are supposedly intended to portray as well as to shape, but the relationship between that archive and the archives of its predecessors on which it is partially built. It is the accurate reproduction of some of the terms of the previous archives, relocated in the offical British network of documents, that is a chief concern. Thirdly, this reproduction and relocation is not so much about translation as about transliteration; it is the orthography (and so the visual appearance) of indigenous terms in the English language which is of prime consideration. Since precise equivalents in English of indigenous terms often cannot be found, inevitably what is important is paraphrase, as well as transliteration. The aim is not to find precise equivalents as such, but rather to reorient languages at the points where they meet so that a kind of working system of equivalences, with the help of transliteration and paraphrase, might be produced. It is reorientations of this kind which characterize the relationships between interacting administrative idioms in the polyglossia of British India.

Wilson's *Glossary* was published in 1855, but some of the preoccupations of his introduction were evident earlier in the East India Company's regulations. These preoccupations were sometimes central to the company's very conception of itself. For example, in the promulgation of 1793, which defined the ideal of a regular code of all regulations enacted for the British territories in Bengal, the first clause declared that such a regular code should also be printed 'with translations in the country Languages'. Clause 18 made it clear that such a translation must not be a 'close verbal' one, but rather must adopt the 'idiom of the native languages'. Furthermore, it would be the duty of the translator to revise the proof sheets of the printed translations, and 'to correct all errors of the press'.[19] In practice, the result was that the company's regulations in English were shaped by an interaction with the previous Mughal idioms of administration. In this interaction, Persian terms were, to adapt a phrase from Wilson, partially 'naturalised', and the regulations in English acquired the character of an idiom stranded between two administrative languages.

Here an example of the English text of a regulation, and its Persian translation, might be a useful illustration. The clause chosen is fairly representative (except in one respect, to be discussed) of the type of language used in the Company's regulations until the 1830s at least. Clause 5 of Regulation 2 (27 March 1795) reads:

> The begah of three dirrahs ilahee, thus established, consists of twenty poles, each measuring eight feet and four inches, and eight-tenths of an inch; the whole length being one hundred and sixty-eight feet, or three thousand one hundred and twenty-six square yards; and the biswah, or twentieth part of this begah, of one hundred and fifty-six yards, and eight-tenths of a yard. On its appearing that several of the Aumils and Canongoes understood that the kesraut, or difference in the length between the former and present measuring-rod, was to affect the assessment on all kinds of cultivation, the resident issued an explanatory notification, on the 12th of May 1789, to the following effect, viz. In the places where the null or rod of 1187 was less than the general standard rod established for that year, such difference was to be taken and calculated per begah on the jumnee or kowlee, i.e. nukdy land, and also upon that known under the denomination of rye kunkooty, or land the produce of which is calculated at a fixed or usual quantity per begah, and the revenues rated thereon accordingly.[20]

There are a few points to note. Some sort of rough elucidation is given for a number of terms, such as 'kesraut', 'biswah', 'null', but sometimes even these involve the use of a Persian word which remains unparaphrased. Such is the case with 'rye kunkooty', which is rendered in terms of land whose produce is calculated per 'begah'. Even so, this clause is slightly unusual in that several terms are paraphrased into English. This is in contrast to Clause 2 of the same regulation, where the vast majority of indigenous words are not elucidated. For example, the second sentence reads:

> In this cabooleat it was stipulated, that the Aumils should pay to the Rajah the jumma for which they had severally engaged, according to the tushkees or account particulars of the revenue funds in their respective aumildarries, including nuzeranna, and the Government's moiety of the bhuray, and russoom khazanah, and exclusive of the articles of the mujray, maafy mamooly, and the kharije jumma . . .[21]

Clause 5 is partly about getting to grips with indigenous units of measurement. This concern extends not just to units of spatial measurement, but also to measurements of time. During this period the preamble of each regulation cited the date of its promulgation in at least six different calendars. In Clause 5 itself it is noticeable that two dates are mentioned, one being 12 May 1789 and the other 1187. Interestingly, the latter is from the Faslī calendar, which, Wilson's *Glossary* explains, was a mode of time measurement that originated with the Emperor Akbar, who tried to simplify existing calendars through its introduction; in practice, however, different chronologies continued to subsist simultaneously.[22] The existence of parallel units of measurement, both spatial and temporal, in the East India Company's regulations is evocative of its engagement and interaction with indigenous idioms in its administrative codes.

The Persian translation of Clause 5 is far more succinct than its English counterpart. This is due mainly to the fact that the key lexical items in the clause are drawn from the Persian Mughal idiom of administration. Consequently, there is no need for terms such as *kasrat, bīswah, nal* or *raī' kankūtī* to be elucidated in any way, as they are in the English version.[23] The result is an administrative idiom which is jargon-ridden with what, from the perspective of English, are rather exotic terms. One might even be tempted to say that while technically the Persian version is a translation of the English one, in effect it is the English version that reads like the translation of a Persian original.

It was Act 29 of 1837, which allowed for the company to dispense with any provision of any regulation, that enjoined 'the use of the Persian language in any judicial proceeding or in any proceeding relating to the Revenue'.[24] The motives behind this act are too complex to discuss in much detail here. Suffice it to say it was clear that the aim was to make the language of administration continuous with the 'vernaculars' of each administrative unit. This was easier said than done, given the highly complex linguistic map of the subcontinent; the problems today of defining Urdu and Hindi as the 'national' languages of Pakistan and India respectively, suggest that this task still remains far from straightforward.[25] At any rate, the company's relationship with previous idioms of administration gradually seemed to move away from one of interaction to that of supplanting them with a different type of administrative idiom. Some of the regulations promulgated in the 1830s continue to contain unexplicated indigenous terms, yet they are much fewer in number. The entire tone is much clearer and sharper, with an emphasis on consistency and uniformity of usage. This seems to accord well with the changes historians have studied in the nature of East India Company rule in India.[26]

'The wonderful jargon of official Urdu'

Thus, English was one player in the polyglossia of India, and, although an increasingly influential player, its importance should not be over-estimated. While the tone of its engagement with previous admin-istrative idioms might have altered, the languages declared to be 'official' by the British continued to engage with these idioms of the past in various ways. This was the case with Urdu as the official language of Bihar, the United Provinces and Punjab. The Perso-Arabic component of Urdu is a key part of the language,[27] but the language of the legal petitions submitted in Urdu to the Faujdari courts is a prime example of a contemporary 'official' language's engagement with previous idioms. A large part of the judicial lexicon of Mughal Persian survived in the language of these petitions, a fact noticed both by the detractors and by the defenders of official Urdu.[28] There is some point to the comment made by one observer that until the abolition of Persian as the language of the law courts, the 'official and popular language had been content to remain apart, now they are to coalesce', resulting in that 'wonderful jargon of official Urdu', which combines Persian and 'Hindustani' in syntax, as well as in vocabulary.[29] However, whether or not the hybrid nature of the language of these petitions can be called 'jargon' is debatable. This is mainly because to define lexical items as 'jargon' is to invoke the norms of a standard of some kind, whereas these petitions reflect how orthography and grammatical structure were yet to be standardized. This is in contrast to English, especially literary English, which had remained relatively stable since the sixteenth century.[30] In effect, these legal petitions constitute a case of 'leaky diglossia', in which one ('Low') variety 'leaks' into the functions reserved for another ('High') variety, creating a new variety that mixes both 'High' and 'Low' – and this in spite of the fact that here the 'Low' variety had technically already replaced the 'High'. That it could do so only partially at this stage is indicative of the difficulty of legislating administrative languages into existence, as well as of the continuing presence of the 'High' Mughal Persian lexicon in the vocabulary of the specialist castes who co-operated in the shift from Persian to Urdu.

A brief consideration of the language of Urdu legal petitions in the 1860s bears these points out. First, there is a predilection for using Persian plurals for human beings rather than Urdu plurals: for example, *sākinān* (inhabitants), *bandegān* (servants), *gavāhān* (witnesses),[31] *namāziyān* (those who pray),[32] *dokhterān* (daughters), *mālikān* (own-ers), *pesarān* (sons) and *vāriṣān* (heirs).[33] This extends to plurals for nonhumans too: *sālhāye darāz se* (for long years), for instance, uses a Persian plural and *izafat* phrase combined with an Urdu postposition.[34] There is also a tendency to use the Persian preposition *ba* as a prefix, instead of an Urdu postposition; as in *banām* (by/in the name of) and *bamakān* (to the house).[35] Persian numbers are also used: *yek, panj, haft, shānzadah* and *do ṣad*, instead of *ek* (one), *pānch* (five), *sāt* (seven), *solā* (sixteen) and *do so* (two hundred).[36] This usage extends to Persian names for days; *yak shamba* (Sunday) and *se shamba* (Tuesday).[37]

Secondly, another characteristic of these petitions is the almost exclusive use of the Persian conjunction *vao* rather than the Urdu *aur*. This conjunction is particularly noticeable in what amount to Perso-Arabic formulae which, in addition to specific Perso-Arabic words for key items such as petitioner (*dād khwāh*), defendant (*mad 'ā alaihi*) and named (*musammā*), are found in most of the petitions. It is in fact these formulae which lend the petitions their compressed and condensed form, among them the address with which all the petitions begin, 'gharīb parwar salāmat' (Cherisher of the Poor, may you be kept in safety!). Another example of the succinct formulae which are central to the language of the petitions is the recurring 'va baṭalab o samā'at-e gavāhān' (and to summon and hear witnesses).[38] A number of other Persian phrases stamp their presence on the style of the petitions, such as 'āmad o raft' (coming and going), 'shud o āmad' (custom, usage), and 'gharīb o ẕa'īf' (poor and weak).[39] This list of Perso-Arabic terms and constructions is by no means exhaustive, and there are a host of instances which space does not permit us to note in detail here.[40]

Thirdly, unlike the orthography of the Perso-Arabic items in the petitions, that of the Urdu items remains undefined. To give some examples, there is no systematic use of *bari ye* for final *e/ai*. Thus, words like *pānī* (water) are spelt with this form of *ye*, while the third person singular of 'to be' is spelt with *choṭī ye*. One of the words for plaintiff, *fidvī*, is spelt with both, and this in the same petition, while the particle *ne* used in the ergative tense is spelt with *choṭī ye*.[41] Similarly, there is no use of the *docashmī he* for aspirated consonants. Only the consonant (h), that is, the *choṭī he*, is used in words like *sāth, thī, bhar, thā, thī*, etc.[42] There is also no use of the *nun ğunnā* for the nasalization of a preceding vowel; *hain, main, nahīn*, etc. As for verb forms, these show the use of unreduced forms with vowel stems; *deven, jāven* and *hoven*.[43]

What this amounts to is that these petitions are a mixture of high and low styles, in which Perso-Arabic formulae are combined with 'Hindustani' forms which have yet to be standardized. The result is often an apparently haphazard word order with a string of items of different resonances which can create what, by contemporary standards, is a comical effect. Thus, the combination of the rather ponderous Arabic phrase 'inda' ul mumān 'at mūsta'id' (upon remonstrance [they] prepared) with the colloquial *mār pīṭ* (thrashing, drubbing) produces a clause which might be translated as 'upon remonstrance they made preparations to give him a good thrashing'.[44] These comic effects that result from a mixture of high and low styles do not undermine the abbreviated form of the petitions as a whole, which stems from combining phrases together in an almost telegraphic mode. It may be that the diglossia in which these petitions are embedded enables them to acquire a more succinct form than they might otherwise have been able to. At any rate, they represent an intermediate form arising from the leakage of a 'low' language into that of a 'high' language, in this case brought about by the abolition of the latter by governmental decree. It is because of this fluid linguistic situation that we are unable to say with any confidence that the language of these petitions is jargon-ridden; the variable orthography and unsystematic grammatical forms make it clear that, as yet, there were no standard forms to invoke in what was an ongoing process of diglossia.

It is worth briefly mentioning the correspondence of Rajab Ali of District Ludhiana in Punjab of the early 1870s, which is indicative of another type of linguistic fluidity. Given that often the letters in this collection switch between Arabic or Persian to Urdu, sometimes in mid-sentence,[45] they seem to constitute a case of bilingualism without diglossia which forms a contrast to the sort of hybrid language of the petitions considered above.[46] None the less, both the petitions and these letters reflect an unstable or transitional phase in the relationship between Persian and Urdu, when the latter was struggling to establish itself as an entity in its own right and to maintain its prestigious links with the 'high' languages of Arabic and Persian.

'Scattered' verse, or *rekhta*

In his famous article on diglossia Ferguson discusses how the status of poetry in the 'Low' variety is very different from the status of poetry in the 'High' variety.[47] The unstable relationship between Persian and Urdu considered above is also evident in some of the writings of indigenous literati on Urdu verse in the preceding century. It is clear that the first substantial literary tradition in Urdu was established in the Deccan, as a double consequence of the conquest of the Deccan kingdoms by the Emperor Aurangzeb and the collapse of central authority after his death in 1707.[48] It was with the decline of the Mughal

Empire that the literary development of Urdu became possible; at the same time, the Persianization of Urdu began to play an important role in the maintenance of cultural identity after this decline as a way of reinforcing links with the Muslim power of the past, and so as a 'prestige factor' in enhancing the status of Urdu.[49]

The complex relationship of Urdu with its Perso-Arabic heritage is evident in the case of two *tazkirās*, both written in the 1750s in Persian. In his *Makhzan-e Nikāt* Kiyām organizes his narrative in three parts: the first considers the poetry of the 'ancient' poets (*mutaqaddimīn*), the second the discourse of the intermediate eloquents (*sukhunwarān-e mutawassitīn*) and the third the poetry and the circumstances (*ahvāl*) of the discursive forms of the moderns (*sukhun tarāzān-e mutakhkhirīn*).[50] For our purposes, there are several points to consider. The very terms the author uses for 'ancients' and 'moderns' have the literal sense of those who preceded or went before, and those who came behind or last. This suggests a sense of a belated posteriority. In his *Muqaddama Sh'ar o Shā'irī* (Introduction to verse and poetry) of the 1880s Hālī used almost exactly the same terms in his periodization of poetry, only here the sense of belatedness is even stronger. One might be tempted to say that this sense of belatedness was central to the original conception of Urdu poetry, composed in the shadow of classical Persian and Arabic verse.

In the first group of poets the author begins with the famous Persian poet Sa'dī. He refers not only to the tradition of his travels in India, but also to some purported verses of his in Urdu ('īn dīyār vaqūf yāfteh yekdo bait rekhta').[51] That in a *tazkirā* on Urdu poets the author should begin with the famous Sa'dī and attribute some verses to him (which are not cited) appears to be a strategy which confers respectability and prestige on the undertaking of the *tazkirā*, as well as on the verses the author considers. This reflects the role of Persian as a 'prestige factor' in Urdu poetry at this stage.[52]

The word the author uses for Urdu is *rekhta*, literally 'scattered',[53] and also 'a mixed language, gibberish'.[54] This term was a common one during this period, and it is one which, among others, Mīr Taqī Mīr also uses in his *tazkirā*. *Rekhta* is evocative of the diglossic nature of this lingua franca as an intermediate form, as is the word 'Urdu' itself, meaning camp, which reflects its origins as the lingua franca of the Mughal army camp. *Rekhta* is often used along with 'Urdu' and 'Hindi' during this period as a designation for what is ostensibly perceived to be the same language. However, Mīr Taqī Mīr's *tazkirā Nikāt ul Shu'arā* (The subtleties of the poets) goes further in actually producing a typology of *rekhta* verse which reflects the complexities of this linguistically unstable context, complexities already evident in that both these works, while their subject matter is *rekhta* verse, are themselves composed in Persian.

At the end of his *tazkirā* Mīr divides *rekhta* verse into six types. Of these four are identified on the basis of the extent and manner of their combination with Persian items. Thus, the first kind is that in which one hemistich is in Persian and one in Hindi ('yek miṣra'-ish farsī va yek misra'esh hindī'); the second consists of verse in which half of a hemistich is in Persian and half a hemistich is in Hindi ('dovvom ānke niṣf misr'a-ish Hindī va niṣf farsī'); in the third kind particles and verbs are in Persian, but this is 'ugly' verse ('īn qabīh ast'); and the fourth type uses Persian compounds ('tarkībāte farsī mī-ārand'). Regarding the latter, if the Persian compounds that are used are in consonance with the language of *rekhta* ('munāsib-e zabān-e rekhta mī-uftad'), then this is permissible ('jāiz ast'), but if these compounds are not familiar in the context of *rekhta* then the verse is defective ('va tarkībe ke nā mānus rekhta mī-bāshad ān ma'qub ast'). In fact, style in poetry is dependent upon knowing this, that is, upon knowing when it is appropriate to use Persian compounds ('va dānistan-e īn mauqūf-e salīqa-ye shā'irī ast').[55]

What we have here is an interesting case of a *rekhta* poet (Inshā in his *Daryā-e Laṭāfat* described Mīr as among the most excellent of *rekhta goyān*, or *rekhta* speakers)[56] attempting to take stock in a Persian work of the imprint of diglossia on Urdu verse. Two tentative conclusions can be drawn from this attempt. First, there is a sense in which *rekhta* verse is as yet still emerging from its entangled relationships with Indian Persian. The term *rekhta* is evocative of the tension that arises between an intermediate form and the 'High' language it has tied itself to. Secondly, this mixture of 'High' and 'Low' varieties in *rekhta* verse is also evocative of a situation in which the 'Low' form, while simultaneously relying on its links with the 'High' form to enhance its prestige, is struggling to establish itself as a corpus of verse in its own right. Mīr's typology of *rekhta* verse is suggestive of this, given that part of his typology is based on the interplay between these forms. It is noticeable, though, that the important strategy in questions of style is to know when to use Persian compounds and when to exclude them. The deciding factor is that these compounds, if they are to be admitted, must be consonant with *rekhta*, so that it is *rekhta* which decides what goes. At any rate, Mīr's *tazkirā* reflects a stage of diglossia which parallels that considered above in the case of the legal petitions of the 1860s. The permeable boundary between Persian and Urdu or *rekhta*, as considered by Mīr, reinforces our scepticism about being able to identify or define what would constitute 'jargon' in the context of the sort of diglossias evident here.

The grand popular language of the East

Who decides what exactly constitutes *rekhta* during this period was a sticking point. It is in part the attempt to answer this question which ties Sayyid Inshā Allah Khān's *Daryā-e Laṭāfat* (The sea of elegance) up in knots. This book, also written in Persian, is part grammar, part potted linguistic and social history and part manual of rhetoric. As already mentioned, its circular and convoluted arguments reflect the complexities of the linguistic situation attendant upon the shift to Urdu from Persian among significant parts of the Muslim community, a shift occurring in the wake of the Mughal decline. Furthermore, given that Fasold has convincingly argued that the distinction between diglossia and most instances of a standard with dialects cannot be maintained,[57] Inshā's detailed concern, even fascination, with varieties of speech affords us another perspective on diglossia and Urdu.

Inshā's interest in varieties of dialect and speech communities is significant, given Urdu/Hindi's status as a lingua franca which supplemented the dialects of north India. Thus, at one point Inshā depicts Urdu as a mixture of languages, when he cites a passage that contains elements of Arabic, Persian, Turkish, Punjabi, Braj and Purabi.[58] At the very start of the book Inshā describes the creation of Urdu as the work of eloquent speakers (*khush bayān*) in the Mughal capital of Delhi, who took 'good words' from the variety of languages current there, and turned various expressions and words to their own use, thereby creating a new language separate from other tongues ('ibārat aur alfāẓ men taṣarruf kar ke aur zabānon se alag ek naʻī zabān paidā kī').[59] Inshā is at pains to catalogue the varieties of speech and slang found in each quarter of the city; chapter 2, part 1, lists the tongues of different groups and neighbourhoods in Delhi. This includes those of Hindu groups, *dalāls*, Mughal descendants, Kashmiris and their descendants, *Pūrabīs*, Afghans, Punjabis and other immigrants, as well as the speech of Mughalpūra, the old city and other areas of the city as a whole.[60] Inshā adds to this list later with sections on women's speech and women's verse,[61] and also on the variety of Urdu in Lucknow, which is compared and contrasted with that of Delhi.[62] Each section cites passages illustrating the relevant speech type or slang and discusses pronunciation, accent, verb forms and use of grammatical gender. At the same time, though, Inshā is anxious to establish who in fact speaks 'proper' Urdu; hence the preoccupation throughout the book with distinguishing between *faṣīḥ* and *ghair fāṣīḥ* (polished discourse and its opposite). It is those who have a command of the latter who have the authority to 'Urduize' a word or invent an idiom (*muhāwara*),[63] but the number of those who have such a command in each neighbourhood of the city of Delhi is limited – in some there are one or two individuals, in others there are three or four.[64] Basically, the kernel of Inshā's argument which can be extracted from his section on the 'Pillars of Elegance in Language/Speech' (Faṣāḥat ke arkān) is that proper speech is the language Proper Speakers use, and Proper Speakers are those who speak the proper language.[65]

This circularity in some of Inshā's formulations is paralleled elsewhere when the author tries to spell out the content of some of the notions he appears to be enchanted with. The attempt to define ṯaksālī (genuine or pure) Urdu is convoluted and obscure, bedevilled as it is with a multitude of qualifications and counter-qualifications at every step.[66] The complexities in Inshā's formulations seem to arise because of a number of problematic areas. At times the text reads as though it tries to conjure up a 'pure' Urdu from a swirl of speech types, slangs and dialects which it merges with. This becomes especially apparent when Inshā contrasts what he sees as elegant and polished Urdu with lower and less proper forms of speech. The former specimen strikes the reader as being an artificial and stilted construct, as well as pretentious, while the latter specimens are not only easier to understand, but also bear a closer resemblance to present-day forms of the language.[67] To a certain extent, then, Inshā's problems partly arise from attempting to capture a lingua franca as an entity independent of the necessarily diglossic context in which it is embedded.

There also seems to be an element of snobbery in Inshā's formulations. This is partly evident in the 'Delhi-centric' view of the text. Inshā is anxious throughout to establish that Delhi, and the remnants of the Mughal court there, set the standards of excellence in elegant discourse and polished etiquette (the two are often linked by the author).[68] Alongside the various speech types, dialects and slangs of Delhi, Inshā also describes the invention of various language games in Delhi, and the rules governing their play.[69] There is some similarity between this sense of a linguistic self-reflexivity in the invention of these games and the self-conscious nature of the specimen of eloquent Urdu which Inshā cites, mentioned above. Both perhaps reflect the ways of speaking of an upper or leisure class, whose cumbersome and archaic usages reflect their social distance from the need for more direct forms of communication.[70]

In fact, the book begins by showing why major cities are also important centres of language; urbanity and urban centres go hand in hand.[71] When Inshā discusses who qualifies for membership of the *ahl-e zabān* or the *ahl-e urdū* (masters of language or masters of Urdu), one criterion is having some sort of link with Delhi, either through one's parentage or through one's training.[72] It is partly because of this 'Delhi-centric' view that Inshā is also keen to expose fraudulent members of the *ahl-e zabān* in other cities; they play upon their previous links with Delhi to market their language as the genuine article, whereas in fact their language is a low hybrid, or, as Inshā charmingly puts it at one point, 'half deer, half dog' (*ādhā hiran, ādhā kuttā*).[73] Even so, Inshā is careful not to tie Urdu too exclusively to Delhi, lest its efficacy as a lingua franca, albeit one now attempting to become a 'High' language, is undermined. Hence the qualifications he often expresses, though it has to be said rather tentatively, in his discussions of who qualifies as a *zabāndān* (one versed in matters of language, in this context, well versed in Urdu).[74] To a certain extent, this area of Inshā's concern hints at another problematic area: namely, the attempt to define for Urdu a geographical region of its own, while at the same time ensuring that it is not tied to any one locality exclusively.

Inshā's problematic formulations lead us once again to suspect that in the context of Urdu during this period it is difficult to speak with any confidence about 'jargon', given that there is no standard language which can be invoked. Indeed, Inshā's problems in part stem from attempting to depict what such a standard form of the language would look like. Since this language is so involved with a variety of speech types and dialects, this attempt begins to strike one as rather quixotic. Interestingly, there are some areas of overlap between Inshā's preoccupations and his depiction of Urdu, and those of the 'Professor of Hindoostanee' at the East India Company's Fort William College, Calcutta, Dr John Gilchrist. His *Anti-Jargonist, or a Short Introduction to the Hindoostanee Language* (1800) was written to rebut George Hadley's *Grammar of a Jargon* (1774). Both Hadley and Gilchrist seem to be using the word 'jargon' in two ways: in the eighteenth century sense of a lingua franca (see Peter Burke's introduction, p. 18) as well as in the sense of cant.[75] That it obviously did carry a pejorative connotation is clear in Gilchrist's determination to argue for the 'importance to us all, of a knowledge of something more in the grand popular language of the east, than the smattering of an imaginary jargon'.[76] In a way, both Inshā's and Gilchrist's work was a form of sociolinguistics, given that both are concerned not just with language, but also with social groups, dialects, etiquette and forms of dress.[77] However, where Inshā had a hierarchy of speech forms, with those of the *fuṣaḥā* in cities, especially

Delhi, setting the standards, there is a hint that Gilchrist's hierarchy was the reverse of this. The latter refers to 'the court or high style, and the country or pristine style; leaving the middle or familiar current style between them, which I have recommended as the most useful and described it also at full length in my work'.[78] It is noticeable that what are styles to Gilchrist are more than just styles to Inshā.

None the less, one significant area of agreement is the identification of Urdu as a marker of Indian Muslim identity. Gilchrist's introduction to his work contains a long and systematic section on differences between Muslims and Hindus in dress, jewellery, etiquette and language, with 'Hinduwee' being the 'exclusive property of the Hindoos alone'.[79] Indeed, Gilchrist makes it explicit that one of the purposes of his work is to enable Europeans to distinguish 'a Hindoo from a Moosulman'.[80] Inshā's work is nowhere concerned in any sort of detail with such systematic differences between 'Hindus' and 'Muslims', but at one point he states that 'by idiomatic Urdu is intended the language of the people of Islam'; characteristically, he immediately qualifies this by saying that 'even in this quality, though, there is much difference' ('muḥāwara-e urdū se ahl-e Islām kī zabān murād he, lekin is ṣifat men bhī bahut ikhtilāf he').[81] Thus, even in Inshā's work there is an identification of Urdu as a marker of Muslim identity, albeit a qualified one.

Urdu as a marker of Muslim identity

By the turn of the century this marker of a north Indian Muslim identity had become more explicit, though not all technical works on Urdu made such an identification. This was the case with Sajjād Mirzā Baig's *Tashīl ul Balāghat* (The facilitation of rhetoric, *c.*1940), which in its chapter 'Defects of Discourse' ('uyūb-e kalām) mentioned the mixing of Urdu and Farsi nouns together, and the formation of Hindi and Persian words on the basis of Arabic words, as practices to be avoided.[82] In the context of considering when borrowing from other languages is acceptable, he argues that it is legitimate in the case of specialist terminologies, where it can be used for more pedantic purposes by the learned, but not in the case of the common discourse of everyday language.[83] It is in this sense of specialist terminologies (*iṣṭalāḥāt*) that the author considers 'jargon'. He places a premium on clarity, and in fact defines *faṣaḥāt* (eloquence) as pertaining to a discourse (*kalām*) which is in accordance with 'common, everyday discourse' (*rozmarrā*), so that clarity is related to discourse from which 'jargon' (in the sense of specialist terminologies) is absent.[84] The use of words which are not in accordance with everyday or

common discourse is one of the faults of defective discourse, a fault
which he calls *ghurābat* (literally oddness, peculiarity).[85] Indeed, *rozmarrā* itself is defined as the discourse which the *ahl-e zabān* (masters of
language) use.[86] At one point the author considers the case where the
use of specialist terms cannot be avoided; his advice here is to ensure
that they are placed between words which, in combination with such
terms, render the latter pleasant in sound.[87] The author's passing
concern with 'jargon' in the sense mentioned above is indicative of a
clear notion of everyday discourse, from which specialist terminologies
are set apart. The author also pays much attention to dialectal variety in
the language, so that it is not assumed that 'everyday discourse' is a
monolithic and uniform form.[88] In the context of considering specialist
terminologies, he further draws attention to the Sanskritization of Hindi
by Hindus and the Persianization of Urdu by Muslims, so there is some
recognition in the text of the communalization of languages. The issue
here is one of authority, that is, the question of who has the authority to
coin new words. The author himself is unambiguous about this particular question; the linguistic inventions of newspapers and their articles
(especially when they reflect the vagaries of new political movements)
and those of lesser writers (*kam liyāqat navīs*) are detrimental to the
language as a whole. It is only the language of the *'ulemā* and of
authoritative writers (*mustanad muṣannif*) which legitimizes the use of
words and idioms.[89] There is thus a hint here of the wider struggle for
authority evident within parts of the Muslim community of the United
Provinces from the early twentieth century onwards, a struggle in which
the main contenders were the *'ulemā* and members of the major political
parties at the time.[90]

The All-India Muslim League papers are eloquent testimony to this
struggle and its connection with language issues. Indeed, some of the
associations which preceded the establishment of the All-India Muslim
League were formed to 'defend' Urdu in the wake of the Nagri
Resolution of 1900. This resolution admitted Hindi in the Devanagri
script to an equal position with Urdu in the Perso-Arabic script as an
official language of the United Provinces.[91] The identification of Urdu
with 'Muslimhood' is clearly evident in the All-India Muslim League
papers (though it is worth noting that there were some dissenting
voices). One resolution at the annual session of 1911 described Urdu as
'besides their religion the only bond of union among the Muslims'.[92] This
was echoed later in the 1941 Report of the Kamal Yar Jung Education
Committee, which had a rather stark view of the politics of language:
'Language and Literature have always been the best means to break or
mould the character of a people.'[93] Interestingly, this report stated the

view that it was the abolition of Persian as the language of the courts in 1837 which led to India's being 'divided by the feuds of the local languages',[94] but the report also makes another comment which illuminates the role of Urdu as a symbol of a Muslim identity: Urdu is described as important because it keeps Muslims in India in touch with Arabic as the language of Islam, and Persian as the historical language of Muslim India.[95] One might be tempted to sum up the nature of Urdu as a symbol in this context by characterizing it not as a 'Dummy High' as such, given that it was extensively utilized for real communicative purposes in speech communities, but as perhaps partly mimicking one. As one symbol among others of a Muslim identity, its significance and the high regard it was held in by some stemmed from its closeness to Arabic and Persian, both of which by this date were not used extensively in the subcontinent (except by the 'ulemā). Urdu in this context derived its power as a symbol through its links with two languages which were 'Dummy Highs' in the Indian subcontinent.[96]

Since the Muslim League papers are themselves mainly in English[97] (and the extent to which some of the League's leaders were at home in Urdu is not clear), there is a curious sense of distance from the worlds of Urdu, both past and present, a sense of distance which may have been necessary in view of the League's projection of Urdu as a symbol of a communal identity. To some extent, this sense has an earlier parallel in Gilchrist's work on Urdu, where the reader catches echoes of the worlds of 'Hindustani'; these echoes need to be deciphered and disentangled from that work's preoccupations, and reconsidered from the point of view of the texts of those other worlds. In this way, some sort of picture can emerge about the different types of interaction between both these different worlds and the ways in which they represented themselves and others.[98] While the first part of this chapter considered the impact of Indian Persian on East India Company English, there is no space here to consider the reverse process of the influence of English on Urdu/Hindi.[99] Suffice it to say that English also had (and continues to have) a role to play in the various types of diglossia which surround Urdu. Fasold has claimed that 'Diglossia never ends; it is a human universal';[100] in the case of Urdu, one might be tempted to say that diglossia is central to its very sense of itself as a language. It is the various types of diglossia considered in this chapter which cast doubt on whether or not a standard language can be invoked when considering jargons in Urdu. A glance at present-day Urdu newspapers shows how the boundaries between Urdu and Persian and Arabic, as well as English, remain permeable. It may be possible to speak of varying degrees of pretentiousness in styles of Urdu, but this is not the same thing as talking about jargon.

Notes

The quotation in the title is from Sir William Jones, *A Grammar of the Persian Language* (1777), in *The Works of Sir William Jones* (1799; Delhi: Agam Prakash, 1979), 5: 181–2. I am grateful to Dr S. Aiyar for her comments on this chapter. Dr Z. A. Shakeb of Christie's was kind enough to discuss some of the issues raised here at an earlier stage. I am also indebted to Professor C. Shackle for his help in the transliteration of citations in Urdu and Persian.

1 The most useful and comprehensive account is by Christopher Shackle and Rupert Snell in *Hindi and Urdu since 1800: A Common Reader* (London: School of African and Oriental Studies, University of London, 1990). See also, among others, Amrit Rai's somewhat eccentric but useful *A House Divided: The Origin and Development of Hindi-Urdu* (Delhi: Oxford University Press, 1991) and Paul Brass, *Language, Religion and Politics in North India* (Cambridge: Cambridge University Press, 1974), esp. ch. 3. For post-independence India, see J. Das Gupta, *Language Conflict and National Development: Group Politics and National Language Policy in India* (Berkeley, Los Angeles, and London: University of California Press, 1970), but for a shorter account see Ralph Fasold, *The Sociolinguistics of Society* (Oxford: Blackwell, 1984), ch. 1. G. A. Grierson's monumental *Linguistic Survey of India*, 10 vols (Calcutta: Superintendent Printing, 1916), while dated, remains useful both in the examples it cites and as a reflection of British attitudes to the polyglossia of the Indian subcontinent, attitudes which had some influence on indigenous perceptions as well. Vol 9, pt 1, deals with Western Hindi and Panjabi.

2 Fasold, *The Sociolinguistics of Society*, 53.

3 For some comments on the role of Persian as the main component of Indo-Muslim rule, see Shackle and Snell, *Hindi and Urdu since 1800*, 3–7; for a linguistic treatment of the Persian component in Urdu, see ibid., 59–78.

4 Ibid., 4. The problem of defining a 'national' language for the purposes of administration and education in the multilingual societies of the Indian subcontinent continues to be complex; see ibid., 14–17, and Fasold, *The Sociolinguistics of Society*, 20–33.

5 Ernest Gellner, *Nations and Nationalism* (Oxford: Blackwell, 1983), chs 2–3. See also Benedict Anderson, *Imagined Communities: Reflections on the Origins and Spread of Nationalism* (London: Verso, 1983), 66–78, for a discussion of the role of language in defining homogeneous communities.

6 Fasold, *The Sociolinguistics of Society*, 41, 52, 54.

7 Shackle and Snell, *Hindi and Urdu since 1800*, 7–8; on the Hindu castes who acted as scribes in the Persian language, see 3.

8 C. A. Ferguson, 'Diglossia', in Pier Paolo Giglioli (ed.), *Language and Social Context: Selected Readings* (Harmondsworth: Penguin, 1972), 232–51.

9 Fasold, *The Sociolinguistics of Society*, 49, citing John Platt, 'A Model for Polyglossia and Multilingualism (with Special Reference to Singapore and

Malaysia)', *Language in Society*, 6 (1977), 373–4.

10 C. A. Bayly, *Indian Society and the Making of the British Empire* (Cambridge: Cambridge University Press, 1988), 14–16, 45–78; C. A. Bayly, *Imperial Meridian: The British Empire and the World 1780–1830* (London: Longman, 1989), 60; J. Majeed, *Ungoverned Imaginings: James Mill's 'The History of British India' and Orientalism* (Oxford: Clarendon Press, 1992), 18–25.

11 On the high regard in which Persian was held by the East India Company in the late eighteenth and early nineteenth centuries, see B. S. Cohn, 'The Command of Language and the Language of Command', in Ranajit Guha (ed.), *Writings on South Asian History and Society*, Subaltern Studies, 4 (Delhi: Oxford University Press, 1985), 287.

12 Fifth Report from the Select Committee on the Affairs of the East India Company (1812), in *Parliamentary Papers* 7 (1812), 20, 70–4.

13 H. H. Wilson, *A Glossary of Judicial and Revenue Terms, and of Useful Words Occurring in Official Documents relating to the Administration of the Government of British India* (London: W. H. Allen, 1855), i.

14 Ibid., iii.

15 Ibid., iii.

16 Ibid., i, v, vi–xxiv.

17 C. A. Bayly, 'Knowing the Country: Empire and Information in India', *Modern Asian Studies*, 27 (1993), 25–9, 33–4.

18 Wilson, *Glossary of Judicial and Revenue Terms*, iv–v.

19 East India Company, *Regulations Passed by the Governor General in Council of Bengal with an Index and Glossary Containing the Regulations Passed in the Years 1793, 1794, and 1795* (London: J. L. Cox, 1828), Regulation 41, 1 May 1793, 345–7.

20 Ibid., Regulation 2, 1795, 418.

21 Ibid., 416.

22 Wilson, *Glossary of Judicial and Revenue Terms*, 158.

23 East India Company, *Regulations Passed by the Governor General in Council During the Year 1795* (Calcutta: The Honorable Company's Press, 1795), Qānūn Dovvom, 1790 īsvī, daf'ā panjam (Act 2, 1790 of the Christian era, clause 5), no pagination.

24 William Theobald, *The Legislative Acts of the Governor General of India in Council 1834–67 with an Analytical Abstract Prefixed to Each Act; Table of Contents and Index to Each Volume; the Letters Patents of the High Courts, and Acts of Parliament Authorizing Them* (Calcutta: Thacker, Spink, 1868), 1: 73.

25 For some of these problems, see Shackle and Snell, *Hindi and Urdu since 1800*, 13–16; Fasold, *The Sociolinguistics of Society*, 20–30.

26 The classic account is Eric Stokes, *The English Utilitarians and India* (Oxford: Clarendon Press, 1963); see also his 'Bureaucracy and Ideology: Britain and India in the Nineteenth Century', *Transactions of the Royal*

Historical Society, 5th series, 30 (1980), 131–56, and Bayly, *Indian Society*, 151.

27 Shackle and Snell, *Hindi and Urdu since 1800*, 46–72.

28 For example, see J. Beames, 'Outlines of a Plea for the Arabic Element in Official Hindustani', *Journal of the Asiatic Society*, 35 (1867), 6–8, and F. S. Growse, 'Some Objections to the Modern Style of Official Hindustani', *Journal of the Asiatic Society*, 35 (1867), 175.

29 Growse, 'Some Objections to the Modern Style of Official Hindustani', 175.

30 W. F. Bolton, *A Short History of Literary English* (London: Arnold, 1972), 24.

31 Government of India, *Collection of Urdu Petitions Made Under the Orders of the Government of India, for Her Majesty's Civil Service Commissioners* (Calcutta: Office of the Superintendent of Government Printing, 1869), Petition 3, 8–9.

32 Ibid., Petition 7, 17–18.

33 Ibid., Petition 11, 27–8.

34 Ibid., Petition 7, 18.

35 Ibid., Petition 3, 8, and Petition 9, 22–3.

36 Ibid., Petition 7, 17–20, and esp. Petition 11, 27–8.

37 Ibid., Petition 3, 8, and Petition 9, 23.

38 Ibid., Petition 3, 9, Petition 7, 20, and Petition 9, 23, where the formula appears as 'āz ṭalab va samā'at ažhār govāhān'.

39 Ibid., Petition 7, 17–19, and Petition 9, 22–3.

40 For example, 'sar qadīm ul ayām se' in Petition 7, 18.

41 Ibid., Petition 3, 8–9.

42 Ibid., Petition 7, 18–19.

43 Ibid., Petition 7, 18–19, and Petition 9, 22–3.

44 Ibid., Petition 7, khulāsā (substance of the petition), 17.

45 For example, see p. 16 of the first volume of the collection, MS 821, Lahore Museum. I am indebted to Dr Z. A. Shakeb of Christie's for transcribing some of these letters from the *shikasta* style into legible Urdu.

46 For the case of bilingualism without diglossia, see Fasold, *The Sociolinguistics of Society*, 41.

47 Ferguson, 'Diglossia', 236–7.

48 Shackle and Snell, *Hindi and Urdu since 1800*, 5; D. J. Matthews, C. Shackle and S. Husain, *Urdu Literature* (London: Urdu Markaz, 1985), 10–11, 36–7.

49 Rai, *A House Divided*, 239–40, 242, 276.

50 Kiyām, *Makhzan-e Nikāt* (1754–5), Persian MS, India Office Library, Ethe 701, fol. 2b.

51 Ibid.

52 For links between Urdu poetry and Persian courtly traditions, see Matthews, Shackle and Husain, *Urdu Literature*, 16. For the travels of the famous poet, see John Andrew Boyle, 'The Chronology of Sa'dī's Years of

Travel', *Islamwissenschaftliche Abhandlungen* (1974), 1–8.

53 Grierson speculates that the name derived from the manner in which Persian words were 'scattered' in Urdu poetry; see his *Linguistic Survey of India*, 10: 45.

54 Steingass gives one of the meanings of *rekhta* as 'gibberish'; Steingass, *A Comprehensive Persian–English Dictionary* (1892; London: Routledge, 1988), S. V. 'rekhta', 601.

55 Mīr Taqī Mīr, *Nikāt ul Shu'arā* (1754; Aurangabad, Anjuman-i Tarraqqi-i Urdu, 1920), ed. with an introduction in Urdu by Habibur Rahman Khan, 186–7.

56 Inshā Allah Khān, *Daryā-e Laṭāfat* (1808; Karachi, Anjuman-e Tarraqqi-e Urdu, 1988), trans. into Urdu by Pandit Braj Mohan, 56.

57 Fasold, *The Sociolinguistics of Society*, 44.

58 Inshā, *Daryā-e Laṭāfat*, 6–7.

59 Ibid., 2 (citations are from the Urdu translation mentioned above).

60 Ibid., 15–38.

61 Ibid., 83–104.

62 Ibid., 104–25. It is interesting to note how vol. 9 of the *Linguistic Survey of India* contains specimens of similar groups and areas, though on a much sounder and more comprehensive basis; see Grierson, *Linguistic Survey of India*, 9: 63ff.

63 Inshā, *Daryā-e Laṭāfat*, 37.

64 Ibid., 36. The author goes so far as to name some of these rare individuals.

65 Ibid., 37–43.

66 Ibid., 280.

67 Ibid., 27, for the specimen of polished and elegant Urdu, and for a specimen of the unpolished language which bears a clearer resemblance to contemporary forms, see 45–6.

68 Ibid., 23, 53–4, 114–15.

69 Ibid., 54–6.

70 P. Burke, Introduction, P. Burke and R. Porter (eds), *The Social History of Language* (Cambridge: Cambridge University Press, 1987), 6.

71 Inshā, *Daryā-e Laṭāfat*, 1–2.

72 Ibid., 43, 52–3.

73 Ibid., 33. See also 3, 34.

74 Ibid., 52–3.

75 It is in the former sense that Jones seems to be using the word when he mentions the 'jargon' and 'idiom' of India. See general note to the chapter, above.

76 J. Gilchrist, *The Anti-Jargonist, or a Short Introduction to the Hindoostanee Language (vulgarly but erroneously called The Moors), comprizing the rudiment of that tongue, with an extensive vocabulary, English and Hindoostanee and Hindoostanee and English: accompanied with some plain and useful dialogues, translations, poems, tales &c. with the view of illustrating the whole on practical principles. Being partly an abridgement of the Oriental*

204   Javed Majeed

Linguist, but greatly altered and improved, embellished with the Hindoo-stanee Horal Diagram (Calcutta: Ferris, 1800), ii.

77 Ibid., xxii, xxv.
78 Ibid., iv.
79 Ibid., iv.
80 Ibid., vi.
81 Ibid., 24.
82 Sajjād Mirzā Baig, *Tahsīl ul Balāghat* (Delhi: Baig Sufi, c.1940), 197.
83 Ibid., 65–6.
84 Ibid., 206.
85 Ibid., 192.
86 Ibid., 60.
87 Ibid., 216.
88 Ibid., 40–55.
89 Ibid., 66–7.
90 For some details, see Brass, *Language, Religion and Politics*, 163–4, 174–7; David Gilmartin, *Empire and Islam, Punjab and the Making of Pakistan* (London: I. B. Tauris, 1988); P. Hardy, *The Muslims of British India* (Cambridge: Cambridge University Press, 1972), 243–5; Jacob M. Landau, *The Politics of Pan-Islam, Ideology and Organization* (Oxford: Clarendon Press, 1990), ch. 4; Gail Minault, *The Khilafat Movement: Religious Symbolism and Political Mobilization in India* (New York: Columbia University Press, 1982); Barbara Daly Metcalfe, *Islamic Revival in British India: Deoband, 1860–1900* (1982; Karachi: Royal Book Company, 1989), chs 4–5; F. Robinson, *Separatism among Indian Muslims: The Politics of the United Provinces' Muslims 1860–1923* (Cambridge: Cambridge University Press, 1974), 353–6; Farzana Sheikh, *Community and Consensus in Islam: Muslim Representation in Colonial India, 1860–1947* (Cambridge: Cambridge University Press, 1989).
91 For the Nagri resolution and the question of Muslim politics, see Brass, *Language, Religion and Politics*, ch. 3, and Robinson, *Separatism among Indian Muslims*, 33–83; see also Grierson, *Linguistic Survey of India*, 9: 50. See the proceedings of the meeting of the Preliminary Committee for the Defence of Urdu, 30 April 1900 (incomplete), in *Muslim League Documents 1900–1947* (Karachi: Quaid-i Azam Academy, 1990), 1: 1–2.
92 Report of the All-India Muslim League 1911, in All-India Muslim League (hereafter AIML) Papers, vol. 65 (resolution on Gokhale's Elementary Education Bill).
93 Report of the Kamal Yar Jung Committee 1941 (AIML Papers), 10–11.
94 Ibid., 82.
95 Ibid., 9.
96 For a discussion of 'Dummy Highs', see Fasold, *The Sociolinguistics of Society*, 49–50.
97 There was some friction early on about which language the league's proceedings should be in. For example, see the letter from Mazharul Haq to

Musa Khan, 11 February 1908: 'It is necessary for our success that the English language shd. be our medium in all our correspondence and proceedings' (AIML Papers, 10, document 24). Even as late as 1945 some were arguing for a greater use of Urdu in the league's deliberations; see the letter of Mohsin Nizami of Anjuman Tahaffuz-i-Urdu, Lucknow, to the secretary of the league, 15 May 1945 (AIML Papers, 471, document 34).

 98 For an excellent discussion of some of these issues, see Aijaz Ahmed, '"Indian Literature": Notes towards the Definition of a Category', in *In Theory, Classes, Nations, Literatures* (London: Verso, 1992), 243–85.

 99 For an interesting treatment of this theme, see Rupert Snell, 'The Hidden Hand: English Lexis, Syntax and Idiom as Determinants of Modern Hindi Usage', in David Arnold and Peter Robb (eds), *Institutions and Ideologies* (London: Curzon Press, 1993).

100 Fasold, *The Sociolinguistics of Society*, 57.

Index